SHAPING WOMEN'S WORK:
GENDER, EMPLOYMENT AND
INFORMATION TECHNOLOGY

LONGMAN SOCIOLOGY SERIES

Series Editor:
ROBERT BURGESS, University of Warwick

Editorial Advisors:
JOE BAILEY, Kingston University
ANGELA GLASNER, Oxford Brookes University
CLAIRE WALLACE, Central European University

LONGMAN SOCIOLOGY SERIES

Shaping Women's Work: Gender, Employment and Information Technology

Juliet Webster

LONGMAN
London and New York

Addison Wesley Longman Limited
Edinburgh Gate
Harlow, Essex CM20 2JE,
England
and Associated Companies throughout the world

Published in the United States of America
by Addison Wesley Longman Publishing Company, New York

© Addison Wesley Longman Limited 1996

First published 1996

ISBN 0 582 21810 1 PPR

British Library Cataloguing-in-Publication Data

A catalogue record for this book is
available from the British Library

Library of Congress Cataloging-in-Publication Data
Webster, Juliet.
    Shaping women's work : gender, employment, and information technology /
Juliet Webster.
        p.   cm. — (Longman sociology series)
    Includes bibliographical references and index.
    ISBN 0–582–21811–X (cloth). — ISBN 0–582–21810–1 (pbk.)
    1. Sex role in the work environment.   2. Women—Effect of technological
innovations on.   3. Information technology.
    I. Title. II. Series.
    HD6060.6.W43   1996
    331.4—dc20   96–459
                                                                  CIP

Phototypeset by 20 in Times 10/11pt
Produced through Longman Malaysia, CLP

Dedicated to Moyra

A most extraordinary woman
and a very dear friend

CONTENTS

SERIES EDITOR'S PREFACE

The Longman Sociology series is a new series of books which are written specifically for first and second year undergraduate students. Each title covers one key area of sociology and aims to supplement the traditional standard text.

The series is forward looking and attempts to reflect topics that will be included in syllabuses for sociology and social policy in the 1990s. It provides a range of volumes that bring together conceptual and empirical material. In addition, volumes in the series also examine key controversies and debates drawing on commentaries using conceptual and empirical material from a range of authors.

Each volume in the series whether authored or edited, will cover an area that would be commonly found in sociology and social policy syllabuses. The focus of each volume will be upon theoretically informed empirical work with policy relatedness.

The volumes are intended for an international audience and therefore comparative material is introduced where appropriate in a form that will be suitable for first and second year students.

There is now a range of writing that contributes to debates about women's work. In this volume Juliet Webster extends the discussion through an analysis of information technologies in relation to women's employment and women's work. Her contribution to this area of study will stimulate the debate among students, teachers and researchers in sociology.

Robert G Burgess,
University of Warwick

ACKNOWLEDGEMENTS

I could not have begun this book, never mind completed it, without the freedom of a sabbatical from my 'day job' in the Department of Innovation Studies at the University of East London. During this period, I was able to read, think, write and consult my colleagues around the world about the material in the book, and I benefited enormously from such a concentrated period of study. This meant, though, that my colleagues at the University – already very heavily committed people – had to cover my duties for a semester, and I am indebted to them for giving me the opportunity to work on this book.

I also received much help and encouragement from Sarah Caro at Longman, and from colleagues and friends in other institutions who discussed ideas with me, or read and commented upon drafts of this book. I particularly want to acknowledge the support of Ruth Carter, Cynthia Cockburn, Clair Drew, Gavin Poynter and Marja Vehviläinen. All these people gave considerable time and expertise to this book, and I thank them very warmly.

Then, in the domestic sphere, my partner, Roger, nurtured me through the writing of this book, and was patient and caring during my long periods of immersion in the subject of women, employment and information technology. He must be the most gender-and-technology-minded geologist in the world, and I thank him very much for his sweet supportiveness.

CHAPTER 1

The terrain of this book

When I trained and then went to work as a secretary in the late 1970s, the technologies of office work were entirely electrical, mechanical or manual. Electric typewriters, addressographs, roneo stencils and shorthand pads were the most advanced technologies I encountered; these were the typical paraphernalia of my job in an office. But even as I was training and learning to use these devices, the world was on the brink of a period of widespread technological change. Information and communication technologies were being ushered in and the face of the workplace was changing profoundly. Word processors, personal computers, electronic photocopiers, fax machines, and computer-based systems of many other kinds are the tools with which we now all work today, not only in offices but throughout the entire economy.

This book represents my assessment of the changes which have taken place in the workplaces of women since these technologies were developed and given application, and of women's place in their development and application. Although my early working life was lived as a secretary, my subsequent employment has been as a researcher and teacher concerned with the social relations and dynamics of information and communications technologies. In one way or another, then, these technologies have been at the centre of my own existence as a woman for some years now. They have been at the centre of many other working women's existences, too. My own experiences, as well as the research of others, inevitably therefore inform and appear in this book.

In the social study of technologies to which I am now a contributor, there has been widespread debate about the social relations and social implications of information and communication technologies, and about the interplay between technical and social changes. The nature of work in computerised society, and the prospects for people's employment, skills and performance of work, number among the central concerns of social scientists, and there is now a huge body of work discussing such issues. Much of this work is the outcome of feminist research, asserting the importance of analysing changes in women's, as well as in men's, work, and changes in the gender relations of the workplace. This is my own agenda; from a fascination with developments in the office which related to my personal experiences of office work I have become increasingly concerned with the nature of women's work in other spheres of employment, and in particular with their experiences of information technologies at work. Feminist research now has much to say about these issues, and it is with the contribution made by such research to our understanding of the contemporary dynamics of women's paid work and of their relationship to information technologies that this book is concerned.

This book, then, is primarily about women and technology at work, and about the ways in which they are mutually constitutive. And here some clarification needs to be made concerning the precise terrain of the book. Many feminist thinkers, particularly those working in a post-structuralist or post-modernist tradition, might argue for a wider focus on 'gender' as opposed to one simply on 'women', in order to introduce an understanding of the shaping of people's (men's and women's) gender identities, experiences and subjectivities into the analysis. This, indeed, is the dominant emphasis of contemporary feminist research. However, this is not my concern here. I am concerned specifically with *women* and their relationship to workplace technologies, rather than with gender and technology in the broader sense. Some would argue that the shift in feminist thinking to a focus on gender rather than on women runs the risk of implying that men and women are equally important subjects of study, whose identities and experiences – as gendered identities and experiences – are of equivalent intellectual interest. This shift in approach carries with it the danger of making 'gender' a very individualistic and apolitical concept, obscuring the power relations which create the differences between the lives of men and women (Richardson and Robinson, 1994; Stabile, 1994). I have chosen not to take this approach, but to focus primarily on women and their relationship to technologies. By focussing on 'women' as opposed to 'gender' in the broad sense of the concept, I am choosing not to focus on men and masculinity. I am less interested in the gender relations of work and technology and their implications for men and masculinity than I am in the gender relations of women's work. Sexual divisions in the labour force are for me so central to its constitution that I have chosen not to engage in analysis of the conditions and relations of work for both sexes. This derives from a view of gender relations as involving not simply difference but inequality and power – male domination and female subordination. In that sense, my view of gender differs somewhat from that of some contemporary feminist accounts in which masculinities and femininities are mutually constitutive and equally interesting. In my view, the position of women in society, and in this case, in employment and in technology, remains one of pressing concern for feminist political analysis, and by no means an issue which has been superseded by gender analysis. For me, it is still the disadvantage which attaches to the position of working *women* – still confined at the bottom of hierarchies, in restricted sectors of the economy and often doing terrible jobs – which is the problematic requiring our attention.

This is not to say that gender relations do not enter into the discussion in this book at all. They are indeed a vital part of the picture, but only in so far as they shape or constrain women's positions in, and experiences of, work and new technologies. They are not the central focus of analysis in their own right. Thus, for example, the book addresses gendered divisions of labour, but it addresses them in terms of how these serve to allocate women to, and usually to segregate them in, particular occupational areas. It is the women who occupy these positions who are of central interest to me here. Similarly, I discuss the gendering of jobs, but in order to show how women come to perform tasks which carry the imprint of their socially constructed roles in the family and in the workplace, in other words, tasks which come to be sex-typed. The gendering of technologies themselves, a discussion of which forms part of this book (in Chapter 3), of course includes the role of men and masculinity. Men, male-dominated institutions, values and culture are central to the shaping of technologies, and thus to the relationship which women have to those technologies. But, again, it is *women's* relationship to technologies with which I want to deal, and I focus on the masculinity of technology only insofar as it illuminates this relationship, and not in its own right.

This, then, suggests an approach to gender which places structural inequalities between men and women at work and in their relationships to technology, rather than the representational or the individual, at the heart of the analysis. I would concur with Kate Figes when she argues that

> We have become preoccupied with the social and cultural manifestations of feminism, with representations of women in the media, with language, with sexuality and with the so-called war between the sexes. Fascinating though these issues can be, they are not the heart of the matter. They are reflections, consequences of the basic economic and political imbalance between the sexes.
>
> (Figes, 1994: 4)

Harding (1986) has proposed three aspects of gender: *individual gender, symbolic gender* and *the division of labour by gender*, and it is with the third of these aspects of gender that I am principally concerned in this book. A similar conceptualisation has come from a Swedish historian, Yvonne Hirdman, who has developed the concept of a *gender system* to denote the consistent segregation, disadvantaging and devaluing of women in all areas of social life (Hirdman, 1988, in Swedish, but quoted in English by Salminen-Karlsson, 1995; Sundin, 1995). The gender system operates in different ways at different social levels and Hirdman distinguishes three such levels: the cultural level (meanings of male and female), the institutional level (conceptions of gender in societal institutions of various kinds), and the individual level (conceptions which regulate interaction between individuals). It is expressed through artefacts, language, work, symbols, and so on, and in this book, I am concerned with its structural expression in artefacts and work and therefore principally with its expression at the cultural and institutional levels. Again, this is not to dismiss the importance of understanding individual women's experiences in the workplace, or the way in which their identities as women, in relation to technology, are formed. Nor is it to reject the idea that technological (and scientific) activities have become symbolised as overwhelmingly (though not exclusively) masculine in important ways which have a profound impact on women's access to skills, to technologies and to technological work. But it is to focus on the *systemic* nature of sexual divisions in occupations and technologies.

An emphasis on the gender structure, or the gender system at work, in the sexual division of labour, need not involve a reductionist or a static view of women's work with technology. As Cockburn and Ormrod (1993) have argued, women are not mere bearers of structures which are immutable. Sexual divisions of labour do not stand still, but are constantly being constructed and reconstructed, dismantled and 'remantled' through individual and collective action (1993: 6). Indeed, the central concern of this book is with the 'remantling' of women's employment through changes in the location, organisation and automation of jobs. Women have not stood passively by as computer-based technologies have been applied to all spheres of their work; women have engaged in various forms of resistance and other forms of industrial protest. Others have worked on projects of reconstruction, not only of the technologies themselves, but also of the masculinity of technological work, women's relationship to technologies, and the interface between computer systems and the design of their jobs.

Technologies and the gender structures which contribute to the shaping of women's work, then, are mutually constitutive (Cockburn, 1983; Cockburn and Ormrod, 1993). Neither are autonomous, immutable or determinate. Both are the outcomes of social arrangements, both with their roots in past human practice. Just as unequal power in the workplace and in society (including power and control over technologies) creates gender structures in which women are predominantly in subordinate employment positions, so too technologies are created out of social processes (including gender structures, relations and meanings) which are negotiated and struggled over between men and women, employers and workers.

For this reason, I also adopt the 'social shaping of technology' perspective, and I discuss the utility of this approach to a feminist perspective on the relationship between women and technology in the next chapter. The 'social shaping' approach defines technology as a social product, but it has a broader conception than technology simply being represented by physical artefacts (although these are important constituents and must not be ignored). Technology also comprises human activities and know-how:

> An object such as a car or a vacuum cleaner is only a technology, rather than an arbitrary lump of matter, because it forms part of a set of human activities. A computer without programs and programmers is simply a useless collection of bits of metal, plastic and silicon. So 'technology' refers to human activities, as well as to objects . . .
> . . . technology refers to what people *know* as well as what they *do*. Technology is knowledge . . . Technological 'things' are meaningless without the 'know-how' to use them, repair them, design them and make them.
>
> (MacKenzie and Wajcman, 1985: 3)

Because I regard technological systems and modes of work organisation as intimately interconnected, in this book human activities and know-how are as much a focus of the analysis as are the artefacts of technology. In the sphere of employment, the activities of men and women, management and labour, which are associated with putting technologies to work are those concerned with the division of labour (social and sexual), the organisation of work by management and the design of jobs and tasks, the wielding of power and control at work, and the allocation of skill labels, skilled status, prestige and rewards. Employees also play a part in shaping the development and application of technologies through their practices in the workplace, by organising in trade unions, by resisting managerial incursions into their control over their own work, and by excluding other groups of employees from access to 'skilled' positions. In these various aspects of work organisation, gender divisions and struggles are central, for example, in allocating men and women to particular jobs, in creating sex-typed work, in restricting access to technological expertise, and in allocating value to men's and women's respective activities. The exercise of power by men over women, as well as by capital over labour, and the allocation of value at the expense of women, are both implicated in technology. In the words of Game and Pringle, then, technology is ultimately the outcome of these 'social processes . . . designed in the interest of particular social groups, and against the interests of others' (1984: 17). This book is concerned with all these aspects of human activity which contribute to 'technology'. It is concerned with how computer-based systems in the workplace form part of, and become embedded within, these human arrangements and with the ways in which men's and women's work activities and work relations themselves are reshaped and reconstituted in the process.

Because technology is the outcome of social processes, including changing gender structures and human activities, it is continually shifting and changing. This is perhaps particularly true of information technologies, which have developed at an increasingly rapid pace over the past twenty years. It is also an important point for an understanding of the relationship between technological change and women's work. Technology is all too often conceptualised in terms of men (Wajcman, 1991). However, seeing technological change as a process, rather than concentrating on the finished artefact, restores an awareness of the centrality of women in technology; they are no longer passive recipients of technologies, as users, but important actors in the process of their development (Berg, 1994: 96). This allows for a feminist conceptualisation, in which the process of development of technologies continues through from design and into the sphere of use, and in which users (who are very often women) play a critical role in shaping technologies, an insight which is central to the social shaping of technology perspective (Fleck, 1988), as we shall see in Chapter 2.

The focus of this book is on computer-based technologies, and specifically those which have been introduced and applied in the workplace. Despite the technologies and social settings which this focus precludes, this is still an all-embracing category. Computer-based technologies have undergone considerable evolution since the first word processors were introduced into offices in the late 1970s. Computers have moved from monolithic mainframe systems administered by centralised data processing departments, to personal computers, to distributed systems linked together in networks. Tijdens (1994) has suggested that such changes in the configuration of systems are potentially very significant for women workers: they may signal the breaking of the stranglehold by data processing personnel over computing facilities, and an increasing ability by end users without any technical background to use their own systems to a certain extent in their own ways. On the other hand, however, it could be argued that a new era of centralised control over computing facilities is being ushered in with the development of computer networks, in which the data processing manager of old has been replaced by a new breed of controller, the network manager. Whether these differences imply substantial change in women's access to, and control over, their computing facilities, is uncertain.

The phrase 'new technology', convenient though it is, now seems inappropriate to describe a series of innovations which have been in use for two decades, and which actually include 'information technologies', 'communications technologies', and a whole range of devices in the office, in the shop and on the factory floor, and often all three areas connected together. In this book, I still sometimes use the term 'new technology' for its convenience, and I also refer to 'computer-based technologies', particularly in relation to manufacturing work, and 'information technologies', particularly in relation to office work. In fact, information technology has been defined as the 'interconnection of technical and organisational innovations in electronic computers, software engineering, control systems, integrated circuits and tele-communications, which makes it possible to collect, generate, analyse and diffuse large quantities of information at low cost' (EC, cited in Rees, 1992: 137), a definition which seems to include manufacturing applications. However, I have tried to distinguish these applications from office applications in the text, because in my view there is an important distinction between office applications in which information is the commodity being worked upon by women, and manufacturing or retailing applications, in which products and goods are the commodities they labour on. Nor am I concerned in this book with communications technologies such as the Internet or the so-called 'Information Super-highway'. There is certainly a growing body of feminist research which examines the use of such network technologies by women and by men, and gendered patterns of communication which are taking place over 'The Net'. Here, however, I am interested in new technologies and their interaction with women's work processes rather than with their patterns of communication outside the workplace, so I confine my discussion of network technologies to those which link workplaces or relocate women's work.

I have to acknowledge, too, that restricting the discussion in this book to one of paid work and of workplace technologies only has some attendant difficulties, of which I am only too aware. For a start, there is an increasingly blurred dividing line between the technologies in use in the workplace and those in use in the home. The telephone and the personal computer are obvious examples of technologies which have a role in domestic and leisure activities as well as in paid work, the constitution (including the gendering) of which is therefore informed by the social and gender relations of the domestic as well as those of the employment sphere (Moyal, 1992; Haddon, 1988). Others, such as the fax machine, indicate a move towards the home as the site of paid work itself, for particular types of employees. Indeed, the workplace, for a number of women, *is* the home, and this is in part a result of teleworking made possible by the capabilities of both information and communications technologies. Teleworking also signals a potentially increasingly intimate relationship between paid employment and the domestic sphere, certainly so far as women are concerned, given their difficulties in 'compartmentalising' their paid work from the demands of their families.

But there is also the more fundamental point that the position of women within the sexual division of labour, and their continuing confinement within a few sex-typed occupations, is in part a product of their position in the home. For domestic responsibilities restrict women's ability to participate fully in the labour market, and shape the kind of work for which women are deemed suitable. More than this, women's role in the domestic sphere is used to confirm and legitimate their marginal status in the labour market. Further, their family roles are often translated into workplace roles, so that women may often be found playing roles of wives and mothers to their colleagues (Benet, 1972; Pringle, 1988). Because women's domestic labour is undervalued, women in general are treated as unimportant in the work that they do and in the work they may aspire to do. Glucksmann (1990, 1995) has articulated the concept of the 'total social organisation of labour', in order to address this inter-relationship between women's paid and their domestic roles. However, I would concur with Liff's (1993) argument that gender segregation in employment is partly the outcome of processes operating *within* the workplace, the evolution of forms of work organisation and gender relations. In my view, the gendering of jobs cannot be reduced to a discussion of women in the domestic sphere, but must be seen as arising out of the interplay between their socially ascribed, and therefore shifting, roles in both the public and the private domains. In this book I have tried to make some of these connections, but my concern is first and foremost with the workplace, with the nature of women's paid employment and with their experiences of new technologies.

As I have already indicated, the main premise which underlies the structure of this book is that the gender/technology relationship is one in which a mutual process of shaping takes place. The book is therefore concerned first with the ways in which gender relations contribute to the shaping of technology and then with the role of technology in affecting women's jobs and gender relations at work. The progression of the discussion in the book reflects this approach. Chapter 2 sets the scene by examining the social scientific conceptual tools which are commonly used to analyse changes in women's work with technologies and which form the basis of the discussion in later chapters, in particular the concepts of labour market and labour process. It also examines debates on the relationship between women and new technologies, particularly feminist responses to technology, and discusses the body of work which has been most influential on my own thinking about this relationship and assessment of empirical research in this area. Chapters 3, 4 and 5 examine research by feminists and others into the dynamics of technological change and women's work. Of these, Chapter 3 deals with the gendering of computing. 'Computing', as I indicated earlier, is not only taken to mean computers as artefacts, but also the expertise and knowledge, culture and values of the computing profession, and the gender divisions and gender relations involved in the production of hardware and software. I also address the ways in which the application of new technology to women's jobs affects the pace and direction of technological change. Does the process of computerisation proceed more quickly when it is women's or men's work that is being automated? Does it proceed in particular ways depending on the sex of the worker? What agendas for the transformation of labour, as a sexually divided commodity, have informed the design and development of computer-based technologies? An examination of the ways in which various aspects of computing embody gender relations, which condition the processes and outcomes of new technological systems, forms Chapter 3 of this book.

In Chapters 4 and 5, the emphasis is reversed, and the impact of technological change upon gender divisions of labour and gender relations at work is examined. First, in Chapter 4, I consider the ramifications of new technologies for women's employment at a societal level, that is, for the broad structure, pattern and location of women's employment (and, to some extent, unemployment) and for the sexual segregation of occupations. To what extent have computer technologies contributed to a change in the level of women's employment? Is the pattern of women's work shifting from permanent to contingent forms of work such as part-time and temporary work, and if so, what is the role of new technology in this process? I also consider the issue of job (re)location away from traditional sites of employment in city centres, areas of industrial concentration and the industrialised world in general to suburban or 'peripheral' areas within the industrialised world, to offshore sites in the Third World, and to the home. In Chapter 5, I examine changes in work processes at the level of industries, occupations and firms, drawing upon case studies of the implementation of new technologies in selected key sites of female labour: in offices, in shops, in banks and in certain manufacturing industries. Here, I draw upon many of the insights and tools of analysis of the labour process perspective, but with a gender perspective that is famously missing from much work in the labour process tradition. In practice, the developments discussed in Chapters 4 and 5 are complementary; I have separated them analytically only for the purposes of my discussion.

Women are not only recipients of technological change in the workplace. In important ways, many have become directly involved in shaping the computerisation process in order to safe-guard, to promote, or to extend their interests (insofar as these can be generalised). In Chapter 6, I review some of the major feminist initiatives which have been launched as interventions in the computer systems development process. These are practical initiatives which aim to redress the exclusion of women from the process of systems development and which aim to address their needs as users more sensitively than 'conventional' methods of systems development succeed in doing. Here I examine the philo-sophical and political roots of such initiatives, and evaluate their success in developing truly novel artefacts and processes which are 'woman-friendly'. In Chapter 7, I review the lessons of this now substantial body of research into new technologies and women's jobs. What have been the overall trends in women's employment? Has the sexual division of labour been altered at all by the process of computerisation? Has the gendering of computing been challenged by the launching of feminist computer systems development projects? What have feminist perspectives on workplace technology contributed to other, 'malestream' analyses (such as labour process and social constructivism), and vice versa?

This book is of necessity a selective review of the research in this area. Women's employment and women's work alone are the subjects of widespread research, as is the subject of new technol-ogies at work. The task of this book is not to review comprehen-sively every single piece of work ever written, but more to highlight the major themes of debate and findings of feminist research. The book is intended to provide a resource which organ-ises and imposes some coherence upon disparate and necessarily incoherent material. My hope is that it has been able to do this in a way which illuminates the terrain and illustrates the direction being taken by feminist thinking on new technology.

CHAPTER 2

Perspectives on women's work and technology

In an era in which women's paid employment is assuming an increasingly important role within almost all economies and in which technological change at work is perhaps more rapid and pervasive than ever before, the task of understanding the nature of these developments and the relationship between them becomes ever more pressing. The nature and quality of women's paid work has long been at the heart of feminist thinking and writing. From the Industrial Revolution and the concentration of women in semi-skilled and unskilled factory occupations, to the exclusion of women from craft unions and therefore from craft skills, to the acceptance of women into engineering jobs during the First and Second World Wars and their subsequent expulsion from them, to their growing presence in offices and in the service sector occupations which were newly created in the twentieth century, these developments have all been explored and evaluated by feminists and other writers as part of their analysis of women's employment.

That analysis has come to include information and communication technologies and their place in women's working lives. It is almost a truism to state that since the late 1970s, the automation of work associated with the computer and associated microelectronic technologies has been one of the most significant features of employment, for both women and men. Comprehending the nature and experience of the work of women in the latter part of this century has therefore centrally involved an analysis of the nature of new technologies, the process of technological change and the rate and direction of technological innovation as it engages with women's work. This has meant developing an understanding of the social context (including the gender relations which surround the emergence and application of these technologies) as well as the employment effects of new technologies. Indeed, in the 'social shaping of technology' tradition, it is argued that only by understanding the social *context*, and consequently the social content, of technological development, (and this must include the gender relations involved in their generation), can we begin to appreciate the *impacts* of them (MacKenzie and Wajcman, 1985; Fleck *et al.*, 1987). This book is about our understanding of women's work in this era of techno-logical change, as the one shapes and is shaped by the other. What are the major features of women's work in the twentieth century and what is the contribution of new technologies to these? In the inequalities between men and women in the work-place, what is the place of technology? What are women's experi-ences of new technologies? And, as Wajcman has asked, does 'the problem' of women's relationship to technology at work lie in men's domination of technology, or is technology in some sense inherently patriarchal (1991: 13)? How does feminist thinking on technology address these issues?

In this chapter, I want to make explicit the concepts of women's paid work and of technology which underlie my discussion of empirical research in the rest of this book, both as technological change uses women's work and as it affects that work. What are the central theoretical issues being addressed in assessments of technlogy in women's work and, indeed, of women's work in technology? How do these conceptual approaches contribute to feminist understandings of technology?

Women in the labour market and the labour process

Women's paid employment, and their relationship in their work to changing technologies, can be understood in many ways. First, there is the position of women in the *labour market*. Women are, we know, contained within a very limited range of occupations in most advanced industrial societies (Hakim, 1979). This segre-gation operates both vertically and horizontally. Women work in particular industries – health, education, retailing, banking and finance, for example – away from men, and also consistently lower down the hierarchies of the occupations in which they are represented. Women are strongly represented in unskilled manufacturing jobs, service jobs (both in the public and private sectors) and in occupations which rely on part-time workers (Bradley, 1989; Rees, 1992). Women are segregated in the work-place to such an extent that the great majority of women work with other women, few entering into male-dominated spheres of work (Blaxall and Regan, 1976; Martin and Roberts, 1984). This gender segregation brings with it a persistent wages and skills gap between men and women, with women's pay on average still less than three-quarters of men's (Figes, 1994, CSO, 1995).

How has this widespread and enduring occupational segre-gation been explained? On the one hand, in radical feminist thinking, the home and the family are seen as the site of gender inequality, in which patriarchal power is established and maintained, and from which it is carried into the labour market. In this conception, women's domestic labour and their role in caring for family members serves to marginalise them as participants in the labour market and to confine them to a narrow underclass within it. Women are excluded from full participation in the labour market by men, both as employers who see women as only fit for a narrow range of work functions, and as trade unionists who develop exclusionary practices against women. On the other hand, in conventional marxist accounts, the sexual division of labour is constructed by capital in its attempt to secure supplies of cheap labour for certain elements of the production process. Here, the source of women's occupational segregation is narrowly located within the employment sphere itself. This kind of emphasis on the purely economic requirements of capital has the opposite problem from radical feminist accounts: here, the role of the domestic sphere is given *inadequate* attention in locating and understanding the labour market position of women.

Although the focus of this book is on gender divisions and gender relations within the workplace, these divisions cannot be explained by a narrow emphasis only on the behaviour of employers; neither can it be explained by focussing simply on the domination of women by men in the family. I take a perspective such as that offered by Eisenstein (1979), in which patriarchal and class relations are separate, but capitalism uses patriarchy and patriarchy is defined by capitalism, so that the two in effect draw upon one another and are mutually dependent. Such a perspective implies that the position and experience of women in employment can only be understood in the context of the wider social relations, not only of the family, but of the state and its policies, the education system and the provision of training, as well as of the social relations operating within the workplace itself. Moreover, it is worth noting that there are both material and ideological factors which contribute to the occupational position of women. For example, the level of childcare provision made by the state may serve to shape women's access to employment in general, while political ideology (sometimes supported by academic research) may contribute to popular notions about the acceptability of women working. Similarly, at the level of employment, occupational segregation rests partly on the objective skills possessed by workers, access to which has largely been denied women; but it also rests very strongly upon ideological processes which confirm the work of some (by no means all) men as skilled simply because it is men who do it (Phillips and Taylor, 1980), while conventionally defining the work of women as unskilled despite the dexterity they may exercise.

It is often pointed out by feminist writers (Game and Pringle, 1984: 15, for example) that a focus on social, or gender, *relations* implies social constructions forged in *relation* to one another; that is, negotiated and changeable, not static and fixed. This is indeed a critical factor to be understood in the analysis of the sexual division of labour and of women's position in the labour market, particularly in an era of technological change. The gender relations within the labour market and also within individual workplaces are in constant tension, and at no time perhaps more so than during a period when the instruments and processes of labour are also in flux. Additionally, in my view, a recognition of gender relations as the site of negotiation and struggle means acknowledging the two-sided nature of gender relations: the agency of women in the constitution of their labour market positions and experiences, as well as that of employers and of men. A problem with many accounts of the position of women at work is that they implicitly treat women as the passive recipients of employers' strategies, or of state policies, or of male domination. While clearly women at work, in periods of technological change, are, in the words of Cockburn, 'more impacted upon than impacting' (1992: 38), women's responses to these impacts also play some role in shaping their labour market position: in their collective organising in the workplace (Women Working World-wide, 1991) as well as in their individual acceptance or rejection of types of work which are numerically or culturally male-dominated. A recognition of women's agency in the shaping of their position and most particularly in their responses to their situation is in my view critical if analysis is not to lapse into another kind of determinism in which women are only objects and never subjects.

In developing an understanding of the work of contemporary women, then, we need to address the issue of whether their position in the labour market has *changed* with the diffusion of new technologies across the economy. Put more broadly, we can ask whether the process of technological change has in any way undermined the sexual division of labour which has conventionally allocated men and women to particular occupational groups at a societal level. And, if the material nature of work has changed with the application of new technologies, has this challenged the ideological basis for the sexual division of labour? To what extent, then, has women's occupational segregation persisted? On the other side of the coin, there is an extreme sexual division of labour in the construction of new technologies themselves. How does this affect the constitution and form of these technologies, and how, if at all, would they differ if the circumstances of gender relations in their construction was somehow other than it is?

What are the *potential* implications of new technologies for women's work which we need to be aware of? First, it has been suggested that women might serve as a source of disposable, flexible labour. It has been argued, for example, that the deskilling of jobs associated with the implementation of computer technologies allows employers to replace skilled workers with cheaper, unskilled ones, chiefly women and untrained young people (for example, Barker and Downing, 1980). This is a variant on the 'reserve army of labour' (RAL) thesis, which was formulated originally by Marx (1954) and refers to a section of the labour force which can easily be drawn into or repelled from waged work at a relatively low cost to capital. This concept has since been used to explain the subordinate position of women in the labour market, which is taken to result from their role in the family and in the domestic sphere (Beechey, 1977). According to this approach, women have been used as a cheap alternative to male labour, and following the introduction of information technology and the deskilling of skilled occupations, women may move into new areas of work formerly done by men.

With the implementation of new technologies, it has been suggested that women can be employed in previously male-dominated, but now deskilled, jobs. Hacker (1990) provides a more complex formulation of this thesis: women may be drawn into previously male craft jobs while they are being simplified, and then expelled when those simplified jobs are subsequently automated. The RAL thesis itself has been subject to sustained critique, on the grounds that women's jobs are so severely segregated from men's that the substitution of male with female labour would not be a straightforward process. Furthermore, women's wages are so much lower than men's that this discourages employers from expelling them from work. However, I examine empirical evidence for information technologies allowing employers to use women as a reserve army in Chapter 4.

The disposability of female workers has been postulated in another form in the 'flexibility debate'. Owing less to marxist conceptions of the behaviour of capital and more to the concept of the 'dual labour market' (Berger and Piore, 1980), the concept of flexibility outlined in the 'flexible firm' model (Atkinson and Meager, 1986) and in the theory of 'flexible specialisation' (Piore and Sabel, 1984) *suggests* (it does not always actually recognise the presence of women in the labour market) a growth in the marginality of female labour. Here, the concept of flexibility is not primarily linked to changes in technology (though the development of flexible automation is seen as supportive of flexible specialisation), but rather to asserted changes in the nature of global markets and therefore in the imperative for firms and economies to reorganise work and make labour more adaptable. This is discussed in rather glowing terms, as offering possibilities for the development of multi-skilled labour and new decentralised production arrangements. But the place of women in these accounts is as marginal workers, married or otherwise dependent on men, whose relationship to the labour market is temporary, uneven and lacking in commitment to work (Jenson, 1989).

The concept of flexibility has been roundly criticised on a number of counts, among other things because of its empirical inaccuracy and because of its ideological legitimation of the informal, secondary economy and the casualisation of labour (see for example CAITS, 1987a; Williams *et al.*, 1987; Pollert, 1988; Jenson, 1989). But a number of feminists have restored a critical discussion of the fate of women's work to the centre of the analysis, and have suggested that the casualisation of work done by women is indeed one of the key developments in the last two decades of the twentieth century, particularly in the United States and the United Kingdom (Walby, 1989; Appelbaum, 1987; Greenbaum, 1995). On the other hand, it is apparent that the use of part-time employment, self-employment, temporary employment and other forms of 'contingent work', which in the flexibility literature are portrayed as being on the increase, are by no means new, certainly not so far as women are concerned. Moreover, the sexual division of labour which places women in semi-skilled and unskilled occupations appears to have changed little, suggesting that any skill gains offered by flexibility have accrued more to men than to women (Pollert, 1988; Jenson, 1989).

Do concepts like the modified RAL or flexibility have anything to offer feminist analysis of trends in women's labour market position in a period of technological change? Do we need other, or new, conceptual tools? The concepts of both the RAL and flexibility have their problems, but I draw attention to them because they both also capture something of the problematic nature of women's relationship to the labour market, and in particular their vulnerability to its vicissitudes under capitalism. The problem lies in their failure to focus beyond the labour market and to locate women's labour market position within the domestic sphere too. In addition, both concepts have an implication of sea-change which may not capture the reality of many women's vulnerability in employment over a considerable period.

My own conceptual approach aims to be both dynamic and complex; to capture incessant change and determinacy from various sources. Analysis of shifts in the sexual division of labour and in the consequent labour market position of women must recognise both continuity and change (Lovering, 1994), and there are also complexities associated with the application of new technologies. The labour market position of women does not have simple antecedents to start with, but is conditioned by many interacting structural and cultural features of twentieth century capitalism. Product markets, the demand for labour, the provision of education and training, the availability of childcare, the employment practices of companies, the exclusionary practices of trade unions, the sex-typing of occupations, and the responses of women themselves to these various conditions all play an important role in shaping, and continually reshaping, the position of women within the labour market and their access or otherwise to particular jobs. Similarly, the process of technological change itself is a profoundly uneven one, with temporal, sectoral, and spatial variations which confound attempts to analyse changes in the work of either sex in a simple or a linear fashion (Elger, 1987; McLoughlin and Clark, 1988). Given these substantial complexities, reducing the discussion of women's work in this period of technological change to one-dimensional analysis is unlikely to be helpful. It is important not to lapse into an essentialism in which technological change affects women's work in the ways that it does simply *because* it is women's work. The gender division of labour and the consequent work situation of women – like gender relations overall – are, as I have already argued, continually being socially constructed, and technological change is a part of this process of construction (and destruction). Furthermore, it is important to recognise the differences between different groups of women, as well as the similarities, for their experiences of new technologies will be as various as women themselves are, in their class position, ethnicities, family circumstances and in many other structural aspects of their lives. These differences and this unevenness – both of situation and of technological outcomes – are illustrated in the discussion of empirical research studies contained in Chapters 4 and 5.

Many feminist studies of technology, including my own, have their origins in industrial sociology, and in particular, in the *labour process* tradition. Labour process thinking is central to analysis of women's work in contemporary capitalism. Moreover, it remains so after many years and considerable debate about its utility for understanding sexual divisions, as opposed to simply class divisions, in the workplace. Debates on the labour process, and on the utility of the concept as a device for understanding the daily detail of work, became widespread after the publication of Harry Braverman's *Labor and Monopoly Capital* in 1974. Braverman in turn drew this concept from Marx's writing, but applied it in the context of changes in the nature of work in the twentieth century, in particular the increasing routinisation of work which he saw as being brought about by scientific management and the scientific-technological revolution. A wave of 'labour process literature' ensued on both sides of the Atlantic, the central concern of which was to analyse developments in job design, skills and management control in various industries and occupations, thus refining the 'labour process perspective' as an explanatory framework for understanding the behaviour of management and labour in constructing work (Zimbalist, 1979; Thompson, 1983; Knights and Willmott, 1990). However, the labour process debate was male-dominated and gender-ignorant: case studies examined 'men's' jobs (for example, in mining, metalworking and other skilled areas of manufacturing), and failed to recognise that many of the characteristics of these jobs (including craft competences and skilled status) were decisively gender divided. They also overlooked the gender relations of technology; technological development was seen solely in class terms, a product of attempts by capital to control the means of production. They recognised the ways in which capital sought to dominate labour through the application of technologies, but ignored the exclusion of women from technology through the gender division of labour and the male domination of skilled work and technical know-how (Arnold and Faulkner, 1985; Cockburn, 1985a; Wajcman, 1991). Finally, they also failed to explore the ways in which technologies were differently applied to men's and women's areas of work, and had a tendency to regard technologies as rippling uniformly through the workplace (Karpf, 1987).

Since these early studies, feminist research has attempted to address this male bias in several ways. First, it has offered a corrective to the predominance of studies which focussed exclusively on the work processes of men. A series of workplace ethnographies in the labour process examined the organisation of work done by women in various spheres of employment, for example, in temporary office work, electrical goods manufacturing, motor components assembly, cigarette manufacturing and hosiery production (McNally, 1979; Herzog, 1980; Cavendish, 1981; Pollert, 1981; Westwood, 1984). Such studies were principally concerned with the oppressive conditions in which women work in unskilled jobs across a range of industries, the intensity with which their labour processes are organised, and with the ways in which they also cope with the burden of families and home. Unlike conventional labour process research into men's work, these studies revealed that women's experiences of, and responses to, the factory regime could not be seen separately from their wider lives: the domestic and the employment sphere combined to shape their world. Though these studies were not specifically concerned with the implementation of computer technologies, in highlighting the specific ways in which women's work is organised and controlled, they offered important insights into women's relationship to production technologies. Pollert's (1981) study of a tobacco factory and Cavendish's (1981) research into the production of components for car assembly both reveal a strongly gendered division of labour based on assumptions about women's 'natural' manual dexterity and their lack of aptitude for handling technology. Pollert describes a strongly segregated long-established division of labour between the highly mechanised, capital intensive tasks performed by men and the non-mechanised, labour intensive work performed by women. In Cavendish's study, the work performed by women, though requiring a considerable degree of manual dexterity, was defined as less skilled than men's work. The contribution of these studies, aside from their ethnographic value, was to call early attention to women's exclusion from technologies, technical know-how and skill. They also served to warn of the vulnerability of women workers in low-grade, low-paid occupations, labour-intensive work which, according to Armstrong (1982), is inherently more insecure than capital-intensive work, due to short-term changes in demand and to long-term pressures for automation.

The concept of the labour process is conventionally used to analyse the detailed features of work and the experiences of workers. A number of central elements recur in labour process analyses: work tasks and their constitution (including the routine of repetitive or fragmentary work tasks), skill use and control over the method and performance of work (including the deskilling of particular jobs and the application of technologies), the intensity of work and the degree of effort exercised by workers in the course of their work, and the level and type of control exercised by management over labour and the labour process. In this sense, then, the labour process is generally understood in terms of a set of structural features which can be identified and described. Feminists with an interest in the labour processes in which women commonly work are concerned with more than these features, however. As well as uncovering the conditions of women's jobs, the gender content of jobs is also central to feminist analysis. A key issue in feminist labour process research has therefore been to develop an understanding of *how* women's work comes to be done by women, that is, how it comes to be sex-typed and what the gender characteristics of sex-typed jobs are. The sex-typing of jobs is traced to the occupational segregation of the sexes within the labour market, which, as we have seen, is in turn variously attributed to the imperatives of employers and to women's reproductive role within the family. But the *expression* of this sex-typing within the workplace is also a central theme in feminist labour process research. Thus, according to Bradley (1989), if occupational segregation by sex is a structural process, then the sex-typing of jobs is the ideological (and, we might add, the cultural) face of that process. The

stereotypes which employers and workers alike call upon to justify occupational segregation by sex, the gender labelling of vacancies, the gender labelling of work with particular characteristics
and the creation of work cultures redolent with gendered roles
and practices – all these have been the subject of labour process
analysis by feminists.

Much of the gender content of women's work seems to relate
to what has been termed 'the production of people' (Murgatroyd,
1985, quoted in Bradley, 1989: 9). By this is meant activities which
contribute to the caring and servicing of others. In the majority
of societies, women are mainly responsible for these activities on
an unpaid basis in the domestic sphere, but in the sphere of wage
labour they often perform commercialised forms of servicing
activities (Bradley, 1989: 9). Thus, the sex-typing of women's jobs
is in part an expression of the playing of domestic roles in the
workplace, a process by which it comes to be seen – by employers
and employees, women and men alike – as appropriate to link
women with these activities within the workplace, because they
perform them outside the workplace. Feminist research into secretarial work, for example, often emphasises the operation of
familial relations within the workplace, so that a secretary may
play the role of 'office wife/mistress' to her boss, notoriously
making him cups of coffee and running domestic errands on his
behalf (Benet, 1972); or she may be cast as a surrogate mother/
nanny, providing emotional support and anticipating his needs, or
even as dependent daughter in a supplicant role (Pringle, 1988).
Lower down the office hierarchy, in the typing pool, women are
linked with a somewhat different, but nevertheless servicing, role
– that of the 'dolly bird/whore' (Barker and Downing, 1980). The
content of many women's jobs, and the overall culture of workplace relations, reflects this translation of women's domestic
labour into the sphere of employment. The domestic aspect of
secretarial labour is now well-known, and in jobs like teaching
and nursing, women are performing obvious domestic functions
as part of their everyday routine.

The sex-typing of jobs as appropriate for women, and their
association with particular gender characteristics, derives not only
from women's reproductive role within the domestic sphere, but
is also the upshot of processes taking place within the sphere of
employment itself. Women's jobs have become sex-typed through
persistent historical employment discrimination crystallised into
the jobs. Thus, in a number of industries, the fast and fiddly
work, the boring work, the sedentary work, or the dirty work, all
of which would deter men, is seen as suitable for women (Game
and Pringle, 1984; Lovering, 1994). Vacancies in these types of
work become gender-labelled. Equally, men contribute to sexual
segregation in workplaces by resisting the entry of women into

their own preserves, either through trade union exclusion (Cockburn, 1983) or simply through collusion with employers that mixed sex teams would be distracting to men (Lovering, 1994).

If technologies are an important element in the shaping of work organisation and work processes, then labour process analysis of women's work has been concerned to examine the role of technological change not only in shaping the structural aspects of women's work, but also in affecting the culture and ideology surrounding women's jobs. New technologies have implications for women's work at both these levels. At a structural level, they potentially affect work tasks and the range of operations which a woman carries out in the course of her working day, the degree of skill and discretion which she is able to bring to bear on her work, the intensity with which she works, and the type of management control which is exercised over her. At the cultural level, the implementation of new technologies may also have important consequences for the gender content (of which servicing tasks are an element) of the work that women do, and for the gender relations of their workplaces. It has indeed been suggested, for example, that the application of new technologies represents an attempt by management to challenge the gender content of women's work in the office, and to replace the old inefficient patriarchal relations of control of both women and men with more direct, technical control (Barker and Downing, 1980). Chapter 5 examines empirical changes in women's labour processes at both these levels.

It is worth pointing out here that feminist thinking on the labour process has undergone something of a shift from its origins in this respect. The focus on women's work grew out of a concern to remedy the sex-blindness of the analysis of Braverman and his followers. However, many feminists now argue that it is not sufficient to simply 'add women in' to conventional labour process analysis (see for example Cockburn and Ormrod, 1993). Instead, it is argued, an understanding of the *gender* relations of work is necessary in order fully to comprehend the dynamics of technological and other forms of change, for it is only by focussing on gender that we can appreciate the ways in which men, and relations of domination and subordination are implicated in the position and experiences of women at work and in the development of technologies. Much feminist research now places 'gender', rather than 'women', at the centre of the analysis of changes in work. In this book, as I have already pointed out in Chapter 1, 'gender' is used to denote sexual divisions of labour and social relations between the sexes, but only as these shape the position of women and not to illuminate the condition of men.

However, the broader feminist emphasis on 'gender' has been important in framing feminist thinking on what we might call 'the technology question'. That is, it has allowed us to unpack the gender relations at work in the constitution of technologies, and thus to examine critically the content and formation of technologies themselves, rather than taking them as given and/or locating the 'problem' with women. This approach enables us to see both technologies and their gender relations as the outcomes of social struggles. It also offers a way out of the impasse which used to dominate feminist thinking on technology, the debate over 'whether the problem lies in men's domination of technology, or whether the technology is in some sense inherently patriarchal' (Wajcman, 1991: 13). Feminist thinking on technology addresses itself to this dichotomy, and to moving beyond it.

Feminisms confronting technology

There is, in fact, not one feminist perspective on technology, but several feminist perspectives, differing in their approaches to the relationship between gender and technology. These perspectives have been exhaustively reviewed in many places (for example, Karpf, 1987; Hacker, 1987; Wajcman, 1991; Van Zoonen, 1992; Morgall, 1993; Grint and Gill, 1995). This book is not centrally concerned with charting the various feminisms of technology as they are elaborated in theoretical terms; rather, it is concerned with assessing the contributions made by empirical studies of new technologies and women's work. Here, I want to situate my own approach within the work of other feminists and to identify the concepts which I have found useful for an understanding of technological change in the lives of women.

To this end, it is, however, worth briefly noting that feminist approaches to technology have generally been categorised as being either liberal feminist, eco-feminist or socialist feminist. These perspectives differ in their views of the nature of technology, the nature of women, and the nature of the gender/ technology problematic. In liberal feminism, technology is taken as given and not subjected to critical analysis, but it is seen as being conventionally dominated by men. In this formulation, the problem lies with women and their sex-typed social roles which create socially accepted notions of what kinds of activity are appropriate for them. Liberal feminism has been highly influential in social policy initiatives, particularly in Britain, where the solution to this situation has predominantly been approached through campaigns to encourage women into technological careers (Henwood, 1993).

In eco-feminism, technology is seen, not as neutral, but as

masculine in its very essence, an outcome of the masculine imperative to control women and nature (which are seen as synonymous because of women's child-bearing capacity). This is most clearly visible in military technologies, and in technologies which destroy the environment in other ways. In the eco-feminist account, the analysis depends entirely upon dualist, essentialist categories of women and nature, men and technology which are redolent with biological and technological determinism (Gill and Grint, 1995). It is also politically disabling because it sees no possibility for women to be agents in shaping technologies (Van Zoonen, 1992).

Both liberal feminist and eco-feminist perspectives have repeatedly been declared to be profoundly unsatisfactory as explanations of the technology/gender relationship (and I count myself among their critics). A third framework is provided by a socialist feminist approach to technology (also dubbed a 'technology as masculine culture' or 'feminist constructivist' approach by Gill and Grint (1995)). This approach conceptualises capitalism and patriarchy as part of a system in which each uses and is defined by the other, such that the sexual division of labour is as central to capitalism as wage labour is, while capitalism is also a defining feature of the sexual division of labour (Eisenstein, 1979; Game and Pringle, 1984). The current sexual division of labour and associated gender relations of technology are therefore historically specific, but a central feature of modern work; conversely, the organisation of wage labour in general is central to the positioning of women themselves. This perspective, then, helps us to uncover the interplay between the position of women as workers, the organisation of their work, and the development and application of technology within the context of contemporary capitalist society. Moreover, unlike the insights of both liberal feminism and eco-feminism, it allows us to acknowledge work-force divisions along the lines of sex (and, we might add, race), but it also reminds us that women are not a cohesive social group simply because they are women. Class and race differences affect their position in the labour force, the work that they do, and their experiences of technological change.

Socialist feminist analysis draws on historical insights into the ways in which, in advanced industrial societies, men have come to dominate technology, and women have come to be excluded from it, from technological know-how and from skill (Cockburn, 1983; Arnold and Faulkner, 1985). And this account again stresses the interplay of capitalism and patriarchy: during industrialisation, the (not necessarily compatible) interests of employers and male craft workers resulted in the progressive mechanisation of skilled trades but the maintenance of a male monopoly over the emerging competences which were required to operate new machinery. Women's exclusion, fostered deliberately by the craft unions, was established and continues to underpin the social relations of technology today. Wajcman has written that: 'Industrial technology from its origins thus reflects male power as well as capitalist domination' (1991: 21). Shaped by male power, technologies 'bear the imprimatur of their social context' (Karpf, 1987: 162), embody patriarchal values, and have become intimately related to masculine culture. Some (but not all) cultures of masculinity have in their turn come to be strongly defined by technological competence (McNeil, 1987b; Murray, 1993). Because this perspective is informed by an historical analysis of the development and use of technology, it demonstrates the specific ways in which technology comes to have its association with men and masculinity, and thus technology emerges in contemporary advanced industrial society as the upshot of struggles between those with power and those without – between capital and labour, and between men and women. Here, technology is not taken for granted or black-boxed, and neither is masculinity and male domination; unlike other explanations, it therefore does not lapse into either technological determinism or biological essentialism.

Moreover, in assiduously demonstrating the specific ways in which, through historical practice, men's and women's relationships to technology have been shaped, this perspective avoids dualist dichotomies. For, although these may be conceptually tidy and linguistically neat, their compartmentalising does not allow for ambiguity: contradictory scenarios, or people who cannot be fitted into dualist categories, for example, women who *do* possess technical competence (Gill and Grint, 1995). Such dualisms tend to suppress thoroughgoing attempts at analysis, and they are profoundly disempowering to the development of new strategies for addressing women's relationship to technology in the workplace (Kirkup and Keller, 1992; Green *et al.*, 1993a).

The role of women's own agency in formulating their relationship to technology must be recognised. Both liberal feminist and particularly eco-feminist accounts have a hopelessness about them: in the first, the main agents for change are public policy makers and campaigners, but not ordinary working women who are seen as simply responsive to policy initiatives; in the second, technology is so hopelessly infused with masculine domination that women can only opt out altogether. Yet as Gill and Grint (1995: 21) have forcefully argued, for many feminists (myself included), the enduring inequalities in men's and women's relationships to technology require explication as part of the emancipatory project – to understand whether and how women can take control over the technologies in their working lives and thus challenge their subordination under capitalist patriarchy.

In assessing the shaping of women's work and of the technologies which they confront in their working lives, I view women's relationship to technology as one of exclusion through embedded historical practice, reinforced and reproduced in contemporary work settings. Women at work suffer the double oppression of being both workers and women, contending with two interlocking systems of domination in which capitalism and patriarchy are by turns prominent in dictating the conditions of women's work. This subordination is reflected in women's relationship to technology (over which capitalism and men struggle for control). But women – both individually and collectively – also resist their subordination and exclusion from technologies. Cultures of women's resistance at work are commonplace, as women find ways of stealing back time and space for themselves from the relentless incursion of managerial and masculine domination (Barker and Downing, 1980; Pollert, 1981; Cavendish, 1981). And women *are* actively challenging their exploitation collectively, in trade unions and in more informal groups of workers with common interests (Women Working Worldwide, 1991). The possibilities for intervention by women in the development of technologies more closely geared to their needs and requirements are also recognisable, as we shall see in Chapter 6, and feminist initiatives have been launched in a number of workplaces worldwide. These are hopeful indications of the potential for countervailing trends to be set in motion by women against what might otherwise be the juggernaut of capitalist patriarchy.

This conception of the relationship of women to technology also draws on the 'social shaping of technology' perspective, derived from the insights of a range of conceptual traditions, including the sociology of scientific knowledge, the sociology of industry, and evolutionary economics (MacKenzie and Wajcman, 1985; Williams and Edge, 1992). This perspective, though traditionally somewhat gender-blind, looks for the social interests and social relations which lie behind the development and use of technological systems. Developed as a challenge to technologically determinist accounts, it argues that innovation is not simply a technical-rational process of solving problems; it also involves building alliances of interests, deploying expertise, enrolling actors (and they tend to be male in conventional social shaping accounts), and negotiating over outcomes. Different actors possess differential, socially-defined levels of expertise. Technological changes are not, therefore, linear processes, but take place across networks of actors in an iterative way. Although the social shaping approach asserts that existing technologies are important preconditions for new technologies, it also argues that equally the form and content of technological change is amenable to *social* analysis. The social relations of technology, then, foster or inhibit particular paths of technological development, so that 'the evolution of a technology is thus the function of a complex set of technical, social, economic and political factors' (Wajcman, 1991: 23).

The 'social construction of technology' (SCOT) approach developed by Bijker *et al.* (1987) is particularly concerned with technological *artefacts* as social constructs, the outcome of nego-tiation between social actors, both human and non-human. It too challenges the 'linear model of innovation', and suggests instead a 'multidirectional' model, in which the development of an arte-fact is marked by negotiation over a range of possible technologi-cal variations, some of which die while others survive (Pinch and Bijker, 1987). Relevant social groups attach meaning to the arte-fact, because they are individuals, institutions and organisations with interests which help to explain its pattern of development. Conflicts occur between different social groups and also between different technical options, and various solutions – either technical or social and moral ones – are possible. The flexibility in the design of artefacts and the variations in the meanings attached to them by social groups are termed 'interpretative flexibility'. However, artefacts ultimately become 'stabilised'; that is, they undergo closure and become fixed in their design for a time until a challenge to that particular technological configuration is made (Pinch and Bijker, 1987: 40–44).

This approach suggests that the process of development of a technology is a long-run affair. The construction of the artefact undergoes numerous iterations in numerous spheres of design and use as competing designs are interpreted, reinterpreted, applied, discarded and stabilised. Nevertheless, despite a clear awareness of the role of 'relevant social groups' in constructing the artefact, the social constructivist approach in its original formulation focus-sed quite narrowly on the design stage and the early development of an artefact (Mackay and Gillespie, 1992; Kline and Pinch, 1995). Yet technological development proceeds beyond the design process; artefacts and technological systems are crucially and sometimes radically reshaped while they are being implemented and used. Fundamental innovations occur as a result of the activi-ties of users, as technologies are, consciously or unconsciously, configured and reconfigured to suit the circumstances and interests of those involved in their implementation (Fleck, 1993; Suchman and Jordan, 1989).

Research into the social shaping and social construction of technologies has examined the social interests implicated in the development and use of a number of technological systems, from machine tools, to robots, to microprocessors, computer hardware and software. Although there are clearly gender relations involved in the evolution of these technologies, they have often been overlooked. Social shaping studies have also been largely unaware of the social relations involved in the development of technologies with which women are more closely associated. However, the social shaping perspective offers a very significant potential for feminist or gender-aware technology analysis.

Focusing on women in social studies of technology

Social studies of technology have, in the main, been concerned with the initiatory moment – invention, innovation. The principal actors therefore have been scientists and engineers, and those entrepreneurs and authorities they must draw into an effective alliance if their technological project is to move forward. Such is the sexual division of labour that few if any women are to be found among these actors. The white-coated scientists, the hard-hatted engineers, the grey-suited business executives – these are almost all men. Women are invisible in the mainstream technology studies partly because of their actual absence from the network as there defined.

(Cockburn and Ormrod, 1993: 9)

First, emphasis on the social relations involved in the creation and development of technologies implies the importance of sexual divisions. Even if these have not hitherto been treated as such, there is a strong argument for requiring that they are articulated as central to the analysis since they represent a central dimension around which societies are organised. Second, the social shaping perspective places a firm emphasis on the construction and enrolment of expertise in the process of technological development, and this coheres with feminist arguments that expertise is gendered and women are largely excluded from social definitions of skill and know-how in technological work. Third, and crucially, the social shaping approach attaches considerable importance to the sphere of technological implementation as a site of innovation, where users 'struggle to get the technology to work in useful ways' (Fleck, 1988: 3). Here, the local contingent knowledge and practices of users provide a proving ground for technologies and thus often the basis for further innovations. Suchman and Jordan offer a similar conceptualisation, but from a feminist perspective, when they state that:

Both design and use of technology involve appropriation. Where technologies are designed at a distance from the situation of their use (as most are), there is an inevitable gap between scenarios of design and circumstances of use. Inevitable, because to some extent technologies have to be designed for unknown users, in unknown circumstances. To get off the ground, designers need to project a scenario of use, the adequacy of which will depend on the adequacy of their understanding of the actual situations of use. However adequate the designers' understanding, the gap will exist and will have to be filled by the user as the technology is interpreted with respect to local concerns and circumstances. *In this sense, design is only fully completed in use.*

(Suchman and Jordan, 1989: 154 my emphasis)

Recognition of the sphere of use as a site where technological development continues to take place makes the role of women and of gender relations in the evolution of artefacts much more visible. Women may be largely absent or marginalised from the design and creation of IT systems in the early stages of their development, but they are very strongly involved in their consumption and use. Feminist thinkers have strongly emphasised the importance of users in the shaping of technologies, albeit mainly in relation to the role of users of domestic technologies (Cowan, 1987; Cockburn and Ormrod, 1993; Berg, 1994; Silverstone and Hirsch, 1992). As far as the workplace is concerned, a similar benefit derives from shifting the focus of analysis beyond the sphere of design. It reveals women and their work, and illuminates the ways in which designers often create IT systems with women's work and gendered divisions of labour firmly in mind. It also allows us to see the ways in which women may actively intervene to configure and deploy the information technologies which they use at work and so leave the imprint of their gender identities at work upon them.

With a few notable exceptions (for example, Arnold and Faulkner, 1985; Wajcman, 1991; Cockburn and Ormrod, 1993; Webster, 1993), the 'social shaping' and 'social constructivist' approaches, while relating the content of a technological artefact to the wider social milieu within which it develops, tend to prioritise the role of powerful groups and individuals, and fail to see the divisions in the social world which marginalise some groups of actors (Winner, 1993). Recognition of gender and ethnic divisions is a particular weakness of these approaches (Liff, 1990; Horn, 1994), an omission which is all the more surprising given the extreme sexual division of labour to which, as we shall see, the creation and consumption of all technologies, particularly information technology, is subject. Attending to this omission has been a key feature of feminist analysis of technologies.

Nevertheless, there remain strong differences of approach, and areas of mutual disagreement, between feminist analyses and social constructivism. Against feminist writings on technology as masculine culture, some of the most sustained critiques have come from recent writings on the social construction of technological systems. In their discussion of the gender/technology relation, for example, Gill and Grint argue that there is an essentialist draft in this approach, because 'men', 'males', 'masculinity' and 'patriarchy' are treated as interchangeable, taken as given and not fully explicated (1995: 12). Similarly, they point out that asserting the masculine culture of technology does not address the issue of precisely how this cultural connection between masculinity and technology is reproduced, and by what mechanisms it perpetuates women's alienation from and domination by technology (1995: 13–14).

This would seem to be an issue for feminist empirical research, and it is an objection which is increasingly being addressed in such research. Studies of the design of artefacts such as the computer (Van Oost, 1992; Shaffner, 1993), of the culture of software production (Tierney, 1995), of the gender relations in the production and use of the microwave oven (Cockburn and Ormrod, 1993), and of the sexual division of labour and organisation of work in the manufacture of electronics (Pearson, 1989; Women Working Worldwide, 1991), all explore the specifics of the translation of abstract masculine culture into concrete technologies, and all chart the particular mechanisms by which women's alienation from these technologies is perpetuated. It would seem that this is a task which can only be undertaken meaningfully at the empirical level, for at the theoretical level it must remain a question of assertion rather than of demonstration. The more feminist empirical research which is carried out in this sphere, then, the more the mechanisms of translation between masculinity and technology can be explicated.

It has also been suggested that 'anti-essentialist' approaches, of which a socialist feminist perspective is one, fall into a trap of *social* determinism (Grint and Woolgar, 1995). In social determinism (as opposed to technological determinism), the effects of technology follow directly from the politics built into the technology. As far as the gender relations of technology are concerned, this argument implies that the capitalist and patriarchal interests which shaped the development and use of industrial technologies and which continue to create a masculine culture of technology, directly result in oppressive effects and experiences of technologies for women. In other words, then, to borrow a phrase from Bob Young (1977), 'technology *is* gender relations'.

This, however, represents a very simple reading of the feminist argument. Much feminist analysis recognises and emphasises the fluidity and variability of the gender relations which inform the development of technologies, and particularly, as we shall see in Chapter 3, the ambiguous nature of masculinity in this respect (Wajcman, 1991; Murray, 1993). In fact, one of the major contributions of recent feminist thinking has been its stress on the complexity of social categories and on the fact that gender

relations arise from *processes* of social construction and interaction rather than being fixed and given (Game and Pringle,
1984; Cockburn, 1992). Like technologies, they are negotiated
and struggled over, but not on an equal basis.

It is my view that structural explanations of technological development continue to offer clear insights into the gender relations
of technology. These focus upon the economic imperatives of
capital and the material interests of patriarchy, the sexual divisions in technological development and use, the exercise of male
power in relation to women at work and the ways in which these
influence the culture of workplaces, the discourses of gender and
technology, and women's experiences of working with technologies. Thus, both gender relations and technologies are constructed as part of these contexts, and not in free floating or
voluntarist ways which are completely autonomous from the
power, inequality and discrimination operating in advanced capitalist societies. Indeed, some social constructivist and feminist
analyses of technology suffer from the opposite difficulty. They
have moved so far into a relativist focus – on identities, subjectivities and interpretations – that they have become deeply indi-
vidualist and apolitical in their explanations. This must surely be
of concern to feminists seeking to analyse the gender relations of
technology partly in order to assess the potential for change. I
would support Kirkup and Keller's critique of

> ... epistemological relativism ... (which) suggests that there are
> as many truths as individual people and that no single truth has
> any claim to be better than any other ... As a position it runs
> counter ... to the aims ... of feminism of the 1970s and 1980s.
> Feminism as a theory, and a political movement, claims that there
> are 'facts' and 'realities' about the position of women, such as rape,
> domestic violence and unequal pay that are a key to understanding
> sexual oppression and that these have been hidden or distorted.
>
> (Kirkup and Keller, 1992: 10)

Consequently, there are elements of feminist theorising about
women, gender and technology which are not explicitly incorporated in this book. In particular, as I indicated in the introduction,
the concepts of gender identities, gender representations and symbols, and the subjectivities of women have become more central
in feminist analyses of the technological experience, for
example, in the work of Haraway (1985), Harding (1986) and
Smith (1987). While I take the position that both technologies
and gender relations are constructed through the activities
and experiences of real individual people, and therefore that
these analyses are very important, I prefer to see those people's

activities and experiences as profoundly grounded in their social contexts – in their work, industry, family, home and the structures of their everyday lives. My perspective privileges these structures and regards cultures and representations, identities and subjectivities as part of, but not separable from, them.

It will be apparent, then, that this book does not set out comprehensively to review all the available theoretical perspectives – feminist or otherwise – on the gender relations of technology. Rather, the perspectives presented in this chapter are those which I have found helpful in selecting and illuminating the empirical material covered in the rest of the book. They are *my* chosen frameworks for understanding the issue of women's relationship to technology in the sphere of paid work which is raised by the steadily accumulating body of empirical research in this area. Ultimately, this book is concerned with evaluating this research in order to shed light on a series of central empirical questions. How do sexual divisions of labour and gender relations of technological work shape the construction and use of information technologies? Through what mechanisms and processes do information technologies come to be gendered, if at all? Are gender relations discernible in actual technological artefacts? What is the role of information technologies in the major contemporary developments in women's employment? How have information technologies affected the detail of women's work, their labour processes? And finally, in what ways can women take charge of the development of technologies in the workplace and how effective might their initiatives be?

These are the central questions which the research discussed in this book has addressed. They also raise a number of related questions. To what extent, for example, can we generalise from the experiences of technologies of women in advanced industrialised countries to those elsewhere in the world? And are the developments in women's work which are described comparable across countries? What are the important variations between women's work in different countries, those which make a significant difference to their experiences of employment and of technological change? And what variations, if any, are to be found between the experiences of women of different classes and races within the same country? Further, are the major developments in women's work peculiar to *women's* work, or are there similarities in the current fates of working women and men?

Finally, we have to evaluate the lessons of research on women and technology in the workplace in terms of the wider intellectual progress to which it contributes. How do the gender relations of technological change in the workplace interact with the other social relations at work? And after two decades of feminist research into technologies at work, will this work at last be brought in from the cold and incorporated within broader social perspectives on the social circumstances surrounding the development and use of information technologies in the period around the turn of the millennium?

CHAPTER 3

Gender relations in the shaping of technologies

The masculinity of technology

Science and technology – the knowledge which constitutes their epistemological fields, the people who inhabit these fields, the artefacts they produce, and the cultures they spawn – are, in a variety of ways, more determined by, and reflective of, the interests of men rather than women.

(Woodfield, 1994: 2.1)

In order to understand how the relationship between gender and information technology in the workplace operates in practice, I want to attend to two aspects of this relationship. First, there are, of course, the ways in which information technologies have affected the sexual division of labour, women's employment, labour processes, gender relations within workplaces, and women's experiences of automation. These are concerns which have been thoroughly investigated, by feminist researchers and by others concerned with changes in work and technology.

However, as we have seen, technologies do not simply have effects (on work, on society, the economy). Their constitution and evolution within a social, and sexually stratified, context has to be interrogated. However, at the moment, the class, and particularly the gender, relations shaping technologies remain less well understood than do the impacts of technologies upon class and gender relations. In this book, I analyse the relationship between technologies and gender relations as a two-way relationship, in which each helps to constitute the other. Indeed, gender relations must be regarded as the context within which information technologies are evolving, assuming the mark of their social and gendered context, and in turn acting upon this gendered social context. I therefore find it appropriate to start by considering the role of gender relations in shaping information technologies, before examining the impacts of information technologies on gendered patterns of employment and gender relations in the workplace.

In this analysis, I draw on the 'social shaping of technology' approach, which emphasises the social relations involved in the development of technologies. This perspective was central to the evolution of my own, and many other feminists', thinking about technological applications in the office and in other work-places, though unfortunately most social shaping studies pay, as I have commented, too little attention to the *gender* relations involved in the creation and consumption of technologies. Yet feminist studies, many of them undertaken outside the social shaping tradition, demonstrate that gender relations and divisions are indeed firmly embedded in the creation and development of information technologies. First, gender divisions of labour are central to the *process* of technological development, in the occupational segregation of the IT industry and in the deployment of female labour in particular parts of the IT production process. Then, the *products* of technological development carry a gender imprint on another level: they are designed for particular categor-ies of work which are sexually segregated (like secretarial work), and the gendering of this work may appear in the construction of the artefact. Thirdly, information technologies are introduced into particular industries and firms within specific contexts of male and female labour use and differentiated managerial control. Such contextual features condition the rate and direction of tech-nological change in these workplaces, often leading, for example, to patterns of IT implementation which are different in sites of women's work from those in relatively expensive, conventionally 'skilled' men's work. It is with these three aspects of the gender-ing of information technologies – the processes, the products and the pace and direction of their implementation – that I am con-cerned in this chapter.

Gender divisions of labour in the construction of IT systems

The processes of production and application of information tech-nologies are at every point shot through with sexual divisions of labour. We can grasp the extent and meaning of the sexual divi-sions operating in the creation of IT by considering the influx and representation of women within the different jobs involved in developing IT systems. IT systems are developed, and therefore IT workers are found, in the computer industry, and also within other sectors, including banking and finance, manufacturing, public services and government.

In the design of IT systems, women are noticeably absent. In Britain in 1991, only 10 per cent of the professional membership

Table 3.1 **Women in IT jobs in the UK**

	Females as % of all		Average age		Female earnings as % of Male	
	1994	1993	Male	Female	1994	1993
IT manager	4	4	45	43	90	90
Other manager	9	8	42	38	92	93
Systems	20	20	38	35	91	91
Analyst Programmer	23	22	33	33	97	98
Programming	23	23	30	31	96	96
Technical Support	11	12	36	34	87	88
Customer Services	28	27	35	33	81	81
Operations	14	14	32	31	88	90
Average	22	21	35	33		

Source: Virgo, P. (1994) *The Gathering Storm: 1994 IT Skills Trends Report*, p. 35.

of the British Computer Society were women, and only 3 per
cent of data processing managers, 20 per cent of senior systems
analysts and 25 per cent of programmers, were women (Beech,
1991). Apart from exceptional cases like women's own small
businesses, or cases like the British company, F International,
which was set up by women to provide consultancy work in
programming and systems analysis, women are still under-represented in IT professional and management jobs (Shapiro, 1994;
Sonnentag, 1994). A survey of women in the industry carried out
by the Women into Information Technology Foundation in 1995
has found that 27 per cent of female employees are trainee
programmers, 28 per cent are junior analysts or designers, and 20
per cent are analysts or designers. Only 20 per cent of development managers are female (*Computing*, 18 May 1995). And, while
men make up around three-quarters of computing professionals,
women occupy nearly two-thirds of electronics assembly jobs.
Nearly 60,000 assemblers in the UK industry in 1991 were women;
32,000 were men (OPCS, 1991). Table 3.1 shows the representation of women in IT jobs in the UK in 1994.

The picture is similarly negative in other countries; for example,
in the Netherlands, women make up less than 15 per cent of the
work-force in computer professional posts (Tijdens, 1991; Falck
et al., 1991). Even in the United States, where federal action
was taken in the 1970s to get companies to improve their equal
opportunities records, and where women's representation has
therefore been increasing during the 1980s, women still only constituted 34 per cent of analysts, and 36 per cent of programmers
in 1990. In Singapore, where there has been concerted state
directed IT training, women are strongly represented (58 per cent
of analyst programmers and 52 per cent of analyst designers in
1987), but disappear from view almost entirely at management

level (Kheng, 1989). Even in Scandinavia where the representation of women in the industry has traditionally been comparatively high, it is now declining (Blomqvist *et al.*, 1994).

In the lower echelons of the industry abroad, as in the UK, sexual and racial segregation is marked. In the United States, 60 per cent of white men in computing occupations were to be found in the top two categories of computer scientist and programmer in 1983; 42 per cent of black men were in these jobs, but only 23 per cent of black women were represented there. However, 77 per cent of black women and 76 per cent of white women were in operator and data entry jobs (Glenn and Tolbert, 1987). By 1990, the representation of white women in these occupations was falling, but black women's share of data entry work had risen (Henwood, 1993).

Of course, over the past two decades, significant changes have taken place in information technology, and thus in the organisation of work in the computer industry. The occupational field is much more diverse than it was in the early days of computers, and a range of new IT functions has emerged within user organisations, including that of a new type of IT manager, the network manager. In addition, a distinction between systems analysis (which is business oriented) and programming (which is technical) has emerged. Meanwhile, the data entry jobs which in the past have been almost entirely dominated by women have slid into obsolescence, while software engineering is now carried out by women, not in the West but in India and other parts of south east Asia (Cast, 1995). There work is subcontracted by the big IT companies to local software houses, and organised along regimented rather than craft lines. In this situation, none of the conventional justifications about the work being unsuitable for women because of its technical content are invoked. Companies recognise the advantages of drawing upon female labour where this is highly qualified and less costly than in the West, but this recognition does not appear to signal the implementation of equal opportunities in the industry overall.

Despite these changes in the organisation and location of computing work, women's position in computing work remains marginal and problematic. A decade ago, Game and Pringle (1984) advanced a number of explanations for the absence of women from computing. First, they argued that the field has a maths/science image which restricted the entry of women but not that of men. Second, they suggested that the computer represents power and control, and that this makes computing particularly attractive to men and particularly alien to women. Third, they pointed out that the industry, though relatively new, has quickly developed its own sex-typed jobs and that these jobs, once sex-typed, have tended to stay that way (Game and Pringle, 1984:

83). Have these factors in the exclusion of women from computing endured into the 1990s, and what additional factors can we
identify in this process?

Research certainly indicates that the gender segregation of
computing work continues, and may even have worsened since
the early days of computing. Have the reasons for this gender
segregation persisted? In order fully to understand (and presumably to address) the reasons for women's *numerical* under-
representation in the field, as Game and Pringle's analysis implies,
we have to examine the *culture* of computing and its alienating
effect upon girls and women. Indeed, as Henwood has argued,
simply increasing the numbers and proportion of women in computing is a very small part of the solution to the 'women and
technology problem' (1993: 35–6). The culture of computing is
alienating to girls and advantageous to boys from primary education onwards, and even before. (The collection of articles in
Kirkup and Keller (1992) provides an invaluable discussion of
the educational factors disadvantaging girls in computing.) In
particular, the location of computing in science and maths classes,
the pupil/computer ratio, the practices of teaching staff and the
conduct of computer clubs have been identified as contributing
to the advantaged position of schoolboys in computing (Hoyles,
1988; Newton, 1991). By the time students reach university, patterns of gender segregation are firmly set, with men far more
likely than women to take up computing at degree level (Gerver,
1989). In Britain, the proportion of female entrants into computer
science degrees is low in the first place; moreover, it steadily
dropped from a low starting point of 24 per cent in 1978 to 13
per cent in 1989 (Rubery and Fagan, 1994: 39). Female students
now make up around 20 per cent of computer science under-
graduates in the UK (Higher Education Statistics Agency, quoted
in *Times Higher Education Supplement*, 29 September 1995).

It is not simply a question of the way in which computing is
taught in schools and universities, or of the fact that computeing
has an image synonymous with mathematics and science which
restricts the entry of women, as Game and Pringle suggest.
Women do enter computing occupations, albeit in relatively small
numbers. However, the structure and culture of employment
within the industry inhibit women's participation in the profession. Women experience discriminatory conditions of work,
an informal culture which they find difficult to penetrate, and
disproportionate stress at work when they do penetrate this culture. Studies by Strober and Arnold (1987), Kraft and Dubnoff
(1983) and Donato and Roos (1987) show that, in each computing
specialism, women's salaries in the US IT industry are on average
71 per cent of men's. There are also substantial disparities
between the earnings of black women and white women in

equivalent occupations (Glenn and Tolbert, 1987). In the UK, a survey carried out by the British Computer Society revealed a salary range of £16,000–£20,000 for women, and a ceiling of £25,000 which did not exist for men (Beech, 1991). This situation is not improving with the passage of time; pay differentials between men and women are in fact continuing to widen (Virgo, 1994: 35).

Furthermore, even where women have acquired comparable (and sometimes superior) IT qualifications to their male counterparts in school and higher education, these skills alone do not necessarily guarantee career progression in the IT industry. Instead, this career progression, particularly at managerial level, seems to be heavily dependent upon informal processes within companies including informal promotion criteria such as 'fitting in' and informal promotion procedures such as networking (Shapiro, 1994). The ways in which men and women learn of these informal processes – men acquire the information as part of their tacit knowledge while women rely on the help of a sympathetic manager – disadvantages women in IT career progression. Woodfield's (1994) research in a software R&D unit in the United Kingdom found that the women were subject to a set of expectations about their natural skills and abilities in which they were assumed to play an indeterminate supportive and palliative role within the process of systems development, facilitating the more productive abilities of their male colleagues. If they did not do so, then they were perceived to be failing at their jobs in ways which the men were not, but at the same time, these non-technical skills were not recognised or rewarded. Their non-technical skills were regarded as natural and were also trivialised. Their male counterparts were able to represent their own interpersonal skills as evidence of their 'hybrid' qualities and so were able to gain managerial recognition and promotion within the organisation.

The importance of a workplace culture which privileges men is also highlighted by Tierney (1995). She identifies a range of informal practices and relationships in software companies which are helpful to career progression and from which women are largely excluded – the lunchtime drinks in the pub to which only men are invited, and the networking amongst the 'lads' – critical parts of getting on and going up in the IT world. In addition, male bonding, conversations, swearing and sexual jokes serve to exclude women from social interactions between IT staff and thus from important sources of information about career progression and opportunities (Cockburn, 1985a). Men in the computer industry have even been found to form exclusive clubs playing commando-type games in local woodlands at weekends (Grundy, 1994). In the IT world therefore, men are groomed and ready for a career which depends less upon formal IT skills and knowledge than we might expect and much more strongly upon adherence to a set of informal 'rules of the game'.

It comes as no surprise, then, to find that men are much more strongly represented in senior IT jobs than women. This is borne out by an insider's account of the industry in Silicon Valley, in which it is stated that women have found it so difficult to get into the senior ranks of companies there, that the two women who first achieved vice-presidential status in Microsoft were in fact hired away from Apple at a time when Microsoft was under federal scrutiny for possible sex discrimination (Cringely, 1992: 115). (This situation has since changed with the appointment of a number of women, including Bill Gates's wife, to senior management positions. However, these appointments were not well-received by male colleagues, who are said to have resented deeply the incursion of so many women into senior posts there. Numerical representation of women clearly does not guarantee a woman-friendly corporate culture.) Moreover, even in equivalent senior jobs to men, women perform fewer complex and responsible tasks involving managing and organising teams, and attend fewer formal and informal meetings where crucial design decisions are taken. They therefore experience such work less positively than men, and they tend to miss opportunities to be influential and to demonstrate their competence (Sonnentag, 1994).

Throughout the computing hierarchy, women are on alien territory. Indeed, the culture and practice of the computing profession is redolent with a myriad of forms of masculinity. This seems to be particularly apparent in programming, where, in the West at least, the work is organised in ways which make it foreign to women. But programming has not always been a male preserve. In the early days of computing in the 1940s and 1950s, programming and operating were not strongly segregated tasks as they are today, and women were to be found in programming/operator jobs. Women worked, for example, on the US military computer, ENIAC, during World War II (Lloyd and Newell, 1985; Van Oost, 1992). Programming was assumed to be similar to clerical work and therefore suitable for women (Donato and Roos, 1987; Van Oost, 1992). A rare reference to women programmers justified their suitability for this work in much the same way as their suitability for menial manual work is often asserted today:

> It has been said that computer programming is the job for the future and the best programmers are intelligent girls who are good in embroidering because they have the patience and conscientiousness that is needed.
>
> (Het Vrije Volk, 1966, quoted in Van Oost, 1992: 242)

Subsequently, women disappeared from programming/operator work. The two functions became segregated and women were concentrated in the latter. In the former, in the 1960s and 1970s, the notion of programming as a craft developed, and the apprenticeship route of the 'master (*sic*) programmer' recreated patterns of skill acquisition and employment which were first established in the manual trades during the Industrial Revolution and which were explicitly developed to exclude women. The programming function, like so many other crafts, was subsequently taylorised and subdivided, and with the deskilling process, women began to re-enter a narrowly defined range of computing occupations (Greenbaum, 1976; Kraft, 1977). As we have seen, many IT companies now subcontract this work to software houses in the Indian subcontinent. However, in the West, men continued to dominate the senior and specialist professional areas of computing: systems analysis, operations research and programming.

Programming is now characterised by a different culture of masculinity from the craft culture. The programmer is now a 'hobbyist' or even a hacker (Turkle, 1984; Håpnes and Sørensen, 1995), in that he acquires skills and knowledge not through systematic training but on a voluntary and informal basis. There is a machismo about working individually, without helping or co-operating with fellow programmers (Hayes, 1989: 84). This kind of activity seems to be based upon an almost obsessional technophilia which is deeply antithetical to social interaction and relationships. Weizenbaum likens the computer programmer to the 'mad scientist', a 'compulsive' person who pathologically 'play(s) out his fantasies' (1976: 126). Emotional stimulation and addictive kicks are gained from working intensely on projects, over long and odd hours under stress in a hermetically sealed world. The 'project mentality' revels in urgently chasing 'milestones, deliverables and objectives' in almost seige-like conditions (Murray, 1993: 73). In Silicon Valley, this 'pressure cooker' ambience in the computing workplace gives programmers 'an addictive sense of control' which substitutes, apparently, for drug use (Hayes, 1989: 83). It also sometimes seems to be geared more to the construction of masculinity than to actually creating output, for Cringely (1992) argues that most of the long hours worked by Microsoft programmers are unproductive, but staying late in the office doing little or nothing has a symbolic importance (as it does in a number of 'masculinized' private sector professions (Collinson and Collinson, 1995)). In some settings, programmers create their masculine self-image by displaying an extraordinary level of élitism and aggression towards the end users of their products, by referring to them as 'peasants' or 'blockheads' (Grundy, 1994: 354). Such sociopathic behaviour has been linked with masculine inadequacy in interpersonal relationships. Easlea

(1983), for example, traces this to men's inability to give birth, while Hacker (1990) suggests that there is a psychological connection between the fascination of the adult engineer with the workings of inanimate objects, and disappointments with family and social relationships in early childhood. For her, the creation of technology is an erotic experience for male engineers, reflecting their desires and 'shot through with passion and excitement', not at all the 'epitome of cool rationality' which it is generally supposed to be (Hacker, 1987: 188). Many women who do work as programmers in the industry actively rebel against this type of relationship with computers; they fight against the emotional thrall of the machine, and distance themselves from its seductive potential by insisting that it is 'just a tool' (Turkle, 1988: 50).

Hippie programmers and nerd programmers

Hippie programmers have long hair and deliberately, even pridefully, ignore the seasons in their choice of clothing. They wear shorts and sandals in the winter and T-shirts all the time. Nerds are neat little anal-retentive men with penchants for short-sleeved shirts and pocket protectors. Nerds carry calculators; hippies borrow calculators. Nerds use decongestant nasal sprays; hippies snort cocaine. Nerds typically know forty-six different ways to make love but don't know any women.

(Cringely, 1992: 22)

Although there are certainly some female nerds, the vast majority are male. As Shaffner (1993: 84) points out, although 'nerdiness' is acceptable in technically skilled men because it is simply taken to mean that they are eccentric, there is no socially acceptable role of female nerd, so women gain no social status from joining a nerd group. In fact, both hippy and nerd cultures are not only alienating but also, and presumably this is the point of Cringely's description, deeply repugnant to many women. Like all technical cultures, they develop systems of language, jargon and meaning which function to bond members together and to exclude non-members (Bloomfield, 1989). These may give emphasis to the degree of technical expertise involved in computing in ways which exclude outsiders, or they may involve aggressive imagery and terminology (Woodfield, 1994). Vehviläinen's female systems developer describes herself as a 'non-entity' (literally, 'no thing') within this world, so unable is she to define the work she does in the terms of the dominant computer systems jargon (1994b: 111). Cockburn (1985b) has suggested that the culture of computing is so unattractive to many women that they opt to reject this kind of work altogether, and this claim is certainly supported by surveys of women increasingly rejecting computer science courses (Hoyles, 1988; *The Rising Tide*, 1994; Blomqvist *et al.*, 1994). According to Turkle (1988), this is not technophobia, but reticence to enter a culture of masculinity that elevates the machine to an object of intimacy. However, as well as being unattractive to them, the structure and culture of computing work is also incompatible with many women's lives. In much computing work, the separation between working hours and leisure time disappears, and the two become seamless (Avner and Gunnarsson, 1992, quoted in Mörtberg 1994: 139). For men without domestic responsibility, this is not a problem. However, many women, for whom 'personal leisure' is not a commodity at their disposal at all, cannot let their paid work encroach into their unpaid time. Responsibility for homes and childcare do not sit easily with the long hours and intensive activity which are characteristic of much of the computing profession.

> At Microsoft, it's a "disadvantage" to be married or "have any other priority at work", according to a middle manager who was unlucky enough to have her secretly taped words later played in court as evidence in a case claiming that Microsoft discriminates against married employees. She described Microsoft as a company where employees were expected to be single or live a "singles lifestyle", and said the company wanted employees that "ate, breathed, slept, and drank Microsoft", and felt it was "the best thing in the world". . . . The real wonder in this particular episode is (. . .) that the manager involved was a woman.
>
> (Cringely 1992: 114–5)

If being female and having a husband is a 'disadvantage' here, how much more disadvantaged are married women with children, elderly family members, or other responsibilities who cannot or do not wish to lead a 'singles lifestyle'? It would seem that even in companies where there is no overt discrimination of the type practised by Microsoft, the work culture favours staff without domestic responsibilities. This is as true in Europe as it is in the United States. Research into software development in Germany and Switzerland reveals that the bulk of female project team leaders are childless women (Sonnentag, 1994). On the other hand, the kind of computing work to which women *do* have access is, according to Grundy (1994), 'messy' and concrete work which is similar to domestic childcare – the work of matching computer systems to reality and attending to the needs of end users. This is work which is often unpredictable, is very concrete and involves considerable organisational labour. Grundy likens messy work to raising children who have unpredictable needs, or to providing secretarial support for a male executive, but in the computing world the father/executive is the programmer who performs pure and abstract labour. In the sexual division of labour of computing, the 'pure' and abstract tasks are monopolised by men and are symbolic of 'proper' work in the public domain.

The 'purity' of abstract computing work

There is a kind of 'pure', abstract computing work which is unadulterated and prestigious and in which men get intensely involved. To move away from this world of pure computing to the real world in which the end-user works, is to move to work which is no longer pure because it is tainted by the demands and exigencies of the more ordinary, work-a-day world. Men see it as their right and prerogative to work in this rarified world of 'virtual reality'.

(Grundy, 1994: 356)

Masculinity, or rather 'masculinities', are central, then, to the construction of technologies. They are also central to the construction of technological know-how. Technologies are created through social processes and negotiations, and so too is the expertise which gives some people and not others access to them. In craft work, men's jobs have come to be defined as 'skilled', because the workers in these jobs have historically organised strongly in defence of their interests and have striven particularly hard to restrict entry (by young workers, or by women workers, or by those not following the strict apprenticeship route) to their line of work. By the same token, women's work, no matter how much technical dexterity is involved (and technical dexterity is one indicator of skill) is not conventionally defined as 'skilled' precisely because it is women – who have been excluded from skilled status – who perform it (Phillips and Taylor, 1980). Technical know-how has similarly been acquired, and largely monopolised, by men at the expense of women (Cockburn, 1985a); at the very least, our culture is redolent with *assumptions* that men are technological and women are non-technological (McNeil, 1987a: 193). Once acquired, even if only ideologically, technological expertise becomes a key source of men's power over women in the sexual division of labour in the IT industry, in the IT development process, in the workplace more broadly, and in society generally. In IT, men dominate access to and expertise about the inner workings of the machines, both hardware and software, though women may use considerable technological competence and technical dexterity in operating information technologies. But using technical dexterity or having contingent knowledge about the operation of computers is not enough to confer power on women if the key to power is flexible, transferable skills and if these are still the property of men (Wajcman, 1991: 39).

> **Gender divisions in technological expertise**
>
> With few exceptions, the designer and the developer of the new systems, the people who market and sell, install, manage and service machinery, are men. Women may push the buttons, but they may not meddle with the works.
>
> (Cockburn, 1985a: 11–12)

This masculine affinity with technology is not inevitable. It is the product of the social constitution of male gender identity, which revolves around technical prowess, and in the case of working-class men, often also physical prowess associated with shopfloor culture (Lie, 1995). This process of appropriation of technology by men has an enormous historical sweep. Cockburn (1985a) traces it back to the late Neolithic period, in which women's position as technologists was first usurped by men. Arnold and Faulkner (1985) identify the Judeo-Christian tradition as the seedbed for the linkage between science/technology and men. In both accounts, women's role in technological work throughout history is shown to be highly sex-segregated, culminating in their deliberate exclusion from technological know-how by skilled working-class men and their unions during the Industrial Revolution, an exclusion which set the stamp on the masculine monopoly of industrial technology and which has been perpetuated in one form or another until the present.

However, today, as in the past, this linkage is not an unambiguous one. Technology, and particularly information technology, is, as we have seen, something which is constantly evolving, and so the connection between technology and masculine gender identity must constantly be remade. Equally, there are many different versions of masculinity and they too are constantly changing. For example, as shopfloor employment for men decreases and service sector work increases in the West, so too that particular cultural tradition which links the dirt and noise of the shopfloor with technical work and technical prowess may be weakened and may ultimately be broken. Also, the broad concept of 'masculinity' is cut across by class and ethnic differences, and not all versions of male gender identity are marked by technological competence. It is worth noting, by the same token, that not all women have an identical relationship to technological knowledge (Wajcman, 1991); many have technical training, and some work in technical professions within the computer industry, as programmers or systems developers. But mostly, as Cockburn's comment suggests, they are the operators rather than the creators of and 'meddlers' with technology. As far as male gender identities are concerned, even where affinity with technology *is* central to them, this can be problematic. Hacker (1989) has, as we have seen, pointed to the power and erotic pleasure which men derive from engineering and technological activity, as they strive to control the natural world. Yet this quest for domination can be viewed in another light. The very personal inadequacy which makes many men feel comfortable with inanimate things and with technological knowledge confers a vulnerability upon their search for a 'controllable world of secure, certain and maintainable boundaries' which renders the partnership of masculinity and technology a troubled and an ambiguous one (Murray, 1993: 78).

Oppositional categories of 'human' (female) and 'technological' (male) do little to advance our analysis of the gender and technology relationship, forcing us as they do back into static, essentialist and technologically determinist assumptions which fail to uncover the *social* processes by which many men come to have an intimacy with technology while women largely experience estrangement from it (Green *et al.*, 1993a; Henwood, 1993). It is important to show, not only the workings of the association between masculinity and technology, but also *how* this association has come about, for it is not an inevitable linkage or one that has necessarily always existed. As we have seen, socialist feminist approaches to information technology point to the historical processes by which men appropriated production technologies and their institutions during the Industrial Revolution (Arnold and Faulkner, 1985). For them, from these beginnings has developed an association between masculinity and technology which endures throughout industrial capitalist society. I want to suggest that this relationship has not automatically been sustained in the case of information technology, but has had to be constantly created and recreated, and has involved struggles between employers and employees, as well as between men and women.

Clearly, a gendered division of labour has developed and a set of meanings has emerged which link competence in information technologies in similar ways to those in which they appropriated technologies during the Industrial Revolution, and they have again created an advantaged category of labour from which women are largely excluded. But, just as capitalism struggled to undermine the basis of conventional craft labour and to constantly deskill and replace it with cheaper forms, so in the information technology world a struggle has taken place over the nature and location of computing work. Employers have constantly sought to rationalise the process of production of computers. First, they have reorganised and deskilled it, such that programming, for example, which carried with it connotations of masculinity, power and prestige, has now been stripped of much of its autonomy and control and become largely formulaic. Second, employers have supported and sponsored initiatives to get women into the computing profession, perhaps partly because of the cost savings offered by employing women rather than men. As we have seen, such initiatives, however, have met with very limited 'success', due not only to opposition of the male incumbents of professional computing jobs but also to the marked reluctance of many women themselves to enter this, to them still unattractive, world. Third, the grip of white Western men on computing jobs has been loosened by IT companies relocating software production to the Indian subcontinent and south east Asia, where the labour force is well-educated but much cheaper to employ than in the West. The relationship between masculinity and information technology continues to be renegotiated, as men in the West are displaced by women in the East and South. However, there are some parts of the process of production in computing in which women in the Third World have always been participants, precisely because they have provided cheap and efficient labour power. It is to the role of these women in computing that I now turn.

Women in IT assembly

Within the global production of electronics, there has always been a sharp sexual division of labour between men, who are principally involved in the design, development, marketing, selling, installation, management and servicing of systems in the First World, and women, who are most strongly represented in low-skilled assembly work, often located in the Third World. The use of female labour for assembly operations in factories owned mainly by foreign capital and producing for the world market has been termed the 'new international division of labour' (Fröbel *et al.*, 1980). However, this concept does not fully illuminate the complex interplay between sexual and locational divisions of labour at work. Production conditions vary from country to country (with particular differences between those in electronics plants in the First World and those in the Third World), and women's labour power is released and utilised in varying and often very particular forms (Pearson, 1986).

Nevertheless, there are some generalisations that can be made about the role of female labour in the process of producing IT goods. Women are to be found doing very specific and specialised tasks with the production process, working for electronics companies which have located their assembly operations in cheap labour areas of the world and in Free Trade Zones: south east Asia, China, India and Latin America. The so-called Tiger countries, in particular, offer a number of financial and infrasturctural inducements to inwardly-investing electronics multi-

Table 3.2 **Stages in integrated circuit production**

Stage	Location
1 *Design of a new circuit* The precise location of each element in the circuit and the connections between them.	*Europe/USA/Japan*
2 *Production of masks* Each mask represents an individual circuit layer and contains hundreds of identical images next to one another.	*Europe/USA/Japan*
3 *Fabrication of wafers* (a) Production of pure silicon crystal. (b) Slicing into wafers roughly 0.5mm thick. (c) Etching of the patterns contained on the masks onto the silicon wafer using photolithography techniques and a variety of chemical 'dopants'. The complete device is built up in layers. (d) Separation into individual chips and mounting into separate package.	*Europe/USA/Japan*
4 *Assembly of integrated circuit* (a) Bonding or wiring of circuits to external electrodes using extremely fine wires. (b) Sealing of packages.	*SE Asia*
5 *Final testing and shipping*	

Source: Dicken, 1992: 321.

nationals, of which female labour is an important element. Apart from the open financial systems without limits on the repatriation of profits and the often excellent transport and telecommunications infrastructures of the Tiger economies, labour in these countries, and particularly female labour, is attractive to corporations which see women workers as cheap, docile, non-unionised, and apparently easily manipulated into performing the boring and repetitive tasks that constitute the assembly process in microelectronics.

The international sexual division of labour works very simply. Electronics components undergo three principle stages in the production process: design, fabrication and assembly (see Table 3.2). They can undergo these successive processes in quite separate parts of the world; there is no technical necessity to locate them geographically close to one another. Design, integrated circuit mask production, and fabrication normally take place in the IT company's host country, require scientific, technical and engineering labour, and are processes predominantly carried out by men. Fabricated components are then air-freighted across continents to assembly plants in Third World countries, assembled into final products by unskilled or semi-skilled women workers, and air-freighted back to their major markets (usually in the West) for final testing, packaging, marketing and distribution. The high-skill, high-knowledge content elements of the production process are retained in the 'host' countries of the electronics firms, while the low-skill operations are sited in Third World countries which offer an attractive and flexible labour force (Henderson, 1989; Goldstein, 1989).

The assembly process in the Third World, then, is the sphere of information technology production in which women *are* strongly represented. In Malaysian plants, for example, 90 per cent of all workers are women, and women similarly dominate the Indian computer industry (Women Working Worldwide, 1991).

Women's assembly work in an electronics company in Japan

Hiroko's first job was bonding integrated circuits. Transistor chips were bonded to aluminium bases 1–2 cm square, then wired and hatched to them. This wire is only 0.25 microns thick, so that this must be done under a microscope. Since it is very delicate work, workers wear white laboratory coats and slippers to prevent outside dust from getting in. Only the microscopes are well lit; the walls are painted light green and the rest of the room is kept as dim as possible. The eyes look constantly through the microscope, moving the mirror with the left hand manipulating the machine with the right. The bonding process is repeated about a thousand times in one day.

(Women Working Worldwide, 1991: 148)

The sexual and the international divisions of labour work in tandem: in one company with plants in France and Brazil, 76 per cent of unskilled assembly workers are Brazilian women, while just one French male is employed. On the other hand, only 7 per cent of supervisors and technical posts in the two countries are filled by Brazilian women; 56 per cent are filled by French men (Hirata, 1989). In Motorola in Malaysia, the work-force is mainly Malay or Indian, from lower classes and castes. Of the 4,500 people employed in the company there, there are 3,500 women, concentrated in assembly and clerical work; the 1,000 men are employed as technicians, engineers, materials handlers or administrators (Women Working Worldwide, 1991). Women may be present in the IT industry, but largely in functions in which their skill, technological know-how or job prospects cannot be developed. Assembly work in the industry is routine and repetitive, commonly involving bonding wires into integrated circuits, or slotting tiny components into final products.

Increasingly, however, the task of bonding wires manually is being automated and handled by computerised production technology, leaving the operator with the tasks of loading machines, monitoring the movement of batches, unloading machines, and in exceptional circumstances, repairing defective chips. And as the transport to and loading of machines is increasingly performed by robots and conveyor belts, even these activities are disappearing (Goldstein, 1989).

The IT companies prefer to employ women in Third World countries for routine assembly operations for a variety of reasons. First, they are cheaper to employ than both their western and their male counterparts. Women doing IT assembly work in the Third World typically earn the same amount in a day as western women in similar work earn in an hour (Fuentes and Ehrenreich, 1983). Hirata's (1989) comparison of wages in a French multi-national's French and Brazilian plants shows that in unskilled assembly work, Brazilian women earn around 25 per cent of what French men and women earn, and 86 per cent of what Brazilian men earn, thus experiencing the cumulative disadvantaging of the international, the social, and the gender divisions of labour (Hirata, 1989: 137–8). Second, for those processes within assembly which continue to be performed manually, companies require manual dexterity and good eyesight from their employees, and they conventionally assume that women have the 'nimble fingers' and patience necessary for the microscopic assembly of minute components. As Elson and Pearson argue, a 'nimble mind' – aptitude and alertness – together with a capacity for endurance and concentration are also important attributes for IT assembly work, yet they have come to be devalued in women because of their subordinate status in society (1989: 2). Third, women's productivity is generally higher than men's working under the same conditions (Pearson, 1986). Fourth, the IT companies see women, particularly those from the south east Asian countries, as docile and easily controlled by management, as well as less likely to organise themselves in trade unions.

This docility is not necessarily an inherent characteristic of female labour in the Third World, but one which has to be created and maintained by employers in order to keep the costs of labour as low as possible (Pearson, 1986). Companies deploy various mechanisms for maintaining control over this female labour force, for keeping it flexible and responsive to changing market conditions, and for keeping it cheap. In Korea, 'short-term' women workers are typically employed by the industry only for the couple of years before they marry, and in Thailand they are employed on 10–20 day contracts, on the basis that they can be more easily fired in response to changes in market demand, and they are less likely to organise (Women Working Worldwide, 1991). However, there is now ample evidence of militancy and resistance, as strikes and industrial action have occurred through-

out south east Asia (Women Working Worldwide, 1991). Third
World women have not entirely been the passive victims of multinationals' strategies (Elson and Pearson, 1989), despite the industry's attempts to *construct* them as a particularly docile labour
force.

Many IT companies located in the Third World prefer to recruit
young, unmarried women with no children, and preferably with
no plans to have children, though there are variations in their
recruitment policies in line with the availability of local female
labour (Pearson, 1986). Some exercise a policy of compulsory
retirement for their women workers when they reach twenty-five
years old, while others insist that they move from full-time to
part-time work when they reach middle age. Japanese companies
on 'Silicon Island' in the rural area of Kyushu, however, make a
point of recruiting 'older' women (35–44 year olds) for part-time
work in certain production line functions. ('Part-time' work in
many of the SE Asian electronics companies in fact differs little
from full-time work; in Japan the only difference is that part-time
workers have no employment contract, while in Taiwan, they
work only thirty-five minutes per day less than full-time workers.)
The IT companies have been anxious to avoid having to pay their
female workers maternity benefits, and have been keen to ensure
that an employee's primary loyalty is to the company, and not to
her family or household (Siegel, 1980). Therefore some companies, for example Philips in the Philippines, have been reluctant to
employ married women at all; others, in Taiwan and in Korea,
have had a policy of insisting upon retirement at marriage, or
of banning married women from their employment altogether
(Women Working Worldwide, 1991). In the Japanese company,
Matsushita, which makes products under the brand names Pana-
sonic, National, Technics and JVC, women are expected to leave
their jobs when they become pregnant, while in others, pregnancy
may result in instant dismissal. In Mexico, employers routinely
administer pregnancy tests to potential employees and demand
declarations of childlessness. Indian companies prefer to recruit
women who have been sterilised, and one company in the Philippines even offers prizes to employees who undergo sterilisation
(Pearson, 1986; Fuentes and Ehrenreich, 1983).

It is not only the costs of employing women with childbearing
potential which makes employers in the electronics industry
actively avoid them. These costs can be and are easily circumvented, as legal requirements for maternity payments are waived
for particular industry sectors inwardly investing in a Third World
economy. What is also important is the flexibility and dispens-
ability of the female labour force, which is critical if workers are
to be easily made redundant after the ceasing or relocation of
production in another country. This flexibility can be achieved by

---

The employment of young women from rural areas

In the Penang FTZ [Free Trade Zone], there is such an apparent labour shortage that companies are causing workers to be bussed in from Kadeh state. The companies say they need young women 18–25 years old because they are more dextrous than men at the fine work of the production line. They also believe that young women from the country will be less likely to join in union activities, especially on a national scale. In fact, there are women available for the work already in Penang but they are no longer considered suitable because they are married, have children, have poor eyesight due to having already worked in microelectronics, or they have a record of union participation.

(Women Working Worldwide, 1991: 128–9)

---

actually building labour turnover into the company's employment policy, avoiding recruitment of pregnant women and terminating the employment of those who become pregnant (Pearson, 1986).

According to Lin (1987), however, in Malaysia and Singapore the proportion of married women in the labour force is increasing, and marriage and childbirth are no longer automatic triggers for dismissal. But, as Pearson (1986) has argued, what really matters to the employers is not the particular circumstances of their employees, but that these circumstances will create a labour force which will incur minimum costs in terms of wages, fringe benefits, management control, discipline and militancy. Thus, in particular labour market conditions, they have made it their prerogative to subject their female workers to a range of particularly draconian policies concerning their private lives – their family and marital status, their fertility, where they may live. And, as Dicken (1992) has pointed out, these management policies seem especially paradoxical in view of the fact that in other respects the industry epitomises all that is new and up to date.

Women's work in IT assembly is repetitive and menial work, redolent with all the worst features of Fordist production. Corporate apologists portray this work as economic and cultural liberation 'compared with the near slavery associated with the production of classical goods, such as batik' (Meier, quoted in Fuentes and Ehrenreich, 1983: 15). Fuentes and Ehrenreich argue that working conditions in the industry are far from liberating. They provide a very different, but very detailed picture of working conditions in the IT companies. Their picture is one of low modern factory buildings, filled with rows of young women, dressed in company uniforms, working on the lines. High volume pop music is piped into the building to prevent talking. The air conditioning that is provided is not for the women's comfort, but to protect the

---

The tedium of assembly work

... assembly uses more sensing (sight, touch) and more mental/
physical dexterity and judgement than most factory tasks. It therefore
calls for aptitude and alertness but is at the same time repetitious
and boring. Without full concentration by the operator, the product
can suffer.

(*Financial Times*, 5 February 1985, p. 22, quoted in
Elson and Pearson, 1989: 2)

Echoes in Marx's description of 19th century factory work

At the same time that factory work exhausts the nervous system to
the uttermost, it does away with the many sided play of the muscles,
and confiscates every atom of freedom, both in bodily and intellectual
activity. The lightening of the labour, even, becomes a sort of torture,
since the machine does not free the labourer from work, but deprives
the work of all interest.

(Marx, 1954: 398)

---

delicate semiconductor parts they work on. The labour process
itself is highly monotonous, and affords little control over the
work. At the same time, the work is detailed and painstaking, so
the worker must concentrate and cannot let her mind wander. It
is also subject to the sort of machine pacing which has been all
too familiar to workers in the automobile industry since the 1950s.
In Philips and Matsushita, in a manner reminiscent of Ford's
assembly lines (Beynon, 1973), line speeds are gradually increased,
and fast workers are used to set standard times for the execution
of tasks and thus provide models for the rest of the work-force to
be evaluated against. In the Signetics plant (owned by Philips) in
Thailand, talking on the line is forbidden because it is thought to
disrupt productivity (Women Working Worldwide, 1991: 107). In
Malaysia, researchers have reported outbreaks of 'mass hysteria',
collective convulsions and screaming by the women on the line,
which are attributed by management to the presence of 'evil spir-
its', but which seem to occur in response to line speed-ups (Fuentes
and Ehrenreich, 1983: 38).

In addition to the mental health hazards of this work, there are
severe physical hazards. In fact, despite its image as a safe and
clean industry, the IT industry is high on the list of high health-risk
industries. Part of the semiconductor production process involves
etching circuits onto wafers of silicon. According to Fuentes and
Ehrenreich (1983: 19), in the Third World open containers of
carcinogenic acids and solvents giving off toxic fumes are commonplace in electronics factories, and the women have to dip the

circuits into these open vats. Burns to the skin are common, and sometimes the women lose whole fingers in the acid. Regular exposure to the solvents used in the production process has resulted in the IT industry having one of the highest illness rates of any, including cancer, liver and kidney damage, and fertility and menstrual disorders. Further downstream in the production process, during the process of bonding the hair-like gold wires to the made-up silicon chips, women peer through microscopes for 7–9 hours a day. This leads to severe eyesight problems after only a short period of employment; chronic conjunctivitis, near-sightedness, and astygmatisms are common complaints.

Although the international division of labour in the IT industry predominantly concentrates research and development and engineering in the West, and has relocated assembly work in the Third World, not *all* female-labour intensive operations are relocated away from the West. In the United States and Europe, women are employed in semi- and unskilled functions in both assembly and packing, but whereas in the Third World, they make up 80–90 per cent of the labour force, in the developed countries there is a much lower level of female intensity, partly because the production processes carried on there are much more capital- than labour-intensive (Pearson, 1986). Nevertheless, in Silicon Valley, the bulk of women employed in the industry are from Third World countries – from Mexico, China, the Philippines, Korea and Vietnam (Women Working Worldwide, 1991: 38) – constituting, as Fuentes and Ehrenreich put it, 'a microcosm of the global production process' (1983: 54).

In the British Isles, inwardly investing IT companies have located in Scotland (Goldstein, 1989), in Wales (Morgan and Sayer, 1988), in the Republic of Ireland (Murray and Wickham, 1982), and most recently in the north east of England. Some indigenous IT companies have also been established. Electronics companies in this part of the world carry out wafer fabrication and testing as well as assembly work, but institute the same gender and ethnic divisions of labour as elsewhere. Scotland has been attractive to inward investors because, apart from the inducements offered by the Scottish Development Agency over the past two decades and the attraction of the European market, the country offers a supply of experienced designers and engineers, and graduates and technicians with qualifications in electronics. Ireland has also gone to great lengths to provide a supply of labour which is skilled and educated enough to attract foreign direct investment.

However, as elsewhere in the world, skilled electronics jobs are male-dominated and cut across by ethnic divisions. In multi-national firms, technical and managerial jobs are filled by Scottish and Irish men, higher managerial jobs are held by English

Table 3.3   **The sexual division of labour in the Irish electronics industry**

Occupational group	Male	Female	Total	Women as % of total
Managers	841	31	872	3.5
Engineers	691	44	735	5.9
Scientists	183	22	205	10.7
Other professionals	307	86	393	21.8
Technicians	1095	78	1173	6.6
Supervisors	535	141	676	20.8
Administrators	321	323	644	50.1
Clerical workers	214	727	941	77.2
Craft workers	269	2	271	0.7
Production workers	1935	4298	6233	68.9
Others	192	145	337	43.0
TOTAL	6583	5897	12480	47.3

Source: G. Rees, 1994: 148.

and American men. In indigenous firms, technical and higher managerial jobs alike are filled by Scottish and Irish men. In both settings, semi- and unskilled production operations are carried out by indigenous Scottish and Irish women. In Ireland, 95 per cent of all assembly workers are women (Wickham and Murray, 1987) (see Table 3.3). But Scotland and Ireland are not south east Asia, and differ from offshore electronics manufacturing in the *relative* level of skill involved in the manufacturing process; here, companies carry out complex product manufacture to final assembly and testing on a batch production basis, rather than simply assembling components on a mass production basis. Since the proportion of electronics workers that is female varies entirely according to the proportion of unskilled assembly workers in the industry's total work-force, the proportion of women in the Irish electronics industry, for example, is lower than in south east Asia, where it is almost exclusively female, but higher than in the United States, where only about 33 per cent of the work-force is female (Wickham and Murray, 1987). Furthermore, since women are ghettoised in assembly work and in companies doing principally assembly operations on a mass production basis, there is little opportunity for them to acquire, on the job, the skills and experiences which can be gained from variable tasks associated with frequent product changes in small batch manufacture. Yet, like their counterparts in the Third World, women's 'natural' manual dexterity and patience are held up as important attributes for these types of tasks, although their jobs are labelled as unskilled. The discrepancy, of course, is primarily a reflection of attempts to construct a hierarchical distinction between the sexes, rather than properly describing the abilities and attributes necessary for electronics assembly work (Mitter, 1986; Elson and Pearson, 1989).

Female workers in the electronics companies in the British Isles are much less restricted than they are in south east Asia, for example, in terms of age, marital and family status. Here, the industry employs workers in a much larger age group, and employs married as well as single women. Again, however, the prime criterion for employment is actually flexibility and compliance (Mitter, 1986). The IT companies, particularly the American multinationals, are deeply suspicious and fearful of labour militancy; in Scotland, therefore, the bulk of the inward investors have located their operations in 'greenfield' sites, in the new towns of Livingstone, East Kilbride and South Queensferry and away from the established centres of industrial activity. It has been argued that this pattern of location has enabled the companies to circumvent the traditions of labour and trade union militancy which have been associated with the coalmining, steel and shipbuilding industries, thus avoiding 'contamination' of their labour forces by the traditionally militant socialism of regions like Strathclyde (SEAD, 1985; Henderson, 1989; Women Working Worldwide, 1991). Certainly the employment of predominantly women has been part of this attempt to bypass possible labour militancy. Another initiative has been to subcontract the making and packing of electronics of sub-assemblies to homeworking women.

Over the past decade, there has been a sharp decline in women's employment within the industry in the British Isles. Two factors are contributing to this decline, which has been in process since the mid-1960s (Findlay, 1989; Goldstein, 1989; Elson and Pearson, 1989). First, there has been the continuing relocation of work from First to Third World, with the consequent erosion of women's employment in the United States and in Europe. Recently, for example, there has been a significant loss of jobs in the Republic of Ireland, as IT assembly has been consolidated in Scotland while also continuing to be relocated to developing countries. Second, some IT companies have sought to automate the entire assembly and packaging process, and to retain it in Scotland in order to speed up turnaround and delivery time (Goldstein, 1989). The automation of the various assembly processes has turned assemblers into machine minders, loading several machines with components and monitoring the movement of batches of work. Mitter (1986) shows that, as a consequence, between 1971 and 1981 in Great Britain, the industry was steadily being 'de-feminised', as unskilled assembly work performed primarily by women was automated and eliminated. In the period 1981–1991, women continued to make up the bulk of assembly workers in the industry, but their numbers remained virtually static at just under 60,000 despite considerable apparent growth of the sector (OPCS, 1991).

There are very few opportunities for women to move out of this occupational ghetto. If they do so, it is to become engineers' aides, production material schedulers and lower level technicians and supervisors, typically collecting production data, keeping equipment supplied with chemicals and scheduling the movement of work-in-progress. Indeed, it is somewhat ironic that the same IT managers who are willing to devise radically new methods of work organisation and recruiting, still cling to highly conventional notions of what are appropriate jobs for women, and typically conceive of technicians as 'guys' and operators as 'girls' (Goldstein, 1989: 125). There is, then, little evidence to suggest that women's work is undergoing any significant qualitative change or improvement, or that the gender division of labour in the industry is being confronted.

Do artefacts have gender?

If the process of production of information technology is highly gender-segregated, what does this imply for the artefacts that result? Do gender-segregated processes produce artefacts which in some way carry the imprint of the gender division of labour that created them? What stories do the design of information technologies tell us about the gender relations captured within them? Do they reflect the gendered labour used to build them, or the gendered labour that will make use of them? And how do gender relations become embedded or crystallised within information technologies?

First, *visions* of technologies which underpin their design and development are formulated by their apologists, by their critics and simply by users. These visions combine both technical elements and social (including, we might add, gendered) relations; not just equipment but social images of that equipment (Fleck *et al.*, 1990: 637). For example, Noble (1984) showed that the design of numerically controlled (NC) machine tools in the United States during the 1950s was influenced by the managerial objective of deskilling craftworkers employed to carry out metal-cutting work. The technical solution which best met this objective was one in which the machine tool was programmed to move through space, and this was prioritised over the magnetic tape 'record-playback' solution by the aircraft industry because NC, in true taylorist tradition, removed the programming of the machines from the shopfloor and relocated it in the office. Similarly, Fleck (1988) has shown how the design of industrial robots was conceived in terms of a universal replacement for routine manual labour, and was partly informed by visions of robots drawn from science fiction.

This approach can reveal visions of technologies which are also gendered. The computer has, of course, had some of the most potent visions, dreams and nightmares associated with it, in particular concerning its omnipotence and ability to supplant the human being. Visions of the all-powerful computer, with a bewildering array of dials, gauges and levers, were commonplace in the early days of computers. Analysis of cartoons of this period reveals that more than this, though, the power was paternalistic (Van Oost, 1992: 240).

> ... the machine in operation must have been the most spectacular in the world. Thousands of neon lamps flashed on and off; relays and switches buzzed away and the tape readers and punches worked continuously. Passing pedestrians affectionately christened it 'Poppa'.
> (Bowden, 1953: 175, quoted in Van Oost, 1992: 240–1)

Shaffner (1993) has shown that people link masculinity and *corporate* power in their thinking about computers:

> I always think of them as male things, and that's probably because I think computers, I think business, I think money-making, and that whole scheme of things, the corporate business world, money-making, Wall Street, I think of men.
> (Quoted in Shaffner, 1993: 60)

Her research has also shown, however, that the gender symbolism of computers is very variable across different contexts. The hardware and software components of computers acquire gender associations which are linked to expertise in the operation of computers and to sexual divisions of labour in the use of particular applications. These are themselves gender-differentiated; that is, men and women attach different meanings to computing expertise, and different meanings in different contexts. For example, one of Shaffner's male respondents distinguished between the 'femininity' of a computer mouse and the 'masculinity' of the keyboard, because a mouse is user-oriented and therefore suitable for unskilled female users, whereas the keyboard use denotes facility with a computer which was assumed to be more common in men. On the other hand, a female respondent labelled the mouse as male and the keyboard as female, because for her, men used the mouse to substitute for their lack of keyboard skills. Similarly, word processing applications were commonly thought to be pink, but spreadsheets and databases blue; graphical user interfaces (such as Windows) were thought to be pink, but command line interfaces (such as DOS) were seen as blue. But Lie's (1995) research shows that the gender symbolism of computers depends critically on the class position of the user or worker. The working class men in her study distanced themselves from computers and computing, which they defined as office equipment (with connotations of women's work). Their own definition of technological expertise was one which centred around manual rather than mental labour:

> Among men who had a background from 'real' machines with nuts and bolts, the computer had not been able to take the same place in their minds ... The computer does not look like the type of machine they are familiar with, it does not have the functions they are interested in, and they cannot master it by getting to know it in their own way ... The computer does not allow these mechanically able men to demonstrate their strength or their specific skills. In sum, the computer stands for the opposite of the technical, which to them is a manual and not a mental task.
>
> (Lie, 1995: 390)

If gender images can be ascribed to a computer by its users, and even by those who have a much more distant relationship to it, in what ways do gender structures inform the actual design of the artefacts of information technology? In the first place, occupational sex-typing, or the gender division of labour, is a major influence on the design of information technologies which are to be applied to particular jobs; designers and developers of technologies have clear ideas about who the users will be. Designers know, or make assumptions, when they design systems, that their products will be used by particular kinds of users in particular contexts and for particular applications. These assumptions, whether conscious or unconscious, become encapsulated in the technologies. The artefacts themselves bear the hallmarks of this; they bear features which of course testify to the sphere of use but also to the sex of their users. Information technologies are often designed and marketed specifically for use by female or by male workers.

The gendering of artefacts

When a new invention arrives in the workplace, it is already gendered by the activities and expectations of its manufacturers and its owners. It may even be ergonomically sex-specific, scaled for the average height or anticipated strength of the sex that is to use it. Even if it arrives apparently gender-neutral it quickly acquires a gender by association with its user or its purpose.

(Cockburn, 1985a: 170)

In the office, the development of the word processor, and indeed its predessor, the typewriter, are examples of the gendering of artefacts. Secretarial and typing jobs have always, and are still to this day, held predominantly by women. However, while assumptions about women's skills and characteristics have informed the design of office technologies, paradoxically, women's *needs* as users have been accorded marginal importance. So the early typewriters, with their typebar arrangements, were very noisy and heavy to operate, and were also extremely limited in their functions – ease of manufacture was the central consideration in their design (Knie, 1992). Experiments with their configuration were commonplace, though none really addressed the problem of their unwieldiness, because the manufacturers rejected innovations which were not directly concerned with reducing production costs, and were not in the least concerned with the wellbeing of those who used them. Subsequently, the concentrated economic power of the Union of Typewriter Companies of America excluded all contributions to typewriter design by independent engineers and companies, and promoted the Standard Remington as the industry-wide standard. Finally, when all suppliers had accordingly moved over to this standard design and it had become utterly 'closed', it was declared 'beneath an engineer's dignity' (Knie, 1992: 170) to show any further professional interest in the design of typewriters, presumably because they were firmly associated with 'women's work'.

Recognition of the established skills of women typists was however, influential, albeit indirectly, in the evolution of the QWERTY keyboard installed first in typewriters, and later in word processors and computers. The original imperative for its development was a technical one – the necessity to overcome the problem of typewriter keys clashing and jamming when, during the 1870s, the up-stroke typebar design was the dominant arrangement (David, 1985). However, with innovations in downstroke and front-stroke machines, some manufacturers experimented with other keyboard arrangements. Nevertheless, the QWERTY keyboard not only continued to exist, it became consolidated in a 'standard' machine in the final years of the nineteenth century. Of course, the alliance of manufacturers united behind the promotion of the Remington Standard (with its QWERTY keyboard) was by now a very powerful economic group. But the domination of QWERTY was also partly due to the fact that typing had quickly become a sex-typed occupation (Davies, 1979) and, by this time, there was an accumulating body of female office workers with QWERTY touch-typing skills. Therefore employers considering purchasing typewriters found QWERTY machines the most viable option for releasing the female labour power and skills available on the labour market. Again, as with the typewriter itself, consideration of user convenience might have prompted acceptance of an alternative keyboard design. Many others were experimented with, including the Dvorak Simplified Keyboard, which was developed in the 1930s.

These were much simpler and quicker to operate than QWERTY, and were also much less uncomfortable to operate because they loaded the keyboard strokes much more evenly between right and left hands (Noyes, 1983, *Washington Post*, 25 March 1985). However, they were never adopted during the lifetime of the typewriter. Indeed, it has only been with growing awareness of repetitive strain injuries in the hands of office workers (and possibly because of a number of successful litigation actions by sufferers against employers) that computer manufacturers have begun to re-examine the options for alternatives to QWERTY (David, 1985; *The Guardian*, 18 November 1993).

There is an important story to be told about the development of typewriting, and subsequently computing and information, technologies as a function of the role of women and the sexual division of labour in the office. However, although social constructivist accounts correctly point to the economic interests which were at work in promoting particular alliances of actors, particular market conditions and particular technical solutions (David, 1985; Knie, 1992), they do not discuss the fact that the recipients of these technical solutions were to be women and nor does their analysis consider whether the very specific sexual segregation of typing and secretarial work might have been an element in the constitution of these technologies, if only in that women's interests as users were totally ignored. It has been left to others to point to the role of gender divisions of labour in the office in the development of office technologies.

The development of the word processor, for example, has a clear link to the sexual division of labour in the office. The early generations of word processing machine were specifically designed to automate and rationalise the work of female typists (Barker and Downing, 1980; Webster, 1993; Hofmann, 1994). A number of possible technological options coexisted (including line editing systems for editing software), from which a form of word processing emerged as dominant which mimicked and automated the typewriting task, rather than bringing the techniques of data processing to the handling of text (Webster, 1993). The immediate precursors of word processors made by IBM in the 1960s were marketed in the United States and in Britain using the concept of 'power typing' (allowing the typist to create rough drafts very rapidly, backspacing and correcting errors as they were made), and the first word processors which were introduced into offices in the 1970s were machines intended for use by trained typists: 'word processing is . . . concerned with the application of 'state-of-the-art technology to an office setting' (EDP Europa Report, quoted in Hofmann, 1994: 132). As such, the dedicated word processors which were launched in the late 1970s and early 1980s included a pad of specialised command keys for inserting and deleting and saving text, and many also incorporated screen designs which mimicked a sheet of paper. (This is in very strong contrast with today's personal computers, which have function keys to trigger certain word processing operations, but as they stand are incomprehensible without an explanatory template.)

These word processors were designed in this way in order to be usable by and familiar to their principal users – female typists. They had to resemble the machines which these typists were accustomed to, so that word processors would be relatively easy to operate with relatively little training. In this, their design reflected manufacturers' and designers' assumptions about the sexual division of labour in the office, the gender characteristics of the users of these new devices, and, critically, the level of intelligence of these female users and their ability to learn by doing. The design of word processors was a 'virtual construct of reality' – notions about the gender and skills of typists, the types of text to be created and the ways in which they were produced all informed their design and were reflected in the user interfaces of the artefacts which resulted (Hofmann, 1995: 1–2):

> The program interface is supposed to take the program's way of working and present it in a way compatible with what the system designers assume to be the competencies and experiential world of the users. To that extent, the user interface of a word processing program reflects the conceptions that the program developers have about the writers, including conceptions of the conceptions that the writers themselves may have about the program. One is dealing, as it were, with multiple reflections of imagined realities. Computer programs contain a generalized idea, a "script", of actions that they digitalize. This user interface is the staging of that script, a presentation intended to help operators find their way into the realities that it simulates.
>
> (Hofmann, 1995: 3)

These 'imagined realities' were not uniform across the design departments of different word processor manufacturers. The manufacturers of dedicated word processors were at pains to construct systems which were simple for novice users to operate: they offered menus and dialogues that could not be circumvented by the operator, even at the expense of the operator gaining speed once she was familiar with the workings of the machine. 'The imagined addressee of the dedicated system was regarded as an eternal beginner' (Hofmann, 1995: 7). However, the designers of word processing programs (for example, WordStar and WordPerfect) had very different images of their products' users. Although they were also aimed at touch typists, their design assumed that these typists would gain expertise in operating them. In fact, to work with fluidity and rapidity using these technologies *required active mastery* of the program's language and commands on the part of the typist. Thus, the designers assumed a level of technical skill on the part of the user, and, unlike their counterparts in the dedicated word processor business, did not seek to 'protect' the computer or the text from the mistakes which the user would inadvertantly and repeatedly make. Despite the fact that the objective of raising typing productivity was common among word processing designers, their images of the typist whose productivity was to be raised were vastly different. In turn, of course, the images of the user's expertise which informed the configuration of the various word processing systems in their turn became real and effective in that they served to structure the operator's actions and thus to define the operators as well as the technical objects they operated (Hofmann, 1995: 14).

These constructions of the sex and skill of the user, and with them the design of word processing systems, have altered again since the early systems were first marketed. Business software applications were developed during the 1980s, and targeted managers and professionals, who were the later subjects of designers' assumptions. With the diffusion of these technologies into offices, word processing has taken its place as one of a number of personal computer applications, while trained touch typists have taken their place among increasing numbers of non-trained operators using computers with word processing and other packages. Thus, the specific association of keyboard operating and text processing with *women's* work has been undermined, and the design of word processing systems is no longer a matter of the virtual construction of women and their skills in the office. Male professionals, managers and executives have acquired the keyboard skills which they once shunned, and women's monopoly over the keyboard has been broken. The established gender division of labour within offices shaped the early evolution of this technology, but has also, in its turn, been transformed by it.

Gender relations were also at the centre of the development and application of computerised typesetting systems in the printing industry. Managerial objectives to deskill and to alter the sexual composition of its work-force underpinned the development of new technology, and its application took place in a context of intense struggles by print workers as they saw threats to their monopoly of skills and challenges to their masculine identities at the workplace (Cockburn, 1983). Computerised photocomposition systems were the culmination of decades of printing innovations designed expressly to depart from the old linotype techniques and thus from the employers' reliance on the labour of compositors who were skilled, well-paid men living in a patriarchal craft culture marked by long apprenticeships, secure employment and strong trade union organisation. Until the 1970s, women were few and far between in this particular area of the printing industry, debarred by a combination of craft organisation, the ideology of a woman's place being in the home, and the compositors' justification for their position that their work required a particular combination of physical strength and manual dexterity.

Computerised typesetting was based upon a number of technical elements which carried very strong connotations of 'women's work' and which were imbued with constructions of 'femininity'. First, there was the replacement of the linotype keyboard with the QWERTY keyboard, which was quite different and which was also associated more with typing than with composition of print. The compositors found themselves being trained to touch-type by typing instructors, which they experienced as an affront to their skill and masculinity.

$\lceil \delta \rceil \cdot$

Linotype and QWERTY – 'men's' and 'women's' keyboards?

The lay of the linotype keyboard, from which the men had come, differs greatly from QWERTY. Not only does it have 90 keys in contrast to 44, it also, in the case of more elaborate models, has optional side magazines. Each of these has its own set of keys which enable the production of occasional type in different faces and sizes. The relative positioning of the letters of the alphabet also differs from that of a typewriter. Vowels are clustered together, for instance. The keys are larger and spaced further apart and the touch is very light. The use now of one set of characters, now of another, means that the operator's hands travel more distance than those of a typist. He taps with his elbows out, more actively ... In contrast, the type writer keyboard seems cramped to ex-lino operators. The men feel it is fiddly.

(Cockburn, 1983: 96)

But why should the QWERTY keyboard have been chosen for this new technology, when there was no technical need for it and when in fact there might have been strong reasons for choosing a completely new keyboard layout which would have made male compositors and female typists equal contenders for the new typesetting jobs? Or electronic circuitry could have been used in conjunction with the old linotype keyboards, and indeed, Linotype did manufacture such a device. Cockburn's argument is that the choice of the QWERTY keyboard enabled the integration of office and printing technologies and also facilitated the use of relatively cheap female labour. Indeed, the transfer from metal to paper which was inherent in the new technology was in Cockburn's view analogous to the shift from factory to office, to cleaner, lighter and less physically tiring work, a shift in which class and gender relations powerfully interact (1983: 95–100). This new technology was designed, then, not to *confirm* the gender division of labour, as it was in other industries, but in order to *undermine* the craft basis and the sex-typing of composition work. Thus, it seems almost to crystallise femininity within its very construction.

> Everything about the work, the keyboard lay, the styled plastic machine, the closeness of the keys, the smallness of the installation, the posture of the operator and the history of typing, all of these things make [the compositor] feel that he is doing 'a woman's job'.
>
> (Cockburn, 1983: 103–4)

While, therefore, the design of new technologies is dominated by men, it does not always coincide with their interests as a sex (Wajcman, 1995: 193). On the other hand, systems can be designed by women with the specific aim of *protecting* male operators from the incursion of 'women's work'. In one of the UK's leading clearing banks, the decision support system which is currently under development by a team of female systems developers, is being designed to involve minimal keyboard operation by the (largely male) middle managers who will use the technology, precisely because keyboard work might be associated with women's work and therefore prejudice acceptance of the system (Darking, personal communication).

This suggests that there is an important distinction to be made between men's domination of the process of technological change, and the class and gender interests that become embedded in technological artefacts. Men's numerical supremacy in the IT industry, their cultural supremacy in the labour process of IT creation and their monopoly of IT skills does not guarantee that they will benefit from the artefacts that result from this labour. Men as a sex are not a unitary group, undifferentiated by class, or by ethnicity, or by age, or by other characteristics. In particular, there are class interests at work in the construction of information technology products, which result in a separation between the beneficiaries of process and product. Just as with earlier generations of technology, such as industrial machine tools, men built technologies which would, on behalf of capital, ultimately work against the interests of other men, so in the case of IT, the *processes* of design and construction may be male-dominated, but the *products* work for their owners, capital, and thus may serve to undermine men's work and skills. Men may have appropriated the products of technological endeavour from women, but they must continually struggle to appropriate them from capital.

Despite their overwhelming absence from the process of technological development, women too can actively subvert the intentions of systems designers, often in the sphere of use. Martin's (1991) study of the development of telephone systems in Canada between 1876 and 1920s and Moyal's (1992) research into the use of the telephone in Australia both illustrate the important role of women's voices in shaping this technology. Despite the intentions of its creators, it evolved as an important infrastructural element in family, community and friendship networks. In Canada, the original agenda of the Bell Telephone Company was not at all to create a system for informal communications, but to create one which was to be geared to the needs and practices of business users: private lines, secrecy of communication and speedy connections in the exchange. This agenda was not unambiguously achieved, and women, both as operators and as consumers adapted the technology to suit their own activities and uses. The industry transformed the occupation of operator into a female ghetto very quickly (Rakow, 1988), but the women resisted attempts to rationalise their work and imbued it with a particular social significance – the glamorous mediator in communications performing a 'labour of love' (Martin, 1991: 168). Although the job was of course eventually destroyed, the women who performed this work challenged the nature of the telephone system which the company wanted to promote in the interests of its business customers, and had a profound countervailing influence on the form of communication generated by the telephone service.

Increasingly the possibilities for more positive intervention by women in the process of technological development are being perceived. A number of feminist researchers in the UK, in Scandinavia and in the United States have responded to the inequality of representation by women in the design process, to the failure of IT systems often to meet their needs, and to the *de facto* reshaping of systems which is done by users in order to take greater control of technologies (Green *et al.*, 1993a; Bødker and Greenbaum, 1993; Suchman, 1987; Vehviläinen, 1986). Their action research approaches rest upon the principle that women can be drawn more fully into the technological development process as users, but *at the design phase* rather than, as conventionally happens, in the sphere of implementation. In developing the possibilities for the active involvement of female IT users, they endeavour to offer alternative methods and culture of systems development, based upon more equitable gender relations, and thus to create IT artefacts that begin to address women's needs and priorities. We look at these initiatives in detail in Chapter 6.

Gendering in design and gendering in use

The process of IT development and the construction of IT artefacts in their different ways carry the imprint of gender divisions
in the workplace. However, there is a 'problem of translation'
(Sørensen, 1992) between the masculine structural and cultural
domination of the IT industry and the predominance of both
Western and south east Asian women in the routine functions of
IT production on the one hand, and the gender images, symbolism
and associations of the artefacts which result on the other hand.
Although there are gendering processes at work, they operate at a
number of different levels between which linkages cannot always
straightforwardly be made. The gendering, or indeed the 'masculinity', of computers as artefacts cannot simply be read off from
the fact that men dominate the management, design and programming of IT systems; as we have seen, men's numerical and cultural
domination of these processes does not necessarily coincide with
the expression of their interests in the artefacts, regardless of the
class interests and economic imperatives which also underlie
the development of new technologies. (The same problem per-
tains to the articulation of 'women's interests' through the introduction of women into the systems development process, as we
shall see in Chapter 6.) Indeed, it would seem that it is in the
sphere of *use* where technological artefacts acquire much of their
gender (and class) significance.

   Studies of technological objects alone may therefore be of
limited use in understanding how the gendering of technologies
works, for the *context* of their development is critical to their
constitution. In any event, to study an artefact alone is surely to
subscribe to a very limited definition of technology, as simply an
item of hardware or software. As I have already commented in
Chapter 1 of this book, I regard the process of putting an artefact
to work through patterns of work organisation and expertise as
central to the notion of 'technology', and this implies focussing
on something broader than just the artefact. But more than this,
if artefact studies overlook the importance of the *context* of technological development, then this would seem to confirm and
amplify feminist insistence on analysis of technologies in use
(Cockburn and Ormrod, 1993; Berg, 1994).

   In use, technologies interact with sexual divisions of labour and
gendered patterns of working, and these are the subjects of the
next two chapters. However, the sphere of use is not only relevant
to understanding the *implications* of technological change. As we
have seen, the use of IT systems, the sexual division of labour in
a workplace or industry, and the sex of the likely users of systems,
all affect the nature and sometimes the design of IT artefacts –
the word processor, the telephone, the computerised typesetting

machine, and the industrial robot are all gendered technologies in operation in workplaces throughout the world. Technological know-how is also gendered; it is held differentially by men and women. The social value accruing to the sort of expertise conventionally held by men is higher than that held by women simply because, like other forms of skill, it is men who hold it (Phillips and Taylor, 1980). Technological know-how also defines and confirms people's gender identities: technological facility has become part of the definition of male prowess (Cockburn, 1985a; Murray, 1993).

Gender divisions in the workplace also condition the pace and direction of technological change. This has been observed of all types of technologies and not specifically of information technologies; if one of capital's prime motives for introducing and using technologies, including information technologies, is in order to cheapen the labour process by some means or another, then the cost of developing, purchasing and applying technology must be offset by the savings to be had from rationalising human labour. This, of course, very much depends on the price of that human labour, something which varies significantly between social classes and also between the sexes. So, for example, the savings to be gained from automating the machine tool crafts and the printing crafts greatly exceed those gained from automating cheaper work – men's unskilled assembly work or women's office work, for example. Though gender-blind in his construction of the question, the American management writer, Philip Taft, correctly identified this issue in the 1960s when he noted that 'Whenever men (sic) are cheap no machinery is used in industry ... It is only when men are dear that wages are high that machinery is brought in (1963: 31).

Decisions to develop and invest in information technologies have been taken with this kind of issue in mind. In the couple of decades since IT first emerged, the process of technological change has taken place much more rapidly in those industries with expensive or strongly unionised labour (Cockburn, 1983; Noble, 1984), and rather more slowly in industries with an abundant supply of cheap women's labour (Cowan, 1985; Webster, 1986, 1990). The printing industry, for example, has since the beginning of the nineteenth century witnessed successive waves of technological innovations aimed at undermining the skill basis of male compositors' labour, culminating, as we have already seen, in the introduction of computerised typesetting in the 1970s and the destruction of the compositing craft (Cockburn, 1983). On the other hand, office employers have been notably slow to apply new technologies, particularly to women's typing activities, such that, as Barker and Downing noted in 1980 with the introduction of the first word processors, until then secretarial workers had been working with the same type of machine for the previous one hundred years – the typewriter (Barker and Downing, 1980: 86).

The relative cheapness of female labour will not necessarily protect women from the vicissitudes of the automation process, however. On the contrary, in some contexts, it may have made them more vulnerable to the rapid application of new technologies. Poorly unionised and organised workers are easy targets for management's searching attempts at work rationalisation. Certainly, early feminist writings on IT anticipated that women's employment would suffer disproportionately from its introduction, because employers would automate women's jobs first and foremost (Huws, 1982; Wernecke, 1983). In her prospective examination of the application of IT to women's jobs, Diane Wernecke suggested in 1983 that because information technology would primarily affect information handling functions, and because women are concentrated in such functions – as typists and clerical workers, as bookkeepers and cashiers and so on – women would be likely to be particularly susceptible to the labour displacing and work routinising effects of information technologies.

Wernecke's fears have not been entirely borne out, because information technologies have in fact been much more widely diffused than simply within the strict information handling functions that she describes. In fact, their remit has spread wider than even the greatest pessimists predicted a decade or so ago. In this process, all classes of worker in a range of industries and occupations, and both sexes have proved highly dispensable by capital, as we shall see in the next chapter. However, Wernecke's analysis is important because she, rightly in my judgement, points out that women's vulnerability to the displacement effects of automation is exacerbated by their poor access to alternative job possibilities, due to their domestic responsibilities, and presumably also due to their segregation into a still very narrow range of occupations. The current restructuring of work on a global scale, as part of which ITs are now being introduced, means that, once displaced, women seem to be being thrown from precarious employment to increasingly precarious employment. In this type of work, the prospects for learning new skills and developing new career patterns are rapidly dwindling away.

CHAPTER 4

Information and communication technologies and the shaping of women's employment

Gender relations play a central role in the creation and constitution of information technologies, which bear their imprint in a host of ways. Information technologies also, in their turn, affect sexual divisions of labour, women's working patterns and the gender relations of workplaces. In this chapter I look at this aspect of the gender/information technology relationship – the role of information technology in shaping and reshaping women's patterns of employment and sexual divisions of labour. This chapter is concerned with developments in employment and information technologies at the level of national global economies, and with large-scale trends in women's work. Here, I focus particularly upon the practices and strategies of employers of women in their use of female labour. The women themselves come to the foreground in Chapter 5, where I examine gendered work at close quarters, and the impact of information technologies on the detailed labour processes of jobs done by women and on gender relations within workplaces.

In this chapter, however, I want to examine the findings of research into the employment patterns of women associated with the introduction of information and communication technologies (ICTs). This involves a journey back to the early 1980s, to the days when much of the discussion on employment change concentrated on men's jobs. Nevertheless, this journey is important because at the time an awareness of the potential employment implications of new technologies for women was creeping onto the agenda, and important studies were undertaken by trade unions, academics and policy makers. Since then, a significant body of research has accumulated to provide some picture of quantitative change, and a firm indication of the qualitative changes which have taken place in women's employment patterns. Both these forms of employment change are the concern of this chapter.

How can information technologies affect the employment of women? In general, there is a variety of ways in which technologies affect employment. First, they may alter employment levels: jobs may be lost through labour displacement by automation, but may be created in new industries associated with new types of technology. Second, employment patterns change as new technology is associated with new types of work organisation and employment contracts – changes in the location of work and in the nature of the working day or week. Third, the balance of employment between social groups can shift, as technologies are used to displace one category of labour and replace it with another, cheaper category of labour. Here, the sexual and racial division of labour may also alter.

New technology and employment levels

When information technologies were implemented in the first European and North American workplaces during the middle and end of the 1970s, it was feared that they would decimate employment levels throughout the world economy. The effect of new technologies on employment was the subject of widespread discussion among trade unions, public bodies and government agencies in the advanced industrial countries (see for example, ETUI, 1979; Sleigh *et al.*, 1979; TUC, 1980). But few attempts were made to evaluate the effects of information technology upon women's employment specifically. In fact, discussions of actual and potential technological unemployment were often gender-blind, differentiating between the possible effects on different groups of labour, for example, but not between the effects upon women and men (Francis, 1986; Daniel, 1987). There were warnings, however, that women would find themselves especially vulnerable to displacement by automation. Three types of reason were commonly advanced for this state of affairs, all relating in their different ways to women's occupational segregation. One explanation related to the *horizontal segregation* of women in jobs where women predominated; it was suggested that the jobs most susceptible to automation by information technology are clerical and information handling jobs, and that because women constituted, and still constitute, the vast majority of clerical workers, they would be especially vulnerable to unemployment caused by information technology (Wernecke, 1983; Swords-Isherwood *et al.*, 1984). A second explanation emphasised the *vertical segregation* of women into low grade jobs throughout the range of industry sectors and across the economy (Huws, 1982; SPRU Women and Technology Studies, 1982; Gill, 1985), and argued that here, too, they would suffer disproportionately from job loss, because routine jobs could most easily be automated out of existence. A third and related argument was that women are under-represented in the scientific and managerial jobs where employment gain through new technologies would be

most likely to take place, that they have poor access to training
in such skills, and that their prospects for mobility into such
employment are also limited by their domestic and family commitments (Leeds TUCRIC, 1982; Gill, 1985). Thus, women would
be ill-placed to take advantage of any new employment opportunities to arise in the development and use of information technologies.

As far as horizontal segregation is concerned, then, as now, the
majority of women worked in service industries and occupations,
and also in unskilled and semi-skilled jobs within manufacturing.
Women were particularly predominant in clerical work, not only
in the service sector, but also in the offices of manufacturing
firms. SPRU Women and Technology Studies (1982) examined
each of these areas of women's employment, and drew conclusions on the prospects for their jobs. Leeds TUCRIC (1982)
conducted similar research into the impact of new technologies
on women's jobs, though this survey was confined to an examination of jobs in the West Yorkshire area of Great Britain. Both
studies identified a number of manufacturing industry sectors in
which women's jobs were potentially at risk. In the engineering
industries, women's concentration in semi-skilled assembly operations, particularly in the electronics sector, made them highly
susceptible to job loss through the automation of electronics
assembly. In clothing, an industry heavily reliant on black
women's labour, the use of CAD/CAM and automated pattern
cutting was identified as having serious implications for women's
jobs. In textiles, job reductions in both cotton and wool textile
production were identified, and the SPRU study confirmed the
earlier forecast of Green *et al.* (1980) that the worst job reductions
would come in the areas in which there was above average
employment of women. In the chemical industry, women's
employment would be disproportionately affected by new
technologies because of women's concentration in the lower level
jobs which were steadily being eliminated by automation. In
printing and publishing, the SPRU study found women concentrated in the most labour intensive office and unskilled production
operations, areas which were likely to suffer the greatest job loss
due to the introduction of new technology. The SPRU study also
signalled a potential for the creation of jobs for women through
the introduction of microelectronics in composing, but anticipated
(correctly, as Cockburn's (1983) research showed) the opposition
of male composers and their trade unions to the feminisation of
this area of work.

In retailing, the steady casualisation of jobs, the progressive
routinisation of work, and massive investment by the retail multiples in innovations like automated warehousing, computerised
stock control and point of sale laser scanning, marked a funda-

mental restructuring of the industry and severely threatened women's jobs. In telecommunications, too, major job reductions were threatened, in switchboard operation, in the postal service, and in other operator services. In banking and finance, successive innovations – automation of back and front office functions, the centralisation of activities and the development of satellite banking and the development of electronic funds transfer techniques – were also treated as signalling reductions in all categories of women's jobs.

Indeed, it was in white-collar work where the most significant potential job losses associated with new technologies were identified. Office workers in both manufacturing and services, private and public sectors, and of all occupational categories, were expected to suffer as a consequence of the introduction of office automation, as Table 4.1 shows. Women, particularly those in office jobs which had previously been under-capitalised yet which were simple to automate, seemed especially likely to be redundant in the automated 'office of the future'. Secretarial and typing work was therefore tipped to be one of the most vulnerable areas of women's employment, suffering severe job losses (Women's Voice, 1979; CSE Microelectronics Group, 1980; Huws, 1982; Wernecke, 1983; Softley, 1985). At the very least, office workers would endure greatly increased workloads, and the sector would be marked by significant 'jobless growth' (SPRU Women and Technology Studies, 1982).

Almost no area of women's work seemed safe from the threat of technological unemployment. But were these fears borne out? What has the introduction of new technologies actually meant for women's employment? Has it indeed been decimated, or have women enjoyed new employment opportunities then unforeseen?

In the event, it has proved extremely difficult to assess accurately the employment effects of new technologies on any jobs. Indeed, there are significant problems in demonstrating conclusively that the introduction of new technologies has destroyed large areas of women's employment, for there are many other factors involved in job creation and reduction. Pessimistic technological determinism, which saw information technology as the direct cause of job loss, has turned out to be very misleading, largely because it is meaningless to attribute job loss to the use of information technologies without situating the introduction and application of those technologies within the context of the overall dynamics of an economy. Women's employment has been threatened not only because new technologies have displaced jobs, but also as a result of a number of other changes connected to a restructuring of working patterns. This chapter examines this restructuring and the role of information technologies in facilitating it.

Table 4.1 **Forecasts of the impact of microelectronics on office employment**

Report	Types of job affected	Number of job losses projected
Siemens, 1978 (Dangelmayer, 1978)	40% office jobs in Germany carried out by computers by 1990. Report revised; only 25% of jobs now expected to be affected	2m typing and secretarial jobs lost
Nora and Minc, May 1978	Banking and insurance jobs in France	30% reduction by 1992
European Trade Union Institute, 1979	Clerical jobs in W. Europe	20–25% job displacement
APEX, March 1979	Typing, secretarial, clerical and authors of letters and documents	1/4m jobs lost by 1983
Barron and Curnow, 1979	Secretaries, typists, clerks and managers	10–20% unemployment levels by 1997
Jenkins and Sherman, 1979	Information processing jobs	30% displacement by 1990
	Banking and insurance jobs	40% displacement in the long term
	Retail and distribution jobs	40% displacement in the long term
Philip Virgo, 1979	Private sector services – clerical and administrative – particularly in insurance, banking and building societies	40% jobs at risk in the 1980s
	Public sector services	Up to 2/3 of all clerical and admin jobs at risk
Sleigh *et al.*, 1979	Insurance	A shift in employment from low grade clerical and data preparation towards higher grade computer systems jobs. If present level of growth not maintained employment could decline by as much as 15% by 1987
	Clerical and counter staff in the postal service	10–15% by 1992 partly offset by growth in engineering jobs
Emma Bird, 1980	Secretarial and typing; WP sales and customer support	1979, 6000 typing jobs lost to WP, partly offset by 14% of that figure in new jobs in WP sales and customer support. By 1985, 21,000 jobs (2% of secretarial type jobs) will be lost to WP. By 1990, the maximum expected job loss to WP will be 170,000

Table 4.1 continued

Report	Type of jobs affected	Number of job losses projected
Anthony Hyman, 1980	Secretarial and typing	WP will make 60–70% of secretarial and typing staff redundant
Metra International 1980 (*The Times*, 11.8.80)	Clerical	60–70% of clerical jobs at risk in the long term
Tom Stonier, 1978	Education sector	90% of working population employed in this sector by 2010

Sources: SPRU Women and Technology Studies, 1982: 55–6; Leeds TUCRIC, 1982: 29–52; Softley, 1985: 233.

Women's vulnerability to new technology in the office

... women are very vulnerable to the impact of new office technology. It is somewhat ironic that the growth of office employment in the Western economies during the 1960s and 1970s opened up a wide range of job opportunities for women to enter the labour market and yet it is precisely those jobs that are most vulnerable to new technology. There may also be a certain irony in the fact that with so much attention paid in the 1970s to reducing the alienation of the blue-collar by work redesign and job enrichment ..., new office technology could reproduce the same routinized, highly structured, controlled and depersonalized work.

(Gill, 1985: 60)

De-industrialisation

The process of 'de-industrialisation' – the decline of manufacturing and the shift of employment into service industries – has been one of the central developments in post-war advanced capitalist economies. It is a process which in some countries began as early as in the first years of the twentieth century, but which, aided and abetted by government economic policies, has gathered enormous pace since. In the UK, over a decade of Thatcherite deregulation and disinvestment has contributed to the loss of approximately a million men's jobs in manufacturing since 1990 alone (Brewster and Hegewisch, 1994). On the other hand, since the Second World War employment has risen in many areas of the service sector, particularly the public service sector.

The service sector has been the source of great optimism about women's employment prospects following the diffusion of ICTs across the economy. But much of the optimism actually related to growth arising from *structural* rather than *technological* change: the shift from manufacturing to service employment in all the advanced industrial economies in the post-war period. There is strong evidence that this employment growth is now being reversed. In the UK, the rationalisation of service industries like banking and insurance, together with cuts in public expenditure on health, education and public administration, affects women's jobs, as we shall see. In Germany, office sector unemployment has become a major problem (Littek, 1987). And in the private service sector, in retailing for example, much employment growth is the result of the creation of part-time jobs, particularly in Britain and in the United States. This numerical 'growth' in employment has not necessarily improved the *quality* of work for women or their future job prospects. Indeed, arguably, by perpetuating menial work and fixing women in often terrible employment conditions, the growth in part-time work has directly diminished their employment opportunities overall. I look at the conditions of women's part-time work in more detail later in this chapter.

In individual firms, job displacement has been an outcome of socio-economic conditions – market imperatives, corporate employment strategies, locational policies, the cost of labour power, the pressure for work rationalisation and work organisation practices – as much as of the introduction of new technology. In this context, companies have had varying approaches to the adoption of new technologies and techniques, rates of technological diffusion have been very variable, and indeed not all companies have found the wholesale use of information technologies to be cost-effective. For example, in cheap labour areas of the advanced industrial economies, employers are often slower to rationalise women's employment through the introduction of new technologies (Webster, 1990). On the other hand, jobs have disappeared from expensive labour areas (such as capital cities) as corporations have used technologies to facilitate the relocation of work 'offshore' and to use black women's labour as a substitute for white women's labour (Posthuma, 1987; Elson and Pearson, 1989; Dicken, 1992). Similarly, both in Europe and in the United States, women's employment in private service sector industries, such as financial services, has been profoundly affected by increasingly deregulated and competitive markets which have led employers to embark upon continuous innovation strategies in order to provide new types of customer service – electronic funds transfer at point of sale (EFTPOS), automated clearing, and home banking and insurance, for example – (Fincham *et al.*, 1994; Senker and Senker, 1994). In the process of pursuing these strategies, banks and financial institutions have made major changes to their branch network organisation, cutting front office functions, closing high street branches, and relocating employment to centralised information processing centres serving satellite branches. Innovations in products and processes have created 'jobless growth' in the finance sector. Indeed, plans for investment in information technologies in banking and finance are at record levels, but the purpose of this investment is to sustain market growth while increasing efficiency and cutting employment (CBI/ Coopers and Lybrand, 1995). In fact, it has been suggested that in Germany, were it not for the use of information technology, employment growth in offices would have been significant owing to the expansion of business activities (Littek, 1987: 224–5). In this and the next chapter, I shall be considering these developments and their implications for women in more detail.

Despite pessimistic predictions of widespread job loss (and some optimistic ones of the creation of new job opportunities for women), we have no overall picture of what has actually happened to women's employment with the widespread diffusion of information technologies. There are no systematic surveys of changes in women's employment worldwide, or even economy-wide. Daniel (1987) assesses retrospectively the impact of new technologies upon the employment of both sexes in the British economy. His work confirms the argument that the employment effects of new technologies are contingent upon the contexts within which they are introduced: the economic sector, the size of firm, the numbers of workers and the level of trade union recognition, and he demonstrates this point through an economy-wide survey of employment change in two thousand British workplaces. However, his survey does not distinguish at all between the employees surveyed by sex, and this is particularly disappointing when we remember that employment is highly segregated by sex, that women's work is concentrated in particular economic sectors, in jobs which are sex-typed (i.e., where the majority of workers are women) and defined as low-skilled, and that women are very poorly represented by the trade union movement (Martin and Roberts, 1984).

Feldberg and Glenn's (1983) research does distinguish gender differences in employment change in the clerical industries of the United States. They identify significant growth in the service and financial sectors of the American economy during the last three decades. Even though office automation reduces the number of workers needed to carry out a given volume of work, growth in the US economy and in corporate business increased the volume of activity so greatly that many more workers were needed. Thus, there was a doubling of clerical employment between 1960 and 1981. However, this employment growth was gender differentiated. The greatest growth was in jobs associated with the new technologies – the professional technical jobs in IT construction and maintenance which are predominantly held by men. On the other hand, they found a dramatic decline in, or total elimination of, categories of jobs displaced by computers – traditional clerical occupations dominated by women. Feldberg and Glenn conclude, like Hacker (1990), that jobs in which women are concentrated, or have been allowed to enter, are most likely to be the ones displaced by technological change (Feldberg and Glenn, 1983: 67).

Although we have no more than a patchy picture of the specific effects of the diffusion of information technologies on women's employment worldwide, we do have an emerging picture of a series of related employment changes currently taking place in the world economy – changes in the location and timing of work which are strongly underpinned by the diffusion of information technologies, and which are also particularly marked in the areas of the economy in which women are prevalent. The rest of this chapter examines these trends, focussing on particular economic sectors, technological developments and corporate strategies for the employment of women.

It is clear that we are in an era of continuing and profound restructuring of employment overall, and this is taking place on a global scale. In a context of volatile and competitive product and service markets, corporate and, increasingly, public sector, managements are rethinking their use of labour – of both sexes – and other resources. The uncertainty and turbulence in product markets is being displaced into labour markets, with companies passing operating risks onto their employees, whose security of employment is becoming ever more tenuous (Appelbaum, 1992). Restructuring and 'downsizing' (a managerial euphemism for streamlining jobs and making staff redundant) are now commonplace corporate techniques (Greenbaum, 1994; Gunter, 1994; Freeman and Soete, 1994). So, for example, the pharmaceuticals company Procter and Gamble eliminated 13,000 jobs in 1993 alone, although this was a *profitable* year (Freeman and Soete, 1994: 57). In the ten years from 1984 to 1994 British Telecom cut nearly 100,000 jobs, and subsequently announced plans to cut a further 50,000 jobs between 1995 and 2000 (*Network Europe*, September 1994). Similar losses in office jobs of all categories have occurred in a range of US companies in the last five years, both in the professional and technical occupations and in clerical and administrative occupations. Computer programmers declined by 27,000 in the early 1990s, office clerks declined by 62,000 between 1990 and 1993, secretaries declined by 400,000 in the same period, financial information processing workers lost 117,000 jobs, and telephone operators declined by 5000 in 1993 alone (Greenbaum, 1994: 305–6).

Greenbaum argues that these dramatic jobs losses represent the culmination of two decades of management strategy to boost the productivity of white-collar workers of all stripes, through a combination of office automation, organisational restructuring and increasingly temporary contracts of employment. The implications of this, she argues, are that the characteristics of jobs conventionally done by men will increasingly resemble those of women's jobs, while the 'temporization' of women's jobs will become increasingly entrenched and the prospects for them to progress up occupational ladders and through glass ceilings will steadily diminish. Her analysis is highly pessimistic, but represents a careful reading of the twin processes of technological and organisational change in US companies. It is also particularly applicable to the fate of women workers across the world economy. Her arguments are therefore worth considering more closely in the light of evidence from selected industry sectors where women are widely employed worldwide: banking and finance, retailing, textiles and clothing, and the IT industry.

Greenbaum identifies a number of aspects to the 'temporization' of jobs in the United States. There are changing time periods of work – the move from full time employment status to part time and temporary status. There is also the changing location of work – from cities to rural work sites, to homes, and beyond national boundaries (Greenbaum, 1994: 296). Although Greenbaum makes no claim to generalise to other countries, her research confirms the findings of studies elsewhere which highlight progressive changes in both the timing of work (affecting principally white women) and the location of work (affecting both black and white women) (Massey, 1984; Mitter, 1986; Posthuma, 1987; Pollert 1988; Breugel, 1989; Wilson, 1994), which have coincided with the implementation of IT in organisations throughout the world.

The 'temporization' of work

The move away from full-time employment towards a variety of temporary and casual employment contracts – towards labour market flexibility – has been an issue of growing comment and concern, particularly in Britain and in the United States (Pollert, 1988; Greenbaum, 1994; Hutton, 1995). The 'casualisation' of work refers to a range of employment phenomena, including part-time working, new patterns of shiftworking, temporary working, subcontracting, self-employment, homeworking and teleworking. None of these are entirely new patterns of working; for example, shiftworking has always existed in the emergency services and where manufacturers have wanted to run expensive equipment continuously so that their investment is recouped as soon as possible, while subcontracting has always been common in the construction industry. Nor is the association of women with 'contingent work', as it is sometimes referred to, a new one; women workers have always been an attractive source of casual labour (Pollert, 1988). However, all these forms of casual employment are increasing, and they are finding their way into new industry sectors. Temporary contracts are a hallmark of the retailing industry; subcontracting is common in the textile and clothing industries, in the computing industry and in local government, while part-timers are increasingly used to bolster the education system. Today, less than 50 per cent of the working population of Britain has a full-time, long-term job (*The Guardian*, 22 April 1995).

Part-time work for both sexes, but particularly for white women, has been growing consistently over the past few decades. In Britain, (as indicated in Figure 3.1) it has been the main area of employment growth since World War II; 4.7 million part-time jobs were created between 1951 and 1987 (Hakim, 1987). By 1994, 45 per cent of women were working part-time in Britain; that is, an army of over five million women (Central Statistical Office, 1995: 25). This represents over 80 per cent of the total part-time labour force (Beatson, 1995: 8; Hutton, 1995: 106). This trend is continuing; 700,000 part-time workers will gain jobs and 200,000 people will become self-employed, while around 450,000 full-time workers are projected to lose their jobs between 1991 and 2000 (Wilson, 1994: 17).

Part-time work has grown particularly dramatically as a proportion of total employment in Britain, in the Netherlands, in Belgium and in Australasia, but it has been growing steadily in almost all the OECD countries over the past decade. In many, it now constitutes between 20 and 25 per cent of total employment (Beatson, 1995). In the European Union, women hold 83 per cent of all part-time jobs. Within the Union, levels of women's part-time working vary considerably; the countries with the highest levels are the Netherlands (59 per cent), the UK (45 per cent), Denmark (38 per cent) and Germany (34 per cent) (*Bulletin on Women and Employment in the EU*, No. 4, 1994). Indeed, part-time work is a marked characteristic of female-dominated occupations, particularly service occupations, where a large proportion of women's employment is on a part-time basis. The rate of part-time employment is, however, much lower in clerical occupations, though it makes up around one-third of clerical employment in Britain and Denmark, and around one-half of clerical employment in the Netherlands, the countries where part-time work is significant throughout the economy (*Bulletin on Women and Employment in the EU*, No. 4, 1994). Part-time employment and its growth is also principally characteristic of *white* women's

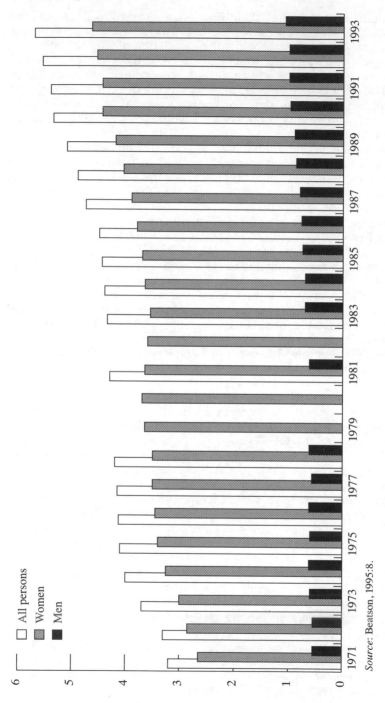

Source: Beatson, 1995:8.

Figure 4.1 Part-time employment (in millions of jobs), 1971–1994

work. Black women continue to be much more likely to work full-time (Roberts, 1994); poverty compels them to do so and black households rely particularly heavily on women's incomes. However, their tendency to work full-time rather than part-time does not protect them from disadvantage, low pay and poor working conditions in the labour market; in fact, they are considerably worse off than white women in these respects (Bruegel, 1989).

Although apologists for labour market flexibility suggest that many (white) women work part-time because they prefer to, it would seem that they are also taking these kinds of jobs because employers are creating them in the fields where these women typically work (Appelbaum, 1987). The increase in part-time jobs is not simply demand-driven by a casual-work-hungry labour force, but is supply-driven by employers and part and parcel of the growth in the service sector (just as the demise of full-time employment is linked to the decline in manufacturing). In the service industries, the managerial response to increasingly volatile market conditions is to rely increasingly on casual labour of one kind or another. In British retailing, the lower echelons of which are staffed almost exclusively by women, the large multiples have over the past decade refined the configurations and permutations of part-time and 'zero hours' contracts which they offer their largely female checkout staff to such a degree that some stores operate more than one hundred different types of employment arrangement each week (CAITS, 1987b: 17). Recent research into employment in UK retailing has uncovered a plethora of different contractual arrangements, with part-time workers of various kinds accounting for 68 per cent of the retail labour force (Neathey and Hurstfield, 1995). These varied employment patterns are often implemented in conjunction with a range of new technologies: electronic point of sale systems which eliminate manual inventory management, accounting and purchasing, EDI systems for electronic ordering and payment, electronic shelf labelling, and most recently, customer-operated scanning technologies which are currently on trial and which reduce the need for the checkout operator and the time spent by customers in checkout queues (Senker and Senker, 1994; Frances and Garnsey, 1995).

> ... three years ago, department managers used to spend ages with pads and pens walking around the store making notes on ordering. Now that we have a store-specific, "just-in-time" ordering system, this work no longer exists – one yoghurt goes out of the store via the till, and the till tells the ordering computer to order another from our distribution centre.
>
> (Quoted from supermarket personnel manager, Neathey and Hurstfield, 1995: 93)

These innovations allow retailing employers to use labour exactly where circumstances require. Staffing needs are determined by computerised 'scheduling engines' which draw on information about the store, sales patterns, the customer profile (or 'footprint'), and about the staff available. Staffing schedules are generated down to person level for fifteen minute periods on a one week- or two week-ahead basis. Employment in British retailing has become a paradigm of casualised, tenuous and automated employment, and female retailing workers in Britain bear an increasingly strong resemblance to the army of 'permanent casuals' (Fuentes and Ehrenreich, 1983) who work in the export industries in the Third World.

The casual nature of women's employment in British retailing

... B&Q, a part of the Kingfisher Group with 279 DIY stores in Britain and 15,000 employees, has 55 per cent of its workers working permanent part-time (of whom 70 per cent are women). Sixteen per cent work Saturdays only, 14 per cent Sundays while the hours of other part-time workers vary according to the needs of the local store and of the individuals concerned. Some work mornings only, others in the afternoon, some a mixture of the two.

(Freeman and Soete, 1994: 113–4)

Part-time and temporary work, though less prevalent, is also becoming an increasingly important feature of the financial services sector, and this is also a major employer of women (Leeds TUCRIC, 1982). The banking industry, for example, employs temporary staff to respond to variations in trade and to correct for persistent understaffing as a consequence of making permanent employees redundant following restructuring programmes. The closure of high street branches, and the reorganisation of branch networks into centralised processing centres (now being outsourced) and satellite branches, together with the development of home banking services (like those offered by First Direct and Bank of Scotland in Britain), are all reducing the banks' reliance on core, full-time workers. Instead, they are increasingly relying on temporary staff, known as 'seatwarmers', to handle the financial details of customer accounts and to work in routine processing jobs eventually destined for eradication by information technology (*The Guardian*, 20 April 1995). Indeed, at one of Barclaycard's processing centres, an employment agency has established an office on the centre's premises. Nineteen per cent of finance sector staff work part-time and 8 per cent are temporary workers. These proportions are rapidly growing, however, as finance sector companies make casual work more and more central to their employment policies (Neathey and Hurst-field, 1995). In the United States, the Bank of America has declared that 'soon, only 19% of the bank's employees will work full-time' (confidential Bank of America memorandum, quoted in Bridges, 1995: 8–9).

The garment industry, which relies on black female labour both offshore and in inner city sweatshops, is renowned for its vola-tility and rapidly changing markets. Clothing companies have developed a strategy of 'quick response' to changing customer demand in order to remain competitive (Rhodes and Carter, 1993). Computerised market information systems, barcode read-ers and EDI networks monitor the turnover of particular product lines at point of sale, transmit the information back to the manu-facturer, and make it possible to gauge the market with speed and accuracy. Consequently, a UK textile company director can boast that he can produce T-shirts with Mickey Mouse on them today and Donald Duck on them tomorrow, if that is what the market demands (Mitter, 1991: 58). The subcontracting of manu-facturing, which is a well-established practice among Japanese retailers, has been taken up widely in Europe, most famously by Marks and Spencer in the UK and by Benetton and Pronta Moda in Italy (Elson, 1989; Belussi, 1992; Mitter, 1991). Small batch production, subcontracted to small firms, allows the industry to respond flexibly and very rapidly to changes in market demand of this sort. In some companies, such as Benetton, the final machi-ning is subcontracted to family networks of female machinists working in small factories or at home, while the skilled parts of the production process (designing, cutting and final presentation) are retained by the main contractor. In other companies, such as Marks and Spencer, the entire process of production is subcon-tracted. In both cases, the rationale is to hold down overheads – the costs and complexities associated with employing small and dispersed work-forces – while at the same time achieving the quickest response possible to market fluctuations.

Temporary work is growing in a number of OECD countries, including Denmark, Finland, France and Belgium. There is a gender discrepancy in temporary work: in all countries the female rate of temporary working is greater than the male rate, and in five EU countries – Belgium, Ireland, Luxembourg, the Nether-lands and the UK – the female rate of temporary working is double the male rate. Again, it is in the feminised service occu-pations where the rate of temporary working is most prevalent. In addition, women on temporary contracts are more likely to have additional part-time employment contracts and this makes their employment position doubly vulnerable (*Bulletin on Women and Employment in the EU*, No. 4, 1994). In Britain, 1.4 million people are now in temporary jobs, and the majority of these (790,000) are women (Beatson, 1995; Central Statistical Office, 1995). The most common types of temporary work which women do is work done under contract for a fixed time period, repeatedly but on a casual basis. In the United States, Manpower (sic), an American temporary staff agency, employs 600,000 workers on call, and this makes it the largest private employer; four times larger than IBM, and Ford's US work-force (Greenbaum, 1994: 297–8). Shiftworking, teleworking, short-term contracting, sub-contracting and franchising are other growing forms of employment – 'all ways of getting work done without actually taking on the responsibility of employing people' (*The Guardian*, 22 April 1995).

In Britain and the US, the resurgence of neo-classical economic policy has made deregulation of labour and other markets a central article of faith in government policy since the late 1970s. This is facilitated by the flexibility of work organisation which is offered by ICTs. Indeed, the current volatility of global market conditions, the strategic responses of corporations to these conditions (which include the use of casualised labour), the deregulation of labour markets by nation states, and the availability of information technologies which can support these innovations, have all coincided to create major transformations in the world of work. It is far from certain that these developments are as beneficial for women as apologists for flexibility suggest. There is strong evidence that forms of employment now being hailed as flexible are in fact long-established patterns of labour market exploitation with which women workers are all too familiar (Pollert, 1988). Institutionalised and legitimated as 'flexibility', they may simply serve to confirm and extend the appalling working conditions of millions of working women, with the low pay, lack of employment protection, lack of equal opportunities and career prospects and insecurity which is commonplace in women's work. In this context, the role of information and communications technologies in facilitating these developments must surely be of profound concern. As Greenbaum has argued:

> Now, in the world of networked computer systems the boundary between time and space is fading. As jobs become temporary in nature, existing for the period of time they are contracted for, expectations about *where* they are done are as fluid as the expectations about *when* they are to be done. The old contract between employer and employee, coming into practice at the start of the industrial period, moved the workplace out of the home, collecting workers under one factory roof and setting a fixed time period for labor. These expectations were carried over into the post industrial period

and stressed the way ... work took shape. Yet now, given a series of changes in global economic conditions, management expectations and, of course, new forms of integrated information technology, the when and where of work are no longer central.

(Greenbaum, 1994: 296)

The decentralisation of work – women's jobs relocated

Together with the growing insecurity and casualisation of women's employment which has been helped along by the implementation of ICTs in a number of industries, the past two decades have witnessed a geographical relocation of jobs and investment between the advanced industrialised countries, and also from the advanced industrialised countries into other areas of the world. There are a number of reasons why corporations locate investment and jobs in particular areas: a need to locate production close to consumer markets, a need to draw upon skilled technical labour, pressure to lower certain production costs by cheapening labour. Corporations have always roamed the globe in pursuit of operational and cost improvements (Fröbel *et al.*, 1980; Dicken, 1992; Henderson, 1989; Magdoff, 1992). The corporate search for new production methods and sites, new production and labour markets is a long-established and well-refined practice, dating back to the earliest days of capitalism itself and involving, at its most extreme, the employment of slave labour in the colonised countries. Today, women in the Third World form the backbone of the cheap labour supply upon which companies seek to draw, in their attempts to lower the risks and costs of their operations. With the use of information and communications technologies, corporate operations have reached new heights of geographical flexibility, a growing range of activities can be relocated, and information can be transmitted around the globe almost instantaneously. As the hype has it, the conventional boundaries of time and space are being overcome. New technologies, then, have facilitated an international and intra-national sexual and racial division of labour of a qualitatively new character. Indeed, few women's jobs seem to be immune to this dispersal of work and to its co-ordination by means of computer and satellite technology.

Offshore processing

In certain manufacturing industries (such as the clothing and electronics industries), multinational companies have for some decades had a strong preference for using Third World female labour for assembly operations (Mitter, 1986). As important employers of women, the locational strategies of textiles and garment manufacturers are of great importance in determining the employment prospects and conditions of black and south east Asian women worldwide. To achieve closeness to consumer markets as well as to reduce labour costs (Elson, 1989), Japanese, American and European companies located plants in Asia and the Far East during the 1960s and 1970s. Since then, many have withdrawn from direct ownership and control of manufacturing facilities there, and now subcontract their manufacturing operations. Women working in textiles and clothing worldwide are therefore today primarily employed in small subcontracting companies and small workshops and selling to multinational customer companies.

The clothing giants subcontract to companies in various parts of the globe. German firms tend to buy from offshore workshops in Eastern Europe and the Magreb countries, British companies from factories in Portugal, Morocco and Tunisia, while US companies have subcontracting arrangements with producers in Mexico and the Philippines, and latterly also with firms in the Caribbean (Dicken, 1992). This means that the clothing industry no longer exploits an international sexual division of labour in the direct sense, but attempts to achieve a balance in its production strategies between the need for close-to-market manufacturing, for skilled labour for technical and maintenance work and for cost containment per unit of output. Clothing companies can in fact derive the benefits of Third World female labour for garment assembly without directly employing it. Typically, therefore, the design and cutting operations in clothing manufacture are performed in the developed countries using high technology and skilled (male) labour, while sewing and garment assembly is subcontracted offshore to small companies in the developing world.

Computerisation and information technology have been critical to the marketing, production and employment strategies of the clothing manufacturers and therefore to their use of female labour. IT networks are used to monitor market demand, and enable companies to co-ordinate international production based on this intelligence; one US company co-ordinates production in south east Asian and other locations through the use of dedicated satellite links which maintain electronic and video-conferencing links with suppliers and customers (Rhodes and Carter, 1993). Levi-Strauss, the American jeans manufacturer, uses a computerised system to keep track of work-in-progress in all of its factories, and to control the overall volume of production on a global basis. In addition, computer-aided design, computer-controlled cutting technologies, robotics and systems of conveyors automate the process of design, making and cutting patterns, and of handling and cutting materials, where the exploitation of technologies has significantly reduced production times (Elson, 1989; Dicken, 1992).

Benetton's use of information technology

Microelectronics technology is vital to the Benetton operation – but in marketing, distribution, designing, pattern laying and cutting, rather than assembly operations. At the Italian headquarters is a computer that is linked to an electronic cash register in every Benetton shop; those which are far away, like Toyko and Washington are linked via satellite. Every outlet transmits detailed information on sales daily, and production is continuously and flexibly adjusted to meet the preferences revealed in the market. Benetton produces entirely to the orders received from the shops.

(Elson, 1989: 103)

With these various technologies, these companies have both improved the efficiency of subcontracting operations overseas, and, at the same time, have improved the cost-competitiveness of their domestic operations. The location of their operations can be very finely organised according to the imperatives of the market and the type of labour required. In fact, information technology has reduced the multinationals' reliance on the female labour of the Third World, with new factories there showing a decrease in employment due to 'modernisation' (Elson, 1989: 98). Garment companies have now begun to reverse the international sexual division of labour, to follow strategies of 'quick response' to customer demand, and stay close to their markets. Western and Japanese companies alike are disinvesting from the Third World and shifting to domestic subcontractors (Mitter, 1991). Even offering cheapness of labour, it would seem, provides no guarantee of employment security for women.

Ironically, the move back to the West has served to reproduce the conditions of work and exploitation of labour traditionally associated with the 'rag trade'. Here, the labour force is predominantly female and largely from immigrant and ethnic minority groups – in Britain, Cypriot, Turkish, Bangladeshi and Vietnamese women (Phizacklea, 1988). Employment is concentrated in particular regions within individual countries and in congested inner city areas, or 'garment districts', where employees live in the immediate vicinity of the factories, or even do subcontract work in their own homes on very low rates of pay (Elson, 1989; Dicken, 1992). In this way, the multinationals have no need of Third World female labour abroad, when they can subcontract within their host countries and just as easily draw upon the labour of ethnic minority women in the West.

The use of subcontracted female labour is also a feature of the software industry, though here, the recent tendency has been to export jobs to the developing countries, particularly India, China, Mexico, Hungary and Israel (Cast, 1995). As in textiles and clothing, outsourcing to software development centres in these countries has allowed the industry to cope with fluctuating markets and labour requirements. (The industry refers to this strategy as 'smartsourcing'). Western managements continue to control the conduct of software development projects, but use overseas labour power as programmers working to their own requirements and design specifications (Heeks, 1993). Telecommunications technologies facilitate the transmission of specifications and completed work between Western client companies and their Third World subcontractors. On this basis, women are deemed quite suitable for the lower-level, standardised and modularised elements of programming. They are attractive, first, because the price of labour power is much lower than in the West, second, because productivity is often higher than in Western companies, and, third, because they are excellently qualified at the same time. Countries like India have a ready pool of labour available for software work, consisting of workers who are well-educated, English-speaking and technically proficient (Heeks, 1993: 242). Here again, in an industry in which the timely delivery of work is becoming increasingly critical to the maintenance of market share, offshore programming labour compares very favourably with Western labour.

The position of programmers in the Third World (of both sexes) is tenuous, however. The automation of software production is steadily reducing its labour intensity, and exactly as in the textile and clothing industry, is reducing the cost advantages which the employers derive from using this sort of labour. Furthermore, at the beginning of the 1990s, a recessionary global economic environment reduced spending on software development and closed the labour demand/supply gap in the developed countries, though the industry is beginning to recover and to grow again (*Network Europe*, September 1994). The market for global subcontracting of software development has shrunk, and the demand for Indian and south east Asian women and men to work on software projects has declined. Like their counterparts in the garment industry, women in the developing countries are highly susceptible to the peaks and troughs in the global economy and to the constant changes of tactics used by multinational and Western corporations in responding to these fluctuations.

In the clerical industries, too, there has been a wholesale export of jobs to the Third World with the aid of new technologies. The pressures of high costs (of both offices and labour) in the First World, the increasing information-intensity of many service industries, and the availability of information technologies and tele-communications facilities have in the last twenty years provided the impetus for service companies to have their data and information processing functions transferred from offices in the industrialised countries to offshore processing facilities. Women in offices are every bit as dispensable as women in manufacturing jobs.

High land and office costs in the capital cities of the industrialised countries have prompted companies to search for cheaper locations for their information processing operations. Labour costs, too, can be considerably lowered by using offshore processing, Posthuma (1987) estimates that the total cost of setting up a facility in the Caribbean is less than one-tenth of the cost of setting up an operation in the United States. In addition, service industries have become extremely reliant upon a rapid turnover of detailed information, and as in other industries where competition is intense, significant added value is achieved by the speed at which information can be processed and transactions made (Dicken, 1992). In many industries, instantaneous transmission of information and continuous transactions are critical to remaining competitive.

The key factor in facilitating the development of offshore information processing has been the availability of information and communication technologies, particularly satellite and telecommunications systems. Offshore processing was first initiated in the early 1970s, when US companies first began sending their data entry operations to overseas facilities for processing by black women in the Caribbean (Posthuma, 1987). They originally sent their information abroad on magnetic tapes, cards, disks or audio recordings via ship, and later by air. By this method, lead times were quite long and so it was only suitable for operations which were not time-critical. Since then, computer-based data processing systems and telecommunications networks have been developing at a rapid rate. Advances in telecommunications technologies have been particularly important for the successful transmission of data irrespective of distance and the digitisation of messages has dramatically increased the speed and reduced the unit cost of transmission over both landline and satellite systems. Digital telecommunications services allow firms to send nearly all business communications – voice, graphics and data – over conventional telephone lines. With these developments, a growing range of operations can be performed offshore, and with increasing efficiency and sophistication.

Offshore processing has been adopted by a variety of service industries, and affects a range of clerical functions performed largely by women. The publishing industry has for many years been sending manuscripts for typesetting and printing to Asia, while the use of offshore labour for data entry in the new service of CD/ROM development and updating is common (Probert and Hack, n.d.). Particularly important in its diffusion has been the financial services sector, perhaps because of its information-intensity and consequently its clerical labour-intensity. This sector has been a leader in the rationalisation of work, the computeris-ation of clerical functions, and the use of satellite and telecom-munications technologies for the separation of back office functions from front office functions and their relocation in areas where the companies have access to large pools of female clerical labour: in Mexico and the Caribbean, south east Asia, China, India and Ireland.

Chairman of Satellite Data Corporation on the role of ICTs in offshore processing

What the airplane was to the garment industry, the satellite is to office work.
(*Business Week*, 15 March 1982, quoted in Posthuma, 1987: 32)

Some companies set up their own offshore processing facilities, while others subcontract this work to specialist bureaux in the Third World which provide office services to client firms in the industrialised world. An example of the first kind of offshore operations is that of American Airlines, which in 1983 opened an offshore processing office in Bridgetown, Barbados, relaying ticket information there to be entered onto a computer system by Barbadan women and transmitted by private satellite back to the company's financial database in Tulsa, Oklahoma. In 1985 the company closed its data entry operation in Tulsa altogether, and in 1986, the offshore processing office was transformed into a separate, profit-making venture (Mitter, 1986; Posthuma, 1987). It has since opened another data processing centre in the Dominican Republic's Free Trade Zone.

Female workers in Third World countries provide a very attrac-tive pool of labour to inwardly investing companies of all kinds, for three reasons. They are, as is well-known, a source of still very cheap labour compared with their counterparts in the indus-trialised countries, and in a global economic climate where competition is intense, this is a key consideration for companies in their locational and investment strategies. But secondly, Third World women stand up well in comparison to Western women in terms of their literacy and general education level. US companies which use offshore processing facilities in the Caribbean do so because there is a high degree of English literacy there, for which they are prepared to pay a premium (Posthuma, 1987). In fact,

many countries in the Third World offer increasingly well qualified labour forces, and this provides a very strong incentive to
companies to locate employment in the lower cost countries
(Patel and Pavitt, 1993; Freeman and Soete, 1994). And finally,
many Third World and developing countries are very anxious to
attract inward investment in information processing centres, in
order to promote rural development and alleviate regional unemployment. The provincial government of Baden-Württemberg set
up a teletext experiment for typing work as part of its regional
employment policy; the Irish Development Authority offered substantial financial benefits to foreign firms in order to develop a
data entry industry on the west coast of Ireland; and Jamaica and
Barbados have explicit strategies to encourage the relocation of
foreign firms there and offer strong financial incentives to this
end (Probert and Hack, n.d.).

What of the experiences of the offshore women themselves?
How do these corporate strategies affect their work processes,
their relationship to technology, and their responses to their situation? Offshore office work compares with factory work in terms
of routine and repetitiveness, and offshore offices are essentially
white-collar factories, in that the women who work there have
only the endless prospect of extremely boring work. A manager
of an offshore office in the Caribbean confirmed this point in a
comment that, 'This data processing is essentially a glorified factory ... These girls are behind computers, but they could just as
easily be behind a sewing machine. All they need to know is how
to type' (Posthuma, 1987: 46). In such establishments, training is
minimal and, beyond touch typing, so are skills requirements.
Technical expertise, of course, is simply not open to these women
and their relationship to the information technology is one in
which they are simply operators of a limited number of routine
functions of the machines.

In this, these women are providing what the inwardly investing
corporations want – a work-force which can process information
dexterously and speedily. However, the benefits to these women
in terms of skills and career development are few. In many companies, there is no internal labour market offshore and so no
prospect of promotion at all. Trade union organisation is discour-
aged, so the chances for contact and interaction with others is
severely restricted. This makes for a very isolating experience of
work. However, according to Posthuma, the women themselves
still regard office work of this type as preferable to the dirtier and
more dangerous forms of manual employment which are available
– a point which it is important to remember when making assessments of this work from the viewpoint of the First World. It is
indicative of the poor options which they perceive as being open
to them, that women in offshore offices feel they must accept

these working conditions. It is a realistic appraisal of the lack of employment opportunities, the risk of unemployment (which is high), and the unattractiveness of manual work which leads these women to prefer this option, wretched though it remains.

The suburbanisation of work

Clerical and data processing functions are also being displaced from metropolitan locations to satellite offices in suburban and provincial areas. These satellite offices provide savings in land and labour costs, yet allow employers to retain day-to-day control over the quantity and quality of clerical work. In some countries, an important impetus for this development has been the regional and labour market policies of governments (Probert and Hack, n.d.). In the north of Sweden, for example, a number of remote office centres have been established to carry out data entry and word processing, in order to create jobs in an unemployment blackspot (Elling, 1985). The impetus for this type of development has also come as much from those organisations seeking a particular kind of labour which they find in suburban women, particularly young, white, married women who have the requisite skills and education for the type of work on offer, and who want to work close to home. In the United States, corporate moves to the suburbs tend to benefit white women at the expense of ethnic minority clerical workers who live in the inner cities (Nelson, 1986; Posthuma, 1987).

Suburban women in an American credit card company

We get a lot of women who get married, and then work here because of the opportunity to work close to home. Most of them have worked before, and most have some college experience. They have families and own homes, so they tend to be more stable workers, with a stronger work ethic ... When we moved out here, we tapped the beautiful source of suburban womanhood!

(Manager of credit card assistance office, quoted in
Nelson, 1986: 154)

The financial industries, which have especially high-volume data processing requirements which can be easily handled away from the inner cities, have been forerunners in reorganising their branch networks and setting up large regional offices dedicated purely to information processing, at the expense of the front offices. In the case of some banks and insurance companies, the use of telecommunications networks enables these suburban offices to deal with customers direct by telephone (often at the cost of a local call), and thus to obviate the need for high street branches or city centre premises. In the UK, there are the well-known examples of the First Direct bank and Direct Line insurance. The industry is also developing 'virtual banking', in which bank staff are located either in an office or at home, interacting with customers via multimedia computer terminals (*Banking Technology*, November 1994).

First Direct's regional operation

Freephone and local call rate allowed First Direct to offer cheap, convenient phone banking to customers ... These services, together with their geography free tariff structures also allowed First Direct to service their target market, *from a single site in a different region*. The services offered over the intelligent network allowed First Direct to locate in Leeds where the most suitable site was available, where there was a large labour catchment area, and where labour was cheaper, and still serve the target market [in the south east of England].

... all the other major banks have launched (or are about to launch) some form of telebanking. In some cases, for example the Banks of Scotland and Ireland, this can be seen as a branchless, and therefore cost effective way, to gain market share in England.

(Richardson, 1993: 18–19)

There are, of course, benefits to be had from the relocation of work which accrue to any company whose business has a high information processing content. British Airways is one such company. It has relocated its telephone sales work away from Heathrow Airport to other cities in Britain (Newcastle, Glasgow, Manchester and Belfast). An automatic call distribution (ACD) system routes customer enquiries to one of these centres, centrally controlled from Heathrow. Although there are therefore five sites dealing with telephone sales, this is a 'virtual single office'. The service to the customer is identical regardless of which site answers the customer's call, and national staff rosters detail the number of staff required at any site at any time. Heathrow itself now only has around a quarter of the staff who once worked there, and British Airways is continuing drastically to reduce staff there (Richardson, 1993).

Suburban processing is also financially attractive to the public sector. The Australian Securities Commission, an industry regulatory body, has opened a national data processing centre in Morwell, Victoria, well away from the head offices in Sydney and Melbourne (Probert and Hack, n.d.). Much of the work there is very routine, involving the entry of information about company activities onto a database in a back office environment. The work is graded very low without the possibility of promotion, though there are sections where the work is a little more varied and where staff also deal with telephone queries and enforce company compliance with legal requirements. Probert and Hack argue that the application of new technology, in combination with the 'back office' nature of the work and the division of labour, has meant that most workers there do not need to understand the significance of their tasks or their place in the overall process. Although tasks have been automated, this has not been done in such a way as to expand the knowledge and skills of the work-force. In addition, there is a considerable degree of temporary contracting which is reducing job satisfaction there. However, as in the Caribbean, many women are grateful for the employment opportunities provided by the centre, mostly because of the lack of alternatives (Probert and Hack, pp. 12–14).

Offshore and suburban processing centres certainly offer the opportunity for relatively clean and safe employment to women who might otherwise be consigned to unemployment or menial manual work. And indeed, employers may rely on the fact that these women have few alternatives, low self-confidence and little conception of what they could do in a different type of work regime. However, white-collar factories, like many blue-collar ones, are not workplaces in which skills and talents are fostered and potentialities are developed, at least, not for the women who work in the low grade jobs at the bottom of the occupational hierarchies of these places. They are workplaces in which people are treated as resources to be moved around in response to the immediate needs of the organisation.

They also, of course, have serious implications for women's employment in cities, reducing opportunities for working class and ethnic minority women who tend to live in such areas. And, like out-of-town retailing centres, offshore and suburban office developments create social and economic wastelands out of what were once city centres. In this sense, the benefits of such employment arrangements both for women in the offshore areas and women in the so-called 'core' areas of the global economy, remain very ambiguous.

Teleworking

Corporate strategies for the relocation of women's jobs are not restricted to the establishment of offshore and suburban processing centres. No potential workplace which cuts the costs of employment is beyond consideration. Teleworking has become popular among organisations which are searching for ways to cut operating costs and the inflexibility of office-based employment, and is eagerly promoted as offering women the opportunity to combine childcare with paid work.

Teleworking refers to many different phenomena, from working at home with new technology, to working in neighbourhood offices ('telecottages'), to working mainly outside the office, but creating a 'virtual office' by transmitting information from a car or from a customer's office. Here, I am concerned with working from home with a computer. The level of teleworking is hard to assess exactly, given that it is not measured in official employment statistics, either in Britain or in the rest of the European Union. In Britain, for example, official measures only cover the broader category of 'homeworking', but this includes all types of working from home, such as garment making, childminding and packing. In spring 1994, there were around 450,000 women working from home (Central Statistical Office, 1995: 29). Of these, only around 130,000 are working from home with computers one hundred per cent of the time (Gillespie *et al.*, 1995: 21). This is confirmed by Phizacklea and Wolkowitz's (1995) study of women homeworking in the UK, which finds a still low incidence of teleworking among those homeworkers. Sweden has the highest level of teleworking in Europe, mostly among male computer professionals (TCO, 1987). In Germany, teleworking has been strongly resisted by both employers and work-force, despite government attempts to promote it (Joeman, 1992).

There still seems to be more rhetoric than reality attached to teleworking (Gillespie *et al.*, 1995). It has been particularly strongly promoted by state and federal governments in the United States, on the basis that it decreases traffic, pollution, work stress and therefore work-related illness. In Europe, it is the subject of European Commission policy. In the White Paper, *Growth, Competitiveness and Employment* (CEC, 1994), it is argued that teleworking promotes economic development and therefore new employment opportunities. In the more recent Bangemann report *Europe and the Global Information Society* (Bangemann Group, 1994), the promotion of teleworking is the first priority for public action; the aim is for 2 per cent of white-collar workers to be teleworkers by 1996 and 10 million teleworking jobs to be created by the year 2000. Pilot projects and exploratory analyses have been set up to evaluate the possibilities for teleworking across borders, and the Commission has shown itself keen to find ways of overcoming constraints to teleworking. In this endeavour, it has the support of the telecommunications and computer companies, which clearly stand to gain significant market growth for their products and services if teleworking is more widely adopted. IBM is one of the major proponents for teleworking in Europe, and

---

BT teleworking consultancy services

- Workshops for senior managers, to help them focus on what can be achieved through teleworking, how they should go about implementing it, and, just as importantly, the best way of keeping the momentum going once you're up and running.
- Feasibility studies and the preparation of detailed business cases.
- Consultancy advice on the human issues, in terms of how you select teleworkers, how you manage them and how you ensure they feel content and comfortable.

Source: BT (1994) *Teleworking – Right for your business, right for your people.*

British Telecom provides teleworking consultancy for businesses in order to promote and assist in its implementation, in addition to running its own teleworking 'experiments' with directory assistance operators in Scotland and employing a growing range of its workers on this basis.

If teleworking holds considerable and obvious advantages for computer and telecommunications providers, it seems to be less clearly advantageous to women teleworkers. In the first place, teleworking is particularly evident in certain industries and occupations which are information-intensive – in media, telecommunications, computing, financial services, printing and publishing, marketing and sales, consultancy and business services, and government. The bulk of teleworkers are therefore involved in the handling of information: consultants, management specialists, computer professionals, media professionals, clerical workers and data processing workers (TCO, 1987; Joeman, 1992; Huws, 1993). The teleworkers in Phizacklea and Wolkowitz's study were doing data entry, computer programming, systems analysis, typesetting, statistical analysis, software production control, consultancy, bookkeeping and secretarial work. But there is a conventional pattern of occupational segregation in teleworking: women make up 90 per cent of teleworking secretarial and administrative workers, 75 per cent of writers and journalists, but just 16 per cent of consultants and 14 per cent of computer professionals (Huws, 1993). In other words, teleworking preserves the sexual division of labour which operates in the wider society, as illustrated in Table 4.2.

Teleworking also reproduces the conditions of work which are associated with conventional working. Huws's (1984) study of clerical homeworking in Britain found that the majority of homeworkers were married women in their mid-30s. In addition to the routine and intense nature of the work itself, the women in her study were low-paid, isolated, non-unionised and uncertain as to

Table 4.2   **A typology of home-based workers**

Type	Commonly found among	Form of pay	Employment status	Occupational progression
Corporate itinerants (Mostly male)	Sales and insurance reps and execs Peripatetic teachers Community nurses, midwives Collector salesmen Mail-order agents Meter readers	Salary/ commission	Direct employees Substantial amounts of time spent away from home	Usually part of a well-established career structure
Freelances	Authors Artists Journalists Architects Consultants Accountants Musicians Actors	Fees	Freelance/ self-employed	High degree of control over nature of product/service and its marketing No formal career structure Progression by peer group and public recognition
Traditional homeworkers or outworkers (Mostly female)	Packers and assemblers Sewers and machinists Typists and secretaries Routine clerical workers Knitters Key punch operators Proof readers	Payment by results (usually piece-rates)	Most are nominally self-employed contractors A minority have direct employee status Mostly work at home	No career structure Some may subsequently return to on-site or direct employment
Self-employed itinerants (Mostly male)	Builders and decorators Photographers Beauticians Hairdressers Taxi-drivers Gardeners Street traders Driving instructors	Usually 'rate for the job'	Sole traders/sub-contractors/ labour-only sub-contractors Substantial amounts of time spent away from home	A minority grow to become small business owner/ managers
Personal services/own account home-workers (Mostly female)	Private tutors Music teachers Bookkeepers Childminders Tailors Dressmakers Telephone canvassers	Usually hourly or weekly paid Some get 'rate for the job' or fees	Self-employed Work at home	Some would subsequently return to on-site direct employment

Source: Stanworth and Stanworth (1989: 51), with additions.

The BT Inverness teleworking experiment

Eleven directory assistance operators were provided with the technical facilities to work from home, on an experimental basis, for one year in order to help the company in developing 'solutions' for other telephone enquiry agent jobs. Each operator was given a computer with a videophone to ensure that she had at least one face-to-face contact with her supervisor each day, software for handling documentation electronically and for receiving urgent information from the directory assistance centre in Inverness, an electronic mail system to allow informal communication between teleworkers, and an ordinary telephone.

Operators gradually lost touch with developments in the directory assistance centre, and complained of receiving less and less support from supervisors. Their feelings of isolation were offset by the communications facilities which they had at their disposal, and particularly the videophone, which was a major factor in maintaining their sense of connection to the workplace.

BT has pronounced the experiment a 'success' (Gray, 1993: 10), and is using the results to develop specific products and services to support teleworking. It has since extended teleworking schemes to other telephone enquiry agents in other parts of the country, and provides consultancy to other companies intending to introduce teleworking.

---

the status of their employment. Routinised and increasingly intense labour processes, together with low pay and lack of unionisation are conditions of work which are typical of women's clerical work in general, but for teleworkers these conditions were exacerbated by their isolation from other workers and their inability to organise collectively in any way.

Although the issue of isolation is universally recognised – by employers as well as by employees – as a central problem with teleworking from home, this is not to say that women's experiences of teleworking have been universally negative (Phizacklea and Wolkowitz, 1995). Many, including the Danish word processor operator quoted, see advantages in not having to travel to work, in having more direct control over their own activities, and in being able to intersperse paid work with domestic tasks. But this very point highlights the gender dimensions of teleworking.

First, sexual divisions of labour in conventional jobs are replicated in teleworking jobs. A survey of teleworking by one of the Swedish white-collar unions found the majority of teleworkers there to be professional men aged between thirty and forty, working at home through their own choice, and in a very strong labour market position (TCO, 1987). When the survey was conducted, teleworking among women in Sweden was quite rare. In Norway, men who telework are also primarily in the computing and data processing profession; women who telework are in their 30s, working from home as self-employed typists, invariably in an attempt to manage their childcare (Lie, 1985). Similarly in Australia, both men and women telework, but there are marked differences in their working conditions (Wajcman and Probert, 1988). Men are mainly in professional occupations (such as management, computer programming and systems analysis) working from home, while women are located largely in clerical occupations, and are married with young children. Like female homeworkers in the traditional sweated industries, they are typically paid at piece rates and earn substantially less than comparably skilled workers working in offices, and in addition, they have to meet their own overhead costs; heating, lighting, and power for machines. Male professionals, on the other hand, are typically self-employed, and are able to exploit the skill shortage in their type of work, earning more working at home than working from an office and with lower overhead costs.

The experience of teleworker in Denmark

In the beginning it was quite fun, you know. My girlfriends often came to watch, for just like me, they did not know these new machines (computers) at all. Then we had a cup of coffee and a chat. Now this has changed somewhat. I must admit that I am sometimes rather bored having to work here alone all day. But I haven't any possibility of getting another job and goodness knows we need the money as my husband also has periods of unemployment.

(Danish woman working from home as a word processor operator, quoted in Vedel and Gunnarsson, 1985: 127)

Second, men and women are being propelled into teleworking for very different reasons: men often becoming self-employed teleworkers after having been made redundant from their jobs or in order to increase their productivity, women taking up teleworking in order to combine childcare with work, since affordable childcare is not available (Lie, 1985; Fothergill, 1994). Survey after survey reports women as putting childcare as the central motivation for taking up teleworking, whereas it is simply not a motivation for men (Phizacklea and Wolkowitz, 1995: 110–11). And due to these differing motivations, teleworking is experienced differently by men and women because of the gender identity of the domestic sphere, which makes women's presence at home seem 'natural'. Women mention domestic responsibilities as a prime consideration in working from home, while men treat the home as a place to be used exclusively for work during working hours (Haddon and Silverstone, 1993).

Teleworking confirms men's and women's different relationships to the domestic sphere. According to Monod (1985), men who work from home establish an office in one room, which they keep plain and functional; women, by contrast, are more likely to work in a room already dedicated to another purpose (such as the dining room), surrounded by their household equipment and domestic items: 'In the home context, the woman loses her professional status, whereas the man holds on to his' (Monod, 1985: 139). Similarly, the gender politics of the household profoundly affect the degree of control which a teleworker has over his or her job:

> ... control is the central problem for households and families. The politics of the household ... nevertheless define the context in which teleworking is more or less successfully adopted. This household politics is a gendered politics. It relates above all to the differential – but remarkably intransigent – responsibilities that men and women have for their household ... the experience of the telework, its meaning and the capacity to manage it within the home, are all fundamentally determined by the gender of the teleworker and the particular gendered politics of the household.
>
> (Haddon and Silverstone, 1993: 144)

Teleworking also fuses women's domestic labour with their paid labour. It is often promoted by employers because of the possibilities which it offers for women to handle better the double burden of paid work and domestic responsibilities. Yet the double burden is not eliminated, nor is the domestic division of labour undermined in any way. Women continue to carry out the two types of labour every day of their lives, and teleworking appears at first glance to ease this burden. However, the matter is less straightforward than this. As Vedel and Gunnarsson have pointed out:

> What is typical of house work and the work related to taking care of a family is that some functions must be performed at certain hours while others may be performed in between when there is time. But a large part of the work tasks, especially those related to child care, consists of being at the family's disposal – being ready to help whenever needed. It is in the period of availability that women are supposed to do the paid home-based work.
>
> (Vedel and Gunnarsson, 1985: 129)

Many women find it very difficult to separate their paid labour from their domestic labour when they telework; they are constantly torn in several directions as they try to juggle the demands of home, children and work which do not neatly dovetail with

---

The attractions of teleworking

Telecommuters have choice; they can choose to work before the commuter trains start running or when offices are long closed. They can commute by telephone or computer link from wherever, can move house without moving job, can revel in the occasional hour of sunshine or take time off to celebrate an anniversary with no one's permission to obtain; they can work fast or work slowly, by the fire or in the attic.

(Handy, 1989: 86)

---

one another. A study conducted among a group of German women found that teleworking precipitated personal crises for most of the women, who were struggling vainly to balance work and home life (Jaeckel, 1989: 46). To cope with this double burden, teleworking women with children work extremely diverse and unpredictable hours, as they seize opportunities when their children are at school or in bed to work without interruptions.

Teleworking has been justified on a number of counts, from the flexibility it affords women to balance work and childcare, to the 'empowerment' it confers on staff, to the reduced demand for new roads, to the protection of the environment which it offers. Yet it seems that the central reason why teleworking is attractive and why it is now being promoted is that it provides employers with a further mechanism for achieving flexibility of labour, and lower overheads. Promoted by the telecommunications, hardware and software providers, it resonates nicely with the aims of corporations which are embarking on 're-engineering' programmes involving organisational rationalisation. So, although it depends upon computer systems and telecommunications networks, the pattern of its development, in Britain at least, suggests these technologies alone are not sufficient to account for this type of change in the organisation of work (Joeman, 1992). Information and communication technologies are the wherewithal for implementation of teleworking, rather than the reason for its emergence. For that, we have to look to the current climate of work casualisation, and to the repertoire of devices being used by employers to restructure organisations and employment. For it is the social, economic and political climate which has been decisive in influencing employers' strategies regarding telework, rather than simply the technologies available to them to achieve this innovation (Haddon and Silverstone, 1993).

There would seem to be little cause for optimism about the quality of women's jobs as teleworking is progressively introduced. Like other current innovations in employment arrangement, it promises to confirm the marginality of much female labour and to rob men and women alike of some of the positive aspects of employment in a conventional workplace. The overall social and economic context within which teleworking is being introduced across the industrialised world is one of cost-cutting and labour displacement across economies, in private industry and in public services. Conventional jobs – for both sexes – are disappearing, and at the same time, lack of proper public child-care provision in many countries represents an additional impoverishment of women's living and working conditions. In this context, teleworking does not solve the 'problem of childcare' for women. On the contrary, it absolves the state from any role in childcare provision, and places the onus squarely on individual women to deal with the conflicting demands of paid labour and domestic work. It thus intensifies the burden on these individuals while releasing employers and the state from any expense or responsibility in this respect. Given this truly pervasive intensification of women's labour, it is hard to envisage any benefit to their working prospects; on the other hand, the role that it can play in the obliteration of sociable, workplace-based, employment, for both women and men, is all too easy to see.

The increasing insecurity of women's work, and the growing sophistication of the corporate and technological practices used to casualise their work creates depressing prospects for women's meaningful participation in the labour market and in technological work, particularly in the Third World. Contingent work of any type is marginalising and restricting, offering few opportunities for skill development, for the acquisition of technical expertise, for personal and career development, for work satisfaction and for the full use of women's talents. On the contrary, the casual employment of women creates 'operating units' (to borrow a term from Robert Boguslaw) – human resources to be used merely to fill in where demand occurs. There is usually scant commitment of a long-term nature by the employing organisations to the women who fill these roles, or to their career development. Human resource management strategies are often formulated far away from the sites in which plants or processing centres are located (Clark, 1993), and once located, they can be, and are, just as easily delocated and relocated. Pollert has argued that the casualisation of employment, or 'flexibility' as it has become popularly known,

> is individual freedom *and* passive obedience to be moved wherever the market dictates. The double aspect of flexibility – freedom and obedience, independence and passivity – gives the term its dual meaning.

> (1990: 86)

This *appearance* of control over working time which women

may now exercise is critical to an understanding of the ideological appeal of the concept. It has been noted that the thrust of labour market development in the European Union in recent years has been towards a type of flexibility which is entirely 'employer-oriented', but which does not involve rights for employees to vary working hours to meet domestic needs (*Bulletin on Women and Employment in the EU*, No. 7, October 1995). Such developments need an ideological underpinning in order to be accepted. Contingent forms of employment, however, do not currently offer a real choice of work to women who have to balance the double burden; instead, they are taken up because of the profound difficulties and anxieties which working women worldwide have in handling this burden. The problem of the double burden does not go away; it persists in almost every society today and is one of the major hallmarks of women's lives worldwide (United Nations Development Programme, 1995). It is disappointing, but not altogether surprising, that the potential of information and communication technologies has been harnessed not to help to address the problems of being a woman at work, but to entrench women's subordination in the sphere of employment.

Contingent forms of employment are not in themselves undesirable developments, and in a few countries, most particularly in Scandinavia, these employment forms are associated with much better conditions than in Britain or the USA. In Sweden, for example, many professional women are employed on part-time contracts which in no way detract from their promotion prospects or statutory rights. Clearly, with adequate pay and childcare provision, 'atypical' employment contracts and homeworking arrangements can be extremely attractive options for women struggling to carry the double burden. However, for these attractions to be realised, political and economic obstacles to fair pay, adequate benefits and childcare need to be overcome. In addition, a shift is needed in the cultural values elevating full-time, workplace-based employment.

There appears to be a less progressive long-term restructuring of the gender composition of the work-force taking place. Women have entered into the labour market in substantial numbers, not merely as a reserve army of labour but on a permanent basis. Capital, meanwhile, is searching for new ways in which to circumvent the employment gains won by the labour movement over the past two decades. The free market, neo-classical economic policies of governments in Britain, the United States, and a growing number of other countries, have been critical to the recomposition of capital which is currently taking place (Pollert, 1990). The old forms of patriarchal closure have been permanently removed and are being replaced by new forms of patriarchal capitalist relations of employment. Employers gain cheap labour, and men retain their domestic labourers (Walby, 1989: 140). Information and communication technologies, I would contend, are essential, but by no means the only, ingredients in this restructuring.

The breakdown of the sexual division of labour?

During the past fifteen years, both substantial optimism and profound pessimism have been the hallmark of social research on technology, and among feminist writers both views are still to be found. However, in my view, the evidence of feminist research on technology does not support great optimism for the progress of women in the workplace.

In the early 1980s, when I embarked on this field of research, explanatory tools for understanding the fate of women workers in increasingly technologically advanced societies were often somewhat simplistic. Women's work tended to be understood by reference to concepts which were not very sensitive to its particularities, and which turned out to be ill-suited to the analysis of technological change. The place of women as a 'reserve army of labour' was one such central concept in feminist thinking on women's work. In the light of evidence about the role of technological change in the shaping of the position of women in the labour market, however, the reserve army of labour thesis now seems to be wanting as an explanation of the dynamics of the current restructuring of employment time and location. Women are not being used as a reserve army of labour – being drawn into the labour market simply in periods of economic growth and ejected in recessions. Their position is much more complex than this and they have become a permanent core of workers, albeit often casual ones, in a number of industries as capitalists find new permutations of employment to circumvent the costs and disadvantages of the old employment patterns. Does this mean, then, that women's prospects of escaping from their old occupational ghettos are improving, and that they will be used to displace men in certain types of work, particularly with the diffusion of information technologies? What is happening to the balance of occupations between the sexes? How, if at all, is the sexual division of labour being transformed?

When ITs were first applied in workplaces, many accounts, particularly those in the labour process tradition, assumed, following Braverman (1974) that the IT application was part of a managerial programme to achieve an increasing degradation of skilled labour and the substitution of this skilled (male) labour with cheap, unskilled (female) labour. Here, then, there was an assumption that new technologies would provide employers with a mechanism for invoking the 'reserve army of labour', and that they would begin to overturn the established sexual division of labour. The point was not always made so explicitly in discussions of technological change, but statements that 'the introduction of new technology can bring about a substitution of female for male labour' (Leeds TUCRIC, 1980: 106) were not unusual.

Although, as we saw in Chapter 2, there is now widespread disenchantment among feminists with the reserve army thesis (Walby, 1986; West, 1990; Rees, 1992; Siltanen, 1994) there is some empirical support for the argument that women are entering previously male-dominated areas. However, they are not entering identical jobs, but changed ones. Cockburn's (1983) research into technological change in typesetting operations described attempts by the print companies to replace hot metal typesetting – work traditionally carried out by skilled craftsmen and from which women had always been excluded – with cold electronic composition. The employers saw this technical change as enabling them to replace the men with cheaper women workers. As we saw in Chapter 3, the very design of the new machinery – with QWERTY keyboards and altogether lighter handling – had built into it the wherewithal to undermine the traditional allocation of skilled jobs to a powerful group of highly unionised male craft workers, and thus their exclusive rights to this craft. The male compositors fought to defend their position by having sole rights to use the computer typesetting equipment, and their strategy of resistance continued to centre around the exclusivity of their skills and the barring of women from the trade. In many work-places, they succeeded, though the old material basis of their craft had now been eliminated. In fact, for the craftsmen these changes were highly emasculating.

Cockburn's later (1985a) research into the automation of garment production identifies a progressive encroachment by women into what were formerly exclusively male areas of the production process. The industry historically had a very strong sexual division of labour: women worked as seamstresses, but men worked as tailors, and it was tailoring which formed the basis of the modern garment industry. As the craftsmen were displaced by factory methods of production and female machinists from the inter-war period onwards, they took refuge in cutting work, which retained its craft basis. However, this too became the object of management attempts to circumvent the wages and the craft basis of the work, and as the work was rationalised, women began to enter this area too. In this context of progressive work rationalisation and the steady breakdown of the established sexual division of labour in the industry, computer-aided design and computer-aided manufacturing systems (CAD/CAM) were implemented in the industry.

Computer technologies provided employers with a further

means to shake off their dependence upon craft labour, to enshrine craft knowledge in the machine, and to move women into the new machine operating jobs. Cockburn concludes that the industry has undergone a 'sex change' (1985a: 69); women are moving slowly into all areas hitherto occupied by men:

> What has happened in the process of technological change in the pattern and cutting rooms, of course, is that men that once produced their consumer goods by means of simple tools (scissors, pencils) entirely under their own control, have been turned into operators (or, more commonly, replaced by women operators) working on machines that are under the technological sway and authority of men with technical skills.
>
> (Cockburn, 1985a: 74)

Cockburn argues that the employers, using the justification that skilled craft labour is no longer readily available, and with the help of automation, are now seeking to create women-only occupational ghettos in areas which were once exclusively male. Female labour is cheaper than male labour, and women 'put less pressure on the wage than men' because they are poorly represented by their unions (1985a: 70). In the long run, she argues, these jobs are destined to become entirely female.

Hacker's (1990) study of technological change in AT&T similarly shows the role of technological change in the reallocation of jobs along gender, and in this case racial, lines. In AT&T, minority men replaced white men in skilled jobs, and women replaced minority and white men in semi-skilled jobs. White women suffered most from the process, and were replaced by minority women who Hacker anticipated would be eliminated in future rounds of technological change. Cockburn's and Hacker's work shows that in particular industries in which craft work and engineering skills are central, the process of technological change has offered employers the opportunity to redesign craft jobs and redefine their holders. The jobs which are created are effectively new jobs; they have much lower status, are defined as lower skilled and require less training. They are more routine, and are more strongly driven by the dictates of technological systems than the old craft jobs which existed before, to which women were always denied access. There are similarities here with the feminisation of office work, which actually represented a radical reorganisation and downgrading of the work, and not simply a substitution of male labour with female labour.

The simple substitution argument assumes that managements regard men and women as undifferentiated groups (Liff, 1986). But women work in occupational ghettos which differentiate them as a resource precisely because of their different relationships to, and ability to participate in, the labour market. Rather than allowing women to move out of these ghettos through the relaxing of the sexual division of labour, it would seem that the process of technological change has rather been part of a reorganisation of particular jobs which makes them more akin to those which women have traditionally performed. Women are not moving into the same jobs which men vacated, but into newly created types of work, the skills and requirements of which are in flux with the process of technological change. The characteristics and skill content of these jobs is the subject of the next chapter.

Studies of occupational shifts, both in the UK (Hakim, 1981; Wilson, 1994) and in the European Union more widely (T. Rees, 1994), show no end to traditional patterns of occupational segregation by sex, despite an overall increase in female economic activity, and despite women's entry into a few new areas of 'feminised' work. There still appears to be a remarkable degree of stability in the sexual division of labour, with women remaining concentrated very heavily in clerical occupations, secretarial occupations, personal service occupations and other low-grade occupations (see Table 4.3). In other words, the existing sexual division of labour has largely prevailed. The continuing employment of women in sex-segregated industries also carries with it the penalty of low pay, and this is so across the European Union. In the textile industry, women may earn as little as 55 per cent of male manual workers' average pay. In banking, which is a relatively high paying sector for women, they may earn only 64 per cent of average male non-manual pay (*Bulletin on Women and Employment in the EU*, No. 5, 1994). Men are less vulnerable to low pay and poverty while in employment, but they have been more vulnerable to redundancy and unemployment. Walby (1989) argues that the current recession is actually a recession for men, in that skilled work is being lost, and new job creation is in semi-skilled and unskilled work. This, of course, does not disrupt the segregation of women in low grade work. The evidence from statistics of employment growth differentiated by occupation and by type of employment contract bears out Walby's contention. Any scope afforded by information technologies for reducing segmentation and gender segregation in the labour market does not therefore appear to have been realised. Women's subordination in the labour market has not, as we would expect, been overcome by the diffusion of ICTs. Rather, it seems to have been confirmed with the use of ICTs to underline a series of employment transformations which have accentuated the numerical and locational flexibility of women but have done nothing to challenge the segregation of occupations by sex.

The casualisation of women's work – in both temporal and spatial terms – is not a new development, but it has become more

Table 4.3 **Women as a percentage of total employment in each occupation**

	1971	1981	1991	2000
Managers and administrators	17.2	20.3	30.5	39.6
Mgrs/proprietors in agric. and services	25.0	27.7	33.0	34.2
Science and engineering professionals	2.5	6.1	9.8	13.4
Health professionals	23.3	25.2	35.0	39.3
Teaching professionals	54.3	58.0	61.1	63.1
Other professionals	17.7	21.7	32.3	34.2
Science and eng. associate professionals	10.8	15.2	22.5	29.9
Health associate professionals	86.4	87.9	88.4	88.3
Other associate professionals	23.7	28.5	38.9	44.0
Clerical occupations	56.5	63.5	68.5	72.3
Secretarial occupations	96.2	95.9	96.6	95.7
Skilled constr., eng. and other trades	24.2	21.0	20.6	15.7
Service occupations	80.0	88.0	93.8	93.5
Buyers, brokers and sales reps	10.1	14.4	24.0	28.7
Other sales occupations	72.3	77.5	79.3	79.8
Industrial plant and m/c operatives	34.9	32.2	29.3	22.3
Drivers and mobile machine ops	4.2	3.7	5.1	4.9
Other occupations in agriculture	22.8	21.8	22.9	21.3
Other elementary occupations	41.9	52.1	56.3	54.8

Source: Wilson 1994: 25.

widespread and pronounced in the IT era, and the options open to employers for creating myriad forms of casual employment seem much greater when ICTs can support more geographically dispersed and flexible systems of work organisation. Of course, the imperatives facing corporations are highly variable across industry sectors and historical periods: some pursue strategies of reducing labour costs, others of reducing costs per unit of output, still others of locating as close as possible to their final markets. These strategies are to a great extent dictated by company perceptions of the central competitive pressures with which they have to engage in any particular period, and they condition corporate applications of new technologies and decisions regarding the location and organisation of employment. The relocation of work, within and between industrialised and industrialising regions of the globe, is one response to the competitive pressures of the contemporary marketplace, and it is one which makes women workers very vulnerable.

However, the relocation of work is not solely a feature of private sector employment. In the public sector, too, information processing jobs (in unemployment benefits and social security administration) are beginning to be outsourced and moved from metropolitan to suburban processing centres. Working women are in danger of becoming increasingly disposable as human resources. Even low paid, unskilled, young women working in appalling conditions with little union or regulatory protection (whether in the Philippines or in the East End of London), are vulnerable as companies move their operations from First World to Third World and back again. And the burden which all women shoulder is crippling, as they take on the breadwinning role in the absence of their men or of jobs for their men.

What of the future for the employment of women? Predictions for Britain indicate that job loss will continue in blue-collar and unskilled work, largely affecting men (Walby, 1989; Wilson, 1994). Some women may benefit from new job creation, but this will favour highly-qualified, white-collar workers who are prepared and can afford to be flexible in their work. But this is not the position of most working women, and even in these professional areas, women remain concentrated in relatively low status service sector areas. For the rest, women and men alike, part-time employment and other forms of contingent work are predicted to continue to increase, though women are predicted to be the main recipients of this increase, and the work involved to be of very low status and low paid (Wilson, 1994: 27). Will black women join the ranks of the increasing numbers of part-time workers, or will their presence in full-time work make them even more vulnerable to unemployment than they currently are? Will the public sector join the private sector in the casualisation of work? There is patchy evidence to show some use of fixed term and temporary contracts in the British public sector since the early 1980s, especially in education and in the Civil Service (Pollert, 1988). However, we still have very little indication of how *women's* public sector employment, for example, in healthcare and in other public sector occupations in which women are concentrated, is affected by changes in economic and political conditions and by changes in the application of technologies.

Projections for the United States show the bulk of employment growth occurring in public service sector jobs such as nursing, on the one hand, and in professional computing jobs on the other, and the former development may benefit women (of all races) (US Bureau of Labor Statistics 1992, quoted in Freeman and Soete, 1994: 62–3). But the signs are that the permanent workforce is dying, and that we are in a period of unparalleled growth in insecure, contingent work in occupations of all kinds. If this trend continues, and spreads in other countries too, then not only will there have been little by way of occupational desegregation or benefits for women in the information technology era, but for both sexes, the worst fears of those who predicted enormous insecurity of work and mass unemployment across the globe will have been confirmed.

The feminisation of work

Work is being redefined as both literally female and feminized, whether performed by men or women. To be feminized means to be made extremely vulnerable; able to be disassembled, reassembled, exploited as a reserve labor force; seen less as workers than as servers; subjected to time arrangements on and off the paid job that make a mockery of a limited working day; leading an existence that always borders on being obscene, out of place, reducible to sex ... As robotics and related technologies put men out of work in "developed" countries and exacerbate failure to generate male jobs in third-world "development", and as the automated office becomes the rule even in labor surplus countries, the feminization of work intensifies ...

(Haraway, 1985: 190)

CHAPTER 5

Secretaries and seamstresses, clerks and cashiers – information technologies and women's labour processes

Employment patterns are undergoing profound and disturbing changes across the globe. Information technologies are heavily implicated in some of the changes we see, particularly in the relocation and decentralisation of work; in other spheres, ITs serve more to underline and support innovations in work organisation and in the use of human resources. This is the global level at which we can analyse the changes taking place in women's (and men's) work. There is also, however, a significant process of change taking place which requires a much more localised analysis – in the *nature* of women's jobs, in their skills, in their relations with their female and male co-workers and in their experiences of work. For jobs can be restructured through changes in the technical as well as in sexual or spatial divisions of labour and, as we saw in Chapter 2, feminist contributions to the labour process debate have examined the reorganisation of women's work through automation. It is with women's labour processes, gendered labour processes, that this chapter is concerned.

What kinds of labour processes and what kinds of gendering are at issue here? In the first place, there are the effects of automation upon the nature and character of 'women's jobs', occupations in which women are strongly represented and which have lent themselves to extensive feminist analysis – secretarial work, clerical work, banking work; women's jobs in the manufacturing industries of clothing, confectionery, and printing; women's work in the functions of assembly, packing, and so on. The sex of the labour forces in these industries is important: it affects the rate of technological change and the ways in which technological work is organised. Thus, the effects of technological change are shot through with gender differences, and these effects are the subject of this chapter. Second, there are the gender relations of those jobs and of the workplaces in which they are carried out. As Liff (1993) has pointed out, occupations become gendered through a complex of processes, not simply because of their disproportionate tenure by women or by men, but also because workplace dynamics create relations of gender which underpin the very organisation of jobs and the roles played by their holders. With the automation process, this gendering of occupations is open to important changes as workplace relations between workers and bosses, men and women, shift and are reshaped. Those gender relations may be transformed in the process of information technology implementation. This chapter therefore considers both women's jobs and the gender relations of those jobs. The area of women's work which has received the most sustained attention since microelectronic technologies were first implemented in workplaces is the office, and this therefore provides the starting point for my discussion.

Office wives and office workers

I qualified as a secretary at the end of the 1970s, at a time when middle-class young women were either directed towards some kind of profession or, if they were not considered to be academically bright (which I wasn't), learnt shorthand and typing, and went to work in offices. For a short period I worked in a variety of offices and organisations, all of which still used a collection of 'old technologies'. Some had not even invested in electric typewriters for their secretaries; the manual versions required considerable strength to operate and a great deal of affinity with the machine. There was no automatic correction facility on these machines and mistakes had to be rubbed or 'tippexed' out; in fact, Tippex correction paper was considered to be the epitome of labour-saving technology for the typist.

I was lucky to have the opportunity to study at university, and my period of undergraduate study was precisely the period during which the first generation of new technologies was making an appearance in organisations. In the process, they were generating frantic speculation about their likely effects on work and on society at large. In an echo of the automation debates of the 1950s, concerns were expressed about the effects of new technology upon the *nature* of work – on working routines, on skills and on job satisfaction. The labour process debate of the 1970s and 1980s generated a stream of research studies into transformations taking place in many spheres of work – in engineering and technical work, assembly line work, and coal mining, for instance. Many of these early studies, however, concerned the labour processes of men; the theorising, conceptual categories and empirical focus of the labour process literature were all male-dominated.

It was, however, widely recognised that with the introduction of new technologies, one of the areas of work most susceptible to automation and to changes in work process would be the office, and that it would witness changes perhaps more dramatic than those likely to take place in factories. Indeed, the key exponent of the labour process perspective, Harry Braverman, devoted a large part of his analysis in *Labor and Monopoly Capital* to the imminent rationalisation of office work, which he saw as a critical element in the transformation of modern work. Yet it was left to feminist writers to point out the gender-blindness of the analysis of Braverman and his followers (West, 1978; Beechey, 1982), to stress that office work is predominantly per-formed by women, and to argue that certain office jobs – especially secretarial jobs – are characterised by peculiar relations of control based on patriarchy which are very different from those operating in other workplaces (Benet, 1972; Barker and Downing, 1980; Pringle, 1988). Changes in women's office work could not simply be read off from a conventional labour process analysis, but required in addition a feminist perspective – an understanding of the nature of 'skill' in women's work, and a recognition of the gender relations creating power and subordi-nation in the office. Office work was thus one of the first and most important foci of feminist analysis of technological change, and it was one of the first sites of the implementation of infor-mation technology, in the form of the word processor. This was a sphere of work which I personally understood well through my own experience of secretarial work. From having worked in an office, I was now investigating other women's work in offices (Webster, 1986, 1990).

The term 'office work' covers several distinct jobs: secretarial work, typing work and other kinds of women's clerical jobs. These are very differently organised and controlled, and also vary across economic sectors, as we shall see. I start with a consideration of the automation of secretarial and typing work. The introduction of the word processor (WP) in the late 1970s seemed set to change fundamentally the work of secretaries and typists in offices across the economy and throughout the world. Predictions about the fate of these workers and their skills fell broadly into two camps. On the one hand, there were those who saw the potential of microelectronic office technologies to enrich women's jobs, while on the other, there were those who were very pessimistic about the likely deskilling and work fragmentation effects, and who essentially accepted and extended a Bravermanian perspec-tive to the implementation of new technologies in the office. If the office, which has historically been the site of considerable social interaction between workers, was to be taylorised with the implementation of IT, then this would also signal 'the end of the social office' (Webster, 1990).

An 'optimistic' analysis of the effects of word processing on secretarial work

The new technology is changing the nature of several office jobs. In some cases staff can move relatively easily into the new posts e.g. the copy typist with a week or so's training becomes the word processing operator. In other cases different skills are required ... There are indications that in some companies the introduction of WP is significantly reducing the amount of time which personal secretaries spend typing, since more of their typing work is completed by WP staff. This should allow the secretary's role to expand into a more varied and responsible position ... WP seems to be having a major impact on the jobs of copy typists and junior secretaries, who would normally spend most of their time on text processing; there is little evidence of WP 'deskilling' the jobs of more senior secretaries ... Seven of the nine management interviewees thought that WP operators found the job more satisfying than the copy typist job and cited the following aspects as contributing to satisfaction:

- reduction of repetitive work on standard texts
- high speed of throughput
- quality of output

(Bird, 1980: 45–9)

A 'pessimistic' approach to word processing and women's office work

With word processors the tasks of a typist are fragmented – no longer does she press keys to print information onto paper; rather she simply presses key to feed information into a memory. The printing is done separately. Thus a word processor operator (WPO) 'keyboards' or 'keys in' ...

The move to word processing removes the need for skill in producing neat, well set out work. The machines can indent, centre, justify margins and tabulate, which, together with touch typing are crucial components of any typing course and basic requirements for RSA typing examinations. In removing the need for these skills, word processing effectively removes an area of control which the typist has over both her work and her typewriter.

(Barker and Downing, 1980: 90–2)

Yet when widespread research into women's office work was undertaken, a much more complex picture began to emerge. Instead of a uniform set of outcomes arising from the automation of women's office work, it became clear that office work is much more varied in terms of work organisation and skills than was being acknowledged, and that the application of IT to women's office jobs is a process with very unpredictable outcomes, complicated by the difficulty of applying notions of 'skill' and 'deskilling' to this type of work. Not all women's office jobs are identical to start with, and in fact the distinctions between secretarial work, typing work and clerical work are critical to an understanding of the effects of word processing and other office technologies (McNally, 1979; SPRU Women and Technology Studies, 1982; Webster, 1990). Generalisations about women's office jobs obscure these distinctions and convey the notion that office automation is reducing all jobs to one and the same level. A variant on this theme is the suggestion that information technology creates a polarisation between professional secretarial workers and routine clerical workers, through the emergence of a two-tier organisation of secretarial work into administrative secretaries, on the one hand, concerned primarily with administrative and non-typing tasks, and correspondence secretaries on the other, concerned primarily with keying in and typing work on a routine basis (Bird, 1980; Machung, 1984).

Of all the information technologies, word processing (WP) has received the greatest attention from researchers interested in transformations in office work. It was one of the earliest and most visible forms of IT to be applied to office work, and was readily comparable with previous generations of office technology – specifically the manual, electric and automatic typewriters – which it started to displace in the late 1970s. Word processing has had very variable effects across the range of women's office jobs and has created widely contrasting labour processes in different settings. Even where managements have introduced word processing or other new technologies into the office in order to reorganise clerical work on a wide scale, this has not always led to the direct deskilling of secretaries and typists. In some settings, it has merely allowed these women to cope better with excessive workloads and to eliminate some of the more repetitive elements of their work. Where it has been associated with deskilling, this has usually been because it has been introduced in tandem with rationalised systems of text production which transform office workers into routine processors of text, usually in pools or segregated WP centres (Softley, 1985; Machung, 1988). Where this happens, WP operators generally work more with their machines than with other people (unlike secretaries) and need to be able to tolerate very repetitive typing, unbroken by social contact. Despite the fact that they are usually gathered in large numbers, all sitting next to one another at terminals, WP operating is isolating work. The job demands constant attention and there is no need for interaction with other operators. In this context, the social office has indeed been destroyed (Machung, 1988).

The monotony of WP operating

You have to be willing to do the work. Some people aren't. They get tired of sitting there and typing and getting somebody's work to do. We have one operator who quit. She got tired of working by the midafternoon, and she'd rest her head on one elbow and type with one hand and not get the work out.

(Lois Flandermeyer, a WP operator, quoted in Machung, 1988: 72)

This scenario is very specific to certain employers in certain sectors, however. It is characteristic of the information processing industries in the public and private service sectors – local and national government, financial services, IT, legal services, for example. It is a pattern of clerical and secretarial work organisation which is particularly common in the financial services sector (Glenn and Feldberg, 1979; Greenbaum, 1979; Webster, 1990). Many women who work in WP pools in highly rationalised environments such as this complain of agonising boredom at work.

Routine information processing in a building society

You know exactly what you are going to be doing in the morning, and at a certain time of day. You know you'll be getting (letters) in the afternoon, and you'll be doing audio (typing). You know exactly what you are going to be doing, and it is the same thing every day of the week, just the same thing all the time.

(Maureen, a WP operator, quoted in Webster, 1986: 157)

In other environments, however, the introduction of word processing seems to have brought about improvements in office jobs (Wagner, 1985; Glogau, 1985; Bradley and Bergstrom, 1986; Microsyster, 1988; Tijdens, 1994). Secretaries working in small firms where work rationalisation has been slow to take hold continue to exercise substantial control over their work. Wagner (1985) describes the savings in effort and the ease of correction, and consequently the satisfaction that many secretaries derive from producing higher quality documents than they were formerly able to do on typewriters, and Liff (1993) also points to positive changes in the ease and efficiency of typing. The pattern that emerges from this is that, overall, routine office jobs have been further deskilled when information technology is introduced, while workers who do use skill and some discretion in the course of their work may acquire new skills or abilities, not least in computer use (Microsyster, 1988; Kraft and Siegenthaler, 1989).

Butler (1988) finds such a polarisation of office workers. Her Australian study indicates that on the one hand, a large proportion of office work has been deskilled with the introduction of word processing technologies, because they have permitted secretarial and typing work to be degraded and parcelled out among workers such that individual typists no longer control the overall labour process. On the other hand, she finds that top secretaries have become increasingly polarised from other office workers, are continuing to use their old skills and also are gaining new skills in word processor operating. Although this conclusion is consistent with other research with a similar focus (Wagner, 1985; Webster, 1986), it is important not to romanticise or overstate the positive changes associated with the implementation of new technologies like word processing. Even in circumstances where some sort of 'enskilling' is taking place, women's jobs are rarely regraded, nor are women given any formal recognition for the new tasks which they often now carry out (Wagner, 1985). Virgo (1994) suggests that a new career path has emerged for secretaries to move into user support or departmental IT management. However, it would seem that the very movement of women into this area has served to downgrade its value:

> ... to most users the management of IT is taken for granted as a semi-secretarial-cum-administrative function which no more merits separate senior management attention than the telephones or plumbing.
>
> (Virgo, 1994: 23)

Meanwhile, the pace of, and stress in, almost all women's office work is increasing, as women are called upon to do a wider range of tasks, more 'emotional work', and their working operations are increasingly being dictated by the requirements of the computer system (Goodman and Perby, 1985; Microsyster, 1988). Many are changing jobs altogether in order to have their new abilities more explicitly recognised (Liff, 1993).

These variations in the outcome of the automation of women's office work can be attributed to a number of factors. First, clearly the nature of work depends partly upon the type of office in question. A useful, if a little dated, classification is provided by Green *et al.* (1980), distinguishing between large- and small-scale clerical operations, offices where clerical work is the 'bread-and-butter' of the organisation and ones where it is merely supportive of the organisation's main activities, and manufacturing and service sector organisations. The rate of diffusion of information technologies also varies enormously between these types of organisation, with the clerical industries adopting ITs most eagerly, and others taking it up much more slowly.

Second, the structural differences between secretarial, typing and clerical work shape the impact of word processing and other forms of office automation. Secretarial work is significantly more varied and offers much greater opportunities for the use of judgement and discretion than either pure typing work or routine clerical work do. In addition, even within the category of secretarial work, for instance, patterns of work organisation vary greatly from one office to another, and these too condition the impact of information technologies (Wagner, 1985). Secretaries can work as personal assistants in their own offices, or in groups servicing several bosses in shared offices and sharing tasks, or in other ways (Silverstone, 1974; Vinnicombe, 1980). In my own research on word processing and secretarial skills in Britain (Webster, 1990), I found very decisive differences in office work arrangements between the different organisations, and these differences were a critical contextual feature of the process of technological change.

General types of office situation

- the 'clerical industries' – including mail order houses, public administration, insurance and banking offices, manufacturing company headquarters, manufacturing company headquarters;
- small 'professional service' offices or local branches of larger concerns – solicitors, bank branches, etc.;
- offices attached to manufacturing facilities

(Green *et al.*, 1980: 25)

Many of the research studies of changes in secretarial work and typing work focussed on the word processor and its effects, while studies of clerical work dealt with data processing and mainframe computers. However, the early generations of both types of machine had varied technological arrangements which are important but which are seldom acknowledged. There were two basic types of word processing system: 'stand-alone' word processing and 'shared logic' (networked) word processing. These were technologies which were configured differently, implied different patterns of access by secretaries to files and information, and used printing systems differently, yet this distinction was often overlooked in discussions of the impacts of word processing on secretarial and typing work patterns and skills. Mainframe computers, too, could be configured in a variety of ways, though they handled only a few types of applications initially. Since then, of course, office computing has come to include a much wider set of functions and technologies than simply word processing and almost all women in offices use computers for some function or another. Personal computing now combines a range of data *and* word processing applications, computer networks have become commonplace, and electronic linkages between machines, between different parts of organisations, and even between organisations themselves, have changed the terrain of women's office work. But despite the spread in the coverage of information technologies in offices, there are few, if any, real-life examples of the 'paperless office' which was the vision of many commentators in the early days; there is still a gap between this vision and the reality of information technology in the office, which has in many cases been much more prosaic and much less dramatic than was often assumed.

The impacts of information technologies upon secretarial and typing jobs have also been mediated by management strategies for organising white-collar work, and these strategies vary between employers in different economic sectors. Again, the classification by Green and his colleagues is helpful, because it shows the centrality of office labour to the overall enterprise. This conditions the extent to which management seeks to use information technology to rationalise the work of their female office staff. The Bravermanian vision of the white-collar factory, characterised by a 'stream of paper processing' (1974: 301), dominated both labour process and feminist analyses of the reorganisation of women's work consequent upon the introduction of office automation. Where clerical work is the business of the organisation, where clerical costs are a large proportion of office costs, or where management strategies for work reorganisation are highly developed in response to market conditions or pressure from shareholders, the introduction of new technologies into the office is indeed part and parcel of thoroughgoing centralisation and rationalisation programmes which confirm some of these pessimistic predictions of clerical deskilling. Usually, such rationalisation involves the integration of word processing and audio typing, centralised typing pools and standardised documents, so that the routine experienced by the women who work in such settings derives from the totality of these arrangements:

> ... You do feel really chained to the WP ... you really want to scream because you are just sat there all the time. It gets sometimes that it just gets so bad, if you are busy you just go to the loo for a break, just for a walkabout because it gets so bad sometimes ... It is terrible ... We don't take it out on each other. We just shout! We don't get at each other because we all feel the same way. We just talk to ourselves, just moan to yourself about it, or to each other.
>
> (WP Operator in a financial services company, quoted in Webster, 1986: 159)

Yet in some contexts, in small manufacturing companies and in parts of the public sector, for example, management strategies are often ill-defined, non-taylorist or non-existent, and this has meant that secretaries and typists may escape managements' most searching attempts at work rationalisation. The secretary speaking here works in a small family firm where managerial control is paternalist, so she is able to retain control of her working patterns:

> Nobody ever says "I want this doing" or "My work is more important". They tried it once or twice and I shot them down, so they don't try it any more. Guy's son, Richard, he tried it once or twice, but I just said to him, "You are not my priority at the moment. Just leave yours with theirs and I'll do it when I get round to it" . . . I think you have got to make it clear.
>
> (Quoted in Webster, 1986: 176)

In white-collar factories, the restructuring and deskilling of clerical and secretarial jobs has been a much longer-term affair, one which in fact predates the application of computer-based technologies (Crompton and Jones, 1984), and which certainly predates the current generation of information technologies (Mumford and Banks, 1967; Rhee, 1968; Olerup, 1985). Indeed, Braverman's own analysis was very clear on this point, for he described the long-running taylorisation of office work operating independently of any given level of technology. Long before the days of word processing or computers in offices, women's jobs in many companies were being intensified and controlled through a combination of technical and organisational innovations. In fact, one of the critical technical elements in the process of deskilling secretarial work was the introduction of centralised audio dictation systems, which permitted the separation of secretaries and typists from their bosses and their grouping together in typing pools. Word processing was conceived by IBM as an application of their magnetic tape typewriting technology which would build upon this centralisation of typing work (Glogau, 1985).

There have been enormous country variations, too, in the application and effects of new technologies on women's office work. Some of the worst accounts of alienated automated office work have come from the United States, where employers, again especially in the financial services sector, have been particularly efficient in creating white-collar factories devoid of personal contact and marked by repetitious, isolated, machine-paced work (Machung, 1984, 1988; Feldberg and Glenn, 1983). Part of the reason for this seems to stem from the fact that taylorised work has historically been more widely implemented in the United States than elsewhere, and the application of office automation appears to have reinforced and extended this form of work organisation (De Kadt, 1979; Appelbaum and Albin, 1989). In other countries, work rationalisation has been taken to lesser lengths and other patterns of skill have persisted; in many countries, companies still employ personal secretaries who are all-round workers (Glogau, 1985; Bergouignan *et al.*, 1989; Webster, 1993). In Germany, secretarial work and secretarial skills are regarded as professional and the secretary continues to be expected to work independently and in France she works as part of a team, whereas in Britain she is a supporter of male superiors (Littek and Heisig, 1987; Felstead, 1995). The model of work and automation widely implemented in the United States has not been the only model for all countries, though through the efforts of US multinational companies, management consultants and business schools there appears to be strong pressure on company managements in other countries to move towards the patterns of work organisation which have been honed in the United States.

Clerical jobs in banking and finance

As we have seen, secretarial and typing work is a central area of women's employment. More routine clerical work, involving less typing and more other information- and data-handling activities, is also an important source of office employment for women. Many of the concerns raised in relation to the automation of secretarial work have also been raised in the context of clerical jobs: the deskilling of work, the creation of white-collar factories, the vulnerability of women – through their concentration in these jobs – to the negative effects of information technologies, and the complex nature of the work with its mixture of routine activities and tasks of a more discretionary and sometimes social character (Crompton and Jones, 1984; Smith and Wield, 1987a, 1987b; Knights and Sturdy, 1987; Crompton and Sanderson, 1990).

The financial services sector has a long-established history of automation. In banking, the automation of operations dates back to the 1960s when the first mainframe computers were introduced. A second wave of automation took place in the 1970s with the introduction of microelectronics-based technologies into back office functions like cheque clearing and funds transfer, and with the development of front office counter technologies like automatic telling machines. Regional operations centres were set up to perform some routine processing tasks, such as cheque processing, and thus, the white-collar factory was well and truly created. Indeed, of all the finance industries, the banks were the earliest to automate and the most zealous in their application of taylorist work fragmentation (Crompton and Jones, 1984; Lane, 1988; Child and Tarbuck, 1988). The way in which the streamlining of work is achieved has to some extent changed with the more recent introduction of distributed, online processing and the separation of élite area offices, which handle business accounts, foreign business and personnel matters, from the branches (Murray, 1987). But the 'routinisation' of the clerical jobs which constitute the bulk of banking employment is still one of the most important tendencies in this work, and it is a long-running process, one which was embarked upon many decades ago, well before the introduction of any new technologies (Crompton and Jones, 1984; Campbell-Kelly, 1993).

The sexual division of labour in banking has endured successive reorganisations of work, and the bringing of successive areas of work – from back office to front office to direct customer handling functions – under the sway of automation. Women and men are distributed unequally throughout the organisations, and women remain at the bottom of the banking hierarchy (insofar as a hierarchy still exists). They are also often physically segregated. In the branches, women predominantly work as cashiers (which are increasingly keyboarding functions), standing order clerks, personal bankers (effectively upgraded enquiry clerks), and in routine back office machine operating functions. In both branches and processing centres, women's relationship to machines is a close one; many more women than men work at machines, deemed appropriate for this work because of their keyboard skills (Smith and Wield, 1987b). Despite the tacit skills which they develop, for want of proper training, in order to use computers, female bank clerks remain partially skilled and massively undervalued – dismissed both by management and by their more technologically-confident male colleagues – even when they acquire some expertise:

> It does go to show that management take for granted the fact that a woman faced with a piece of machinery and a manual coming in the next day can get on and do it. We'd prefer to have the proper training but we'll get on and do it. You don't get recognised for being able to do that ... I'd like to know a list of alternatives so as not to bring the system crashing down. But they don't give you much credit. You get frightened of doing things. Then you ring the computer centre staff and they think you're idiots because you don't know what to do.
>   (Bank clerical worker, quoted in Murray, 1987: 17–19)

Women do not stand to gain a great deal in promotional terms from such a system of work organisation in the branches. At the same time, some of the previous features of clerical work with which women identified their femininity have vanished with computerisation. For example, the manual process of producing 'neat' ledgers was in the past a source of job satisfaction; the chance to display skill in this area has been lost:

When I first started here there were massive ledgers – I was given responsibility for two of them. There was much personal pride in keeping these straight, neat and accurate – competition between the girls about who's got the best ledger. Now you just 'blame the computer'.
(Bank employee, quoted in Crompton and Jones, 1984: 73)

Other 'feminine' skills have come to the fore in the modern bank branch, as routine functions are automated, yet contact with customers continues to necessitate 'interpersonal skills' (Child and Tarbuck, 1988: 31). This could potentially represent upskilling, enabling bank staff to diversify away from routine and repetitive tasks towards a new range of duties where the emphasis on customer service is much greater than before (Senker and Senker, 1994). However, the argument that banking employment requires 'interpersonal skills' seems to have replaced 'nimble fingers' as the justification for employing women in certain positions; the key issue, however, is whether these skills are acknowledged, valued and paid for, whether women attract the status and pay of the enskilled. It does not seem, to date, that they do. Indeed, the process of technological change appears to have done little to improve the ghettoisation of women in banking clerical work, although it may have changed its justification.

Despite the use of the 'qualifications lever' by women to progress through firms' internal labour markets (Crompton and Sanderson, 1990), the opening up of career structures to women has coincided with the dismantling of job opportunities wrought by the automation process (Game and Pringle, 1984), and with a progressive 'delayering' of organisations which has closed off career paths which formerly existed. 'Careers' are still largely enjoyed by professional men, while 'jobs', including, as we saw in Chapter 4, an increasing number of part time, peripheral jobs, are still carried out predominantly by women (MacInnes, 1988).

Lower-grade clerical workers have experienced more unambiguous deskilling; this, together with decreased options for job rotation, the growth of part-time jobs and branch network reorganisation programmes, does suggest an overall degradation of this type of clerical work (Crompton and Jones, 1984). The banks' growing centralised processing centres, where the work is completely regimented and almost indistinguishable from batch processing in manufacturing, are totally female dominated; here, women work as machine-room operators.

The implementation of information technology confirms this degradation of work. The design, configuration and implementation of IT in banking and in a number of other industries has moved towards the linking of islands of automation into integrated technological systems, and this facilitates a much more pervasive restructuring of clerical work than took place in the

---

Data processing centres in Australian banks

The main activity is clearance operations. As the computer runs 24 hours a day, this work is performed in shifts, the night shift consisting almost exclusively of married women, many of whom are migrants ... if deskilling and degradation apply anywhere in the banks it is here. The women work under assembly line conditions with no possibility of advancement.

(Game and Pringle, 1984: 55–6)

---

days of simple, discrete automation. Of course, the design and configuration of information technologies in banks is in itself a function of the objectives of corporate management, though these objectives do appear to become crystallised in the machinery.

The degradation of women's clerical work and the diminution of promotion prospects (which has in fact been noted in relation to both men's and women's jobs (Smith and Wield, 1987b)), has to be seen in the context of overall developments within the finance sector over the past two decades. In Britain, in Australia, and in a number of other countries, the sector has been dramatically deregulated, and this has brought intensified competition between different players in the sector. In other countries, most notably Germany, the trend has been somewhat different; a more highly regulated product and labour market has led to banks attempting to preserve clerical skills and use them to increase flexibility between job tasks (Lane, 1988). Changes in employment are therefore part and parcel of overall corporate strategies which in a number of countries have recently focussed on measures for maintaining and improving market position (Rajan, 1985; Fincham *et al.*, 1994). To address these market pressures, the financial institutions have made a series of innovations which have had profound implications for women in clerical jobs. The creation of a 'second wave' of back offices performing functions previously performed in branches, the application of telematics technologies to permit the reorganisation of clerical activities, and the automation of managerial control functions, all carry the deskilling, intensification and isolation of clerical labour in banks – still predominantly performed by women (Storey, 1987) – to new heights.

A growing number of banks, insurance companies and other corporations have reorganised their operations around 'telemediated' back offices, in which business is dealt with over the telephone and personal contact is completely eliminated (Richardson, 1993). 'Agents' receive calls via automatic call distribution systems which route customer calls according to pre-programmed instructions. Attached to the system by headphones and a monitor, the individual agent has access to customer data, and deals with a narrow range of activities relating to that customer. In line with the general trend towards the fragmentation of work in the industry and its allocation to specialist workers (Storey, 1987: 52), an agent may be dedicated to new customer business, or to domestic policies, or to company business, but within that restricted range of activities, all agents have access to the same data, and so are completely interchangeable. Furthermore, used effectively, these arrangements give management substantially increased control over the labour process. In First Direct bank, for example, the automatic call distribution system provides real-time information on the performance of agents which is supplemented by the taping of all calls. The tone and style of conversations with customers are monitored, as are the subjects of these conversations and the performance of 'banking representatives' in selling additional services (Richardson, 1993: 8).

This work is regimented and isolated. Most routine services are automated, and the agent merely takes the customer through a set of transactions prescribed by a system menu, the responses to which are also recorded. It is not work that is considered appropriate for people with a background and skills in conventional banking and finance; these are not needed because operations are, literally, 'systematised' (Richardson, 1993: 18). Instead, recruitment is based on behavioural skills and personality traits such as telephone manner and ability to work as part of a team, again, the kind of 'interpersonal skills' which women are particularly held to possess.

In the UK, the retail banks are now embarking upon the 'outsourcing' of clerical operations to back office service providers, using IT networks to transmit data between bank and subcontractor. Cheque processing, for example, is one operation which has been mooted as ideal for outsourcing. With this arrangement, the direct employment contract between bank and clerical worker is broken. So too are career or promotion possibilities which might potentially enable women to progress out of clerical work and into other banking functions. Their employment in organisations which specialise, not in offering a banking service to the public but in processing information, cuts them off from customers and keeps them away from the customer service work for which it is often argued that women are so suitable. Indeed, the pool of clerical labour from which the subcontracting banking services companies draw may need to have no experience or background in banking whatsoever, but may simply need some task-specific training in entering cheque details onto a computer system. Certainly, outsourcing cuts the connection between clerical workers and the banks for whom they ultimately work, and requires no understanding on the part of these workers of the significance of their work within its organisational context.

Of course, information technologies in financial services do not need to be used in this way. They can have the reverse implications, allowing the creation of clerical functions requiring product knowledge and the exercise of judgement and discretion. Appelbaum and Albin report on clerical workers in one US firm who handle a range of customer service functions, including selling insurance, explaining rating procedures to customers, answering their queries, and responding to complaints (1989: 253). However, even here, the possibilities for promotion into managerial jobs are slim, as the stripping out of management layers is reducing the potential for upward mobility. The trend has been for the creation of routine data entry jobs in the industry, and the employment of married women as part-time low-paid workers who receive no training, have no promotion prospects, and 'who require very few skills beyond the typing accuracy they must demonstrate to be hired' (1989: 252)

Managerial control of the clerical function with the aid of office automation

Several monitoring systems keep track of the work done by each clerk. An automatic call distributor distributes phone calls and records the number of calls answered and those lost (by customers hanging up) on each line. The clerk's code, entered into the computer terminal, with every transaction, provides a tally and an error count on information processed. In this more rationalized system, each part of the job must be handled according to specific procedures and within a specified time frame.

(Feldberg and Glenn, 1983: 72)

Glenn and Feldberg's research into clerical work in the United States supports this conclusion (Glenn and Feldberg, 1979; Feldberg and Glenn, 1983). Their analysis of developments in clerical work organisation identifies the different effects on different segments of the labour force, and in particular differences along the lines of sex. There have been several effects associated with the computerisation of clerical work. In addition to the overall decline in female employment within the industry, at the level of firms, women's prospects for upward mobility have diminished as the higher-level, more complex clerical jobs which they might aspire to are eliminated. At the level of the organisation of work within firms, Feldberg and Glenn argue that technological change has not had uniform effects across jobs and segments of the labour force. Women have been differently and more negatively affected than men by the changes accompanying office automation (1983: 73). Feldberg and Glenn cite the case of a utility company, in which a computer system has permitted the centralisation of customer files to which the clerks have instant access. This in itself is a positive change for both clerks and customers, because clerks can now immediately access customer information while dealing with telephone queries, and set up procedures to deal with problems. However, the job is also more closely monitored and regimented, and the scope for deploying specialist knowledge has disappeared.

The shift from batch to online processing is also identified as significant in research into the automation of British insurance work (Knights and Sturdy, 1990; Sturdy 1992). Clerks can now perform their tasks more quickly and smoothly than in the early days of batch computer systems, and thus eliminate the frustration of the backlogs of work which were created, but these gains are double-cdgcd:

> ... You can get work 'shifted' by 'punching' in ... used to have to wait for ages and you were always looking for files ... I'm always telling other departments how great it is ... you can see your own work and errors but it is not terribly interesting – I don't like sitting in front of the screen all day.
>
> (Annette, a clerical worker in the motor insurance industry, quoted in Knights and Sturdy, 1990: 143)

Fearfull (1992) is more optimistic, and emphasises the tacit skills which are still necessary in many clerical jobs, particularly in small organisations and outside the financial services sector. She finds that office automation has not removed the requirement for specialist knowledge and experience of customer circumstances and organisational procedures. However, Feldberg and Glenn argue that these highly-graded customer service elements of clerical jobs are transferred into the male domain, so that the grading of the clerical job itself is changed with the feminisation and automation of the work. In their research, men with practical knowledge have retained seniority, while the female clerical job has become a routine and regimented function. Overall, it seems that women's clerical work is becoming increasingly specialised and downgraded, and increasingly being organised around little other than task-specific knowledge. Routine clerical work shares with secretarial work the status of women's speciality; women in this sector are being firmly fixed in low-grade jobs (Crompton and Jones, 1984: 137–48; Lane, 1988: 87; Crompton and Sanderson, 1990: 166).

This low status is underlined by the abysmal level and quality of training in new technology which is given to secretarial and clerical workers. This was particularly true in the early days of computerisation, but it remains the case even today. In many cases, the needs of clerical workers are so seriously overlooked that they are given no training at all on the new machines; in other cases, they are given the barest minimum of training, enough to give them a brief résumé of the machine's functions before starting to work with it (Cindio and Simone, 1989; Senker and Senker, 1994). To women in offices, the first computers and word processors were unfamiliar devices, and the human/computer interfaces of the early machines were not always user-friendly. Operating manuals, too, were invariably opaque and impenetrable, so offered little by way of support to the novice user. In addition, many women have had, and some still have, a severe lack of confidence with operating computers.

In this context, the process of computerisation has been a profoundly upsetting experience for many women in offices, in which they were faced with unfamiliar technologies and given little support in getting to grips with these new machines. 'We had tears initially', I was told in 1982 by a company manager who had just bought his personal secretary a word processor and left her to learn for herself how to use it (Webster, 1986: 274). The secretary, a very competent and conscientious woman, felt extremely anxious about her ability to cope with the new technology, and in this anxiety she was by no means alone. Many women were introduced to computer technologies in a similar way; implementation was conducted without the slightest attention to their needs.

Yet, contrary to the notion that women do not 'meddle' or experiment with technologies, there are many instances of office workers developing enormous resourcefulness in their use of computers – using manuals, teaching themselves, and often teaching their colleagues as well – (Lie and Rasmussen, 1985; Microsyster, 1988; Lehto, 1989; Jones, 1995). Indeed, the fact that office workers managed to get these early computer systems to work in such hostile conditions is testimony to the patience, adaptability and also the technical facility of the women concerned. However, such a piecemeal approach to their training by office managements has done nothing to advance their skills base or job mobility (Liff, 1993), and their own resourcefulness has also gone unrecognised in the promotion stakes. Overall, the implementation of computer technologies in the office has been done without regard for the needs of office workers, and has done little or nothing to advance their skills or prospects. To get their needs for appropriate computer systems, work design and training addressed, women have had to embark upon their own systems development projects, which put their needs at the forefront of the development process rather than on the sidelines. I examine some of these initiatives in Chapter 6.

Clerical work – if not craft labour, then what?

Craft labour forms the starting point for a labour process analysis of deskilling. But can secretarial and clerical skill changes be compared to craft skill changes? Craft labour came to be defined as skilled as much because of the bargaining power of those who perform it as because of the technical requisites of the work; clerical and secretarial labour has not enjoyed this label or this bargaining power, despite the fact that typing, for example, calls for manual dexterity and abilities which require training and time to perfect (Barker and Downing, 1980; Webster, 1986). Because clerical labour is performed by women, it does not carry the label 'skilled', and is conventionally downgraded. Phillips and Taylor expressed this point very eloquently some time ago (1980); it has been widely substantiated since then (Cockburn, 1985a; West, 1990; Liff, 1993). In addition, the use of 'deskilling' to describe changes in tertiary sector work is problematic because of the connotations of *manual* dexterity which are embedded in the concept of 'skill'. Assessment of skill changes in women's office jobs therefore becomes a very difficult process, in which the precise meaning of 'skill' and 'deskilling' has to be clarified. Murray (1987) and Butler (1988) have distinguished three aspects of skill in relation to women's office work: the skill held by the worker, the skill necessary to do the job, and the socio-political component of skill (which in the case of secretarial work misleadingly confers 'unskilled' status on the work). Crompton and Jones (1984) define 'skill' as the degree of control and autonomous action which the worker exercises in the course of her work.

It has been argued that, in addition to these abilities, the 'interpersonal' work which many women do in a range of occupations – in clerical work, in secretarial work and even in software teams in the computing industry, for example – must be regarded as skilled because it is critical to the effective undertaking of many jobs (Goodman and Perby, 1985; Davies and Rosser, 1986; Woodfield, 1994). Conventionally, it is, of course, very rarely acknowledged as a skill, except when it is exercised by men, in which case it is treated as a primary and productive, rather than as a secondary and supportive skill (Woodfield, 1994).

The gendering of 'skill'

Skill definitions are saturated with sexual bias. The work of women is often deemed inferior simply because it is women who do it. Women workers carry into the workplace their status as subordinate individuals, and this status comes to define the value of the work they do. Far from being an objective economic fact, skill is often an ideological category imposed on certain types of work by virtue of the sex and power of the workers who perform it.

(Phillips and Taylor 1980: 79)

In secretarial work, the concept of 'skill' is most laden with gender bias. The technical competence of touch-typing is not conventionally defined as skilled, while other secretarial tasks are very obviously ones which require abilities 'learnt through an apprenticeship in womanhood' (Barker and Downing, 1980: 75). These have been variously articulated as expending 'emotional labour' (using diplomacy, negotiating with people and managing feelings in the workplace) (Goodman and Perby, 1985; Machung, 1988), 'rendering service' (interacting with customers and others inside and outside the firm), and 'caring' (taking responsibility for maintaining good social relations in the workplace) (Lie and Rasmussen, 1985). The work is underpinned by gender relations characteristic of the domestic sphere, in which women perform a variety of roles, from wife to mother (Benet, 1972; Pringle, 1988). Such relations are not easily amenable to analysis in terms of conventional notions of skills and deskilling, yet they are profoundly implicated in the process of technological change. Barker and Downing (1980) have argued that both secretarial and typing work are gendered jobs in which control of workers has traditionally been achieved through patriarchal relations in the office:

> Flattery and praise, the engendering of a sense of indispensability, as well as an underlying, albeit sometimes explicit, sexual innuendo, are all forms of patriarchal control. As in society generally, (women in the office) are encouraged to fulfill their roles as 'real women', both as 'office wife', caring and servicing groups of or individual men, and as whore/prostitutes, the conventional dolly bird/sex object – and in this latter role, they frequently become the object of sexual harassment, even if in the guise of a joke.
>
> (Barker and Downing, 1980: 74–5)

These relations of control, however, provide loopholes which allow secretaries and typists to evade the direct and thoroughgoing control of management. Word processing, according to Barker and Downing, therefore represents a managerial programme to transform these patriarchal relations of control into more taylorised and mechanical forms of control. Though their analysis of secretarial labour and of the relations of control at work in offices is very rich, Barker and Downing fall back upon a Bravermanian analysis in which all secretarial and typing jobs are ultimately conventionally deskilled and reduced to one and the same level following the automation process. This has not been borne out by detailed studies of women's experiences of the transition to word processing and other information technologies in offices. Women's office work turns out to be far more complex, and still very variable across industry sectors and types of organisation, despite the advent of information technologies and despite moves in many companies to systematise the work of secretaries, typists and clerks. Moreover, the labour which is expended by women in offices is one of the clearest examples of 'gendered labour' (Davies and Rosser, 1986). This means more than that it is work carried out by a predominantly female work-force within a gendered office hierarchy. Gendered labour is also labour which is underpinned by the roles which women play in society generally and by the expectations which are made of them to fulfil their roles as carers and servicers, decorative objects and sex symbols. A gendered job is 'one which capitalised on the qualities and capabilities a woman had gained by virtue of having lived her life as a woman' (Davies and Rosser, 1986: 103). How-ever, because the skills used by women in gendered jobs are not acquired through training or within the workplace, they are not acknowledged as skills and go unrewarded in financial terms. According to Berg and Lie (1995), it is precisely the existence and persistence of this gendered labour in all its complexity which explains why the computerisation of offices has not been more dramatic in its effects upon women's office tasks and skills. Female office workers, they argue, have largely continued to be consigned to the performance of tasks involving communication, interpretation and servility; their ability to do so is regarded as a natural aspect of femininity and thus is rendered invisible. A classic deskilling analysis, though useful for an understanding of the job degrading aspects of technological change and of the re-organisation of many offices, fails to capture the complexities of these processes or the gender relations of office work. It fails to address the ambiguities and variations in these processes, and significantly fails to consider the reasons for variability across industries in terms of specific managerial strategies and practices, and specific responses of female office workers.

Flexible Fordism? Women under squeeze

What of women's work outside the clerical industries? How have manual and manufacturing jobs been changed, if at all, by the progressive implementation of computer-based technologies? Have there been discernible effects on manual skills? And if so, has the sexual division of labour been upset by shifts in skill patterns?

Outside of the office, one of the most important and long-established employers of women is the clothing industry. Here, women's employment dates back to before the Industrial Revolution when they worked as spinners, weavers and seamstresses in the home. With the Industrial Revolution and the growth of mass production, women's employment shifted from the home to the factory, and today women still make up the bulk of labour in the manufacturing process – more than three-quarters of its workers throughout the world, and around 90 per cent in the UK (Coyle, 1982; Truman and Keating, 1988; Rhodes and Carter, 1993). But, as I showed in Chapter 4, the industry has undergone significant changes in the last few decades – both in manufacturing technologies within firms and in inter-firm patterns of organisation and innovation. Both developments have had profound implications for women's labour processes as well as for patterns of women's employment.

The clothing manufacturing industry has always been highly sexually stratified. It has historically been craft-based, and the craft element of garment production (the 'making through' of the entire garment initially, and subsequently discrete operations like grading and cutting fabric) has been monopolised by male craft workers. Through the strenuous defensive organisation of male skilled workers in the industry, women have been confined to 'assembly' and routine machining jobs. As in so many other branches of work, the clothing industry has been the arena for the creeping rationalisation and automation of labour processes over the years; in this process, the skills of men and women, and the role of machinery in the production process have fundamentally altered.

The clothing industry is notorious for its low pay, and because of its reliance on cheap labour (often ethnic minority women), it has a tradition of low capital investment and application of technology. The rationalisation of garment production was initiated with the application of scientific management as late as the interwar period. The 'making through' of a garment, which had previously been carried out by a single tailor, was subdivided into multiple processes which were then progressively mechanised (Coyle, 1982). This simplification and mechanisation process provided the basis for the deskilling of operations and the entry of female machinists who assembled sections of sewn fabric into complete garments (Cockburn 1985a). They were employed to perform a vast range of sewing operations – stitching pockets, sleeves and collars, for example, and at high speeds – and were classified as semi-skilled. Skilled male workers gradually retreated, until they were to be found only in the small, and as yet still skilled, enclave of fabric cutting.

In the 1970s and 1980s, the introduction of CAD/CAM (computer-aided design/computer-aided manufacture) which took place in the large firms that could afford this level of capital outlay (Phizacklea, 1990), threatened again the tenure of skilled men and facilitated the deskilling of the cutting function. Before laying and cutting fabric was computerised, it was a manual and mental process, the transformation of which Cockburn (1985a) documents in some detail. It involved laying the cloth, laying the pattern on the fabric, marking the fabric and cutting the fabric. It required judgement of how to juxtapose pattern pieces in the optimum way so as to maximise cloth use and minimise wastage, tacit knowledge of fabric, grain and nap, and considerable experience.

These decisions are now computer-assisted; they are carried out using machines which are operated not only by the men who used to do this work in their heads, but also by women who have been employed as technicians. Lay-making by computer involves entering into the computer the style number of the garment, and the width of the material that the operator knows the lay must fit. She then positions each pattern part which appears on the computer screen into the displayed length of cloth. The computer eliminates all unnecessary space between them, but ensures that they do not overlap, and that certain constraints such as grain lines, nap or pattern in printed fabrics are not abused. The computer then either activates a plotter which prints out a paper marker, or alternatively produces a magnetic tape to drive the off-line automated knife in the cutting room (Cockburn, 1985a: 58).

There is still some competence necessary to operate this equipment, and this is a competence that has been acquired by women. But the cutting job is now a machine-minding job and is performed by both men and women. Moreover, an understanding of the whole labour process, which was one of the hallmarks of the craft, has been destroyed by the fragmentation of the work, so that men and women now work according to a routine and pace prescribed by the computerised system. And the move from human to machine control makes the whole process much more readily amenable to managerial control, both of labour and of materials:

> 'It puts management in the driving seat', one senior manager told me. For instance, it is possible to check the computer record and retrace every step in the production of pattern, lay and cut to detect the source of an error. Employees' time-keeping and output can be monitored. The computer reduces the employer's dependence on his employee's memory and co-operation ... The employer is delighted to shake off his dependence, as one ... manager put it, upon 'the time-served man who thinks he is a cut above the rest' and to operate instead with a flexible, semi-skilled team, responsive to management demands.
>
> (Cockburn, 1985a: 61)

The feminisation of the hitherto male-dominated areas of the garment industry (pattern laying, cutting and sewing), then, has coincided with the deskilling of the tailoring craft, and this has compromised the male workers' sense of masculinity and thrown the sex-typing of the work into flux. Craft control over the labour process has been eliminated, and control, both machine-based and patriarchal, has been eagerly assumed by management. Indeed, the presence of women has given rise to a particular expression of patriarchal control which is common in industries making extensive use of female labour:

> One of the attributes of a manager working with women was the ability to know how to get the best result from a woman – to pinch her bottom, or kick her bottom . . .
>
> (Cockburn, 1985a: 264)

> For many operations we can already take the human skills acquired over time by those directly involved in producing garments and trans-late them into instruction sets which direct a computer controlled machine to perform the same function as a skilled operator. The skill is thus memorised, transferable and can be replicated indefinitely.
>
> (H. Joseph Gerber, president of Gerber Scientific Inc., quoted in Phizacklea, 1990: 63)

The assembly of garments has traditionally been done by women and it too is being reorganised and computerised in the large firms sector of the industry. There were various skilled elements of the assembly process (for example, sewing buttonholes) which are being replaced by computer-controlled processes. Both dedicated and programmable automation create a highly monotonous and very intense job for the operator, who controlled every stitch on manual sewing machines, but is now reduced to loading and unloading the garment piece from the computerised machine (Truman and Keating, 1988: 25). With dedicated machines, the operator is tied to the machine's pro-gramme and pace of operation, and this has its attendant health and safety hazards too, because the machine cannot always be stopped if a problem occurs. With programmable automation, the operator instructs the machine in a particular operation, and it then repeatedly carries out this operation – and again the oper-ator must follow the movements of the machine rather than the machine following the movements of the operator.

The implementation of computer-based technologies within clothing firms is helping to deskill jobs and to reshape the gender profile of garment production. But, as Phizacklea (1990: 67) argues, the sexual division of labour and the deployment of female labour in the industry is by no means a closed issue. It is part of an ongoing process of the transformation of garment production. As in so many other industries, the new-found position of women in previously skilled jobs has not brought them technical training or competence, simply access to work which has been deskilled and degraded. This makes these women vulnerable to further rounds of labour-displacing automation.

In the large clothing companies, computerised production technologies have served to bring women into areas of the workplace from which they were previously excluded, and to provide them with access to jobs which are computer-aided and computer-controlled. At firm and industry level, the introduction of information systems is also significant for women, for the growth of networks of firms linked by computer networks have very important implications for the labour of female garment workers.

The industry is highly polarised between a few very large household name companies mass producing garments, and a mass of small firms, many of them family businesses in the Third World, many small sweatshops in inner city areas of the industrialised world (Dicken, 1992). In the last few decades, the industry has had to respond to a world recession in the 1970s, competition between producers in the First World and much cheaper producers from the Third World, and the increasingly volatile and quickly-changing market conditions of the 1980s and 1990s. It has done so by moving towards a much more flexible approach to the organisation of production across the entire supply chain: reduction of product development times, reduced inventory, and quick response (QR) to the demands of the market, driven by the retailers (Rhodes and Carter, 1995).

This pattern of production organisation has been referred to as the 'Benetton model' (Mitter, 1991). It is, as we have seen, a highly flexible, highly technology dependent, system of subcontract production. Retailers use electronic point of sale (EPOS) technologies to gather sales information which they transmit to their suppliers over computer networks. Suppliers are generally small manufacturers, either in Europe or in south east Asia and other locations, who have been selected by the retailers to work for them on a long-term basis, supplying on the terms dictated by the retailers (Webster, 1995). Production is driven by the sales information gathered by the retailers and transmitted to suppliers and is done on a small-batch basis. These arrangements have enabled the industry dramatically to reduce order-to-delivery times and levels of inventory, and to extend product differentiation and market segmentation (Rhodes and Carter, 1993).

This system is sometimes supposed to offer new opportunities for women in the clothing industry. First, it has been suggested that subcontracting networks allow them to set up as 'mini-entrepreneurs' with much greater control over their work and lives than they would have as employees (Gaeta *et al.*, 1992). Second, it is claimed that women are particularly well-suited to the team-working arrangements which characterise small batch flexible production, because they are socialised to be more attuned to group work (Chiesi, 1992) and to use their intuitive skills to manage complex relationships and systems with dexterity. Such characteristics should prompt clothing industry employers embarking on new production systems to look again at the hidden talent which their female workers offer (Rhodes and Carter, 1993).

This may be the potential of flexible production in the clothing industry; whether it is the reality is less certain. There are several aspects of women's work in this industry which do not conform to this vision. First, in addition to the smart new subcontract high fashion houses of the Third Italy, women work in rural family firms in the Third World and in the migrant labour sweatshops of the inner cities of the First World (Hoel, 1982; Coyle, 1984; Dicken, 1992). The ability of women in these conditions to transform themselves from low paid workers and homeworkers into 'dynamic small business women' (Mitter, 1991: 59) is doubtful.

The fate of female illegal immigrant workers in the black economy of garment production in the Netherlands

The way illegal immigrant workers get exploited in contract clothing firms is criminal. They are frequently housed beneath or above the workshop in which they work ... they work 7 days a week up to 19 hours a day for a mere 400 guilders. It is a modern form of slavery.

(Quoted in Mitter, 1991: 60)

Second, even in this apparently flexible system of work organisation, there is still a firm sexual division of labour in operation. In Benetton, there is a huge chasm between the women who are largely concentrated in the labour intensive parts of the production process, for instance, working as machinists very intensively on the floor of a small factory or at home, and the technically oriented core male workers who carry out many of the skilled processes in-house using high technology. Indeed, we might conclude, as Belussi (1992) does, that, notwithstanding the flexibility afforded by programmable automation, in fact as far as its women workers are concerned, this system shares many of the worst characteristics of classical fordism. It has a dual labour force, a highly taylorised labour process and continuing low pay and appalling working conditions. Belussi has dubbed the Benetton model 'decentralised fordism' (1992: 88).

Further downstream in the retailing industry, similar transformations in technology and organisation both within and between firms affects women's work. In the large retail multiples, supermarkets, and in the mail order warehouses, both production and consumption increasingly resemble an assembly line. Nor are the similarities merely superficial. Warehouse picking work, sexually segregated into picking, order assembly and packing (women's work) and truck driving and heavy goods despatch (men's work), is being progressively fragmented and automated, with 'lights out' warehousing the ultimate objective. Where human labour remains, in order picking, for example, it is confined to a fixed spot on the shopfloor and to a few simple movements – reaching and lifting items from a moving carousel, putting boxes of items on conveyor belts. As well as being repetitive, this is difficult physical labour which takes its toll of women's nerves and mental well-being, causing breakdowns and valium dependency (Cockburn, 1985a).

The picking job in a mail order company

Although you've got that much space between your machine, your bench and the belt, you've got to turn round all the time. You do get a bit ... a bit *funny in the head*. Turning round and coming back. You have to turn round to press the number you want on the machine. Then climb up one step, reach for something out the bin, the top, then the bottom bin, then come back out the door again. You aren't just stood there. You are in one spot but you are still moving. And the belts, you have to stretch to put a box on the top belt. Bend under the bench to get things. I'm a fit person. But ... the only thing is I do get *dizzy* on there sometimes. The lights are bright and glaring. Yes, I get dizzy. There's a couple of girls complains of that. And headaches.

(Picking worker, quoted in Cockburn, 1985a: 93)

The similarities with assembly work in manufacturing, and with its hazards, are obvious here. But even in jobs involving direct customer contact, the work increasingly resembles an assembly line. In food retailing, the work is fragmented into checkout work, shelf replenishment, and store management. Retailing work is strongly sex-segregated. Managerial work is male-dominated (except where women manage other women, when it is labelled 'supervisory' rather than managerial (Smith, 1988: 150)). Checkout work is done largely by women. Over the past two decades, this work has also been deskilled – in the technical sense – and wretchedly intensified. The retail employers have achieved this both through the use of point of sale technology and by using techniques of store layout which maximise customer throughput and thus financial turnover. Electronic point of sale (EPOS) technologies have made the process of entering items into the check-

---

The use of EPOS for the surveillance of checkout operators

EPOS systems can be used to monitor individual staff performance in detail. Management can measure the average time it takes for each checkout operator to handle the average item; how long they take to deal with each customer, the amount of time taken between scanning the last item and taking payment for the transaction, the amount of down-time between customers, takings per hour per operator, number of miss-scans and so on.

(Smith, 1988: 150)

---

out simply a matter of passing them over a barcode reader, and many high street retailers intensify this process by laying down targets of numbers of items per minute which must be read. Staff who fail to achieve targets for processing items are 'retrained' until they do so.

Checkout operating is therefore highly regimented and very stressful, and the only 'skill' involved in the work is in the turn of the wrist with which the woman passes the barcoded item over the scanner's 'eye'. Training is therefore on this modest level in most of the retail sector. This is true of a number of European countries, where the bulk of retailing jobs require low-level skills (Senker and Senker, 1994).

It is not only the women on the checkouts who are vulnerable to deskilling and work intensification. Clerical work in stores involves less variety and discretion over inventory handling and payment processing when EPOS systems are implemented to support the centralisation of inventory management and the elimination of store-based stock control (Smith, 1988). Indeed, electronic funds transfer at point of sale (EFTPOS) systems eliminate altogether the clerical effort in processing customers' payments (Howells and Hine, 1993). The development of teleshopping is also likely to have a significant impact on the employment and skills of retail staff, eliminating direct contact with customers, reducing the more personal and variable elements of the jobs and increasing its computer-based nature.

Classic taylorian deskilling – associated with the fragmentation and subsequent automation of discrete functions – represents only one aspect of the complex transformations which have been experienced by working in the retailing sector. The impact of the technologies of electronic point of sale and electronic data interchange, coupled with moves towards quick response (QR) to customer demand and business process re-engineering (BPR) not only are felt within discrete functions or within individual companies, but reverberate across organisations throughout the retailing sector, not only in the stores themselves but also upstream in the organisations which supply goods to the retailers. The apparel industry is one area of supply which, as we have seen, has undergone radical process transformations – if not necessarily improvement of working conditions – in order to meet the strictures of its customers. Similar developments are evident in the food and agricultural sectors. Responding to information on sales patterns transmitted over computer networks from supermarkets, food growers and suppliers have had to initiate growing-to-order programmes and quality control improvements in order to keep their supplier status to the large retailers (Frances and Garnsey, 1995). Labour scheduling has also been affected by these innovations. Maintaining a permanent 'just-in-case' work-force to meet customer orders is now untenable, and workers are instead hired on a casual – daily or even part-daily – basis using labour agencies. The demand for labour may either be poor (when supermarket orders fall or when weather conditions are unfavourable), or conversely it may be intensified when orders are high:

> I would say an average day would be an eight hour day. Ten to twelve years ago an average day would probably be a five to six hour day, because they want to start at nine and finish at half past two to three o'clock which obviously tied in with the schools and children. We find that difficult now with some women, we've got farmers and packers crying out for women but they want them to work from half past six in the morning to six o'clock at night.
>
> (Spokesperson from an agricultural labour agency, quoted in Frances and Garnsey, 1995: 22)

While on the one hand, therefore, the women's work is casualised, on the other hand, when they *are* required to work, their labour is intensified and increasingly sweated. Either way, Frances and Garnsey argue that their position, both as labourers and as final consumers of the food sold in supermarkets, has become increasingly a reactive one in a system in which change is largely initiated by the strategies of the big retailers to control very tightly the supply both of goods and of female labour.

Conclusions on women's work and its transformation

In the early days of the implementation of IT, in the late 1970s and early 1980s, there was some evidence to suggest that employers had yet to turn their most searching rationalisation programmes in the direction of their female work-forces, concentrated in unskilled and semi-skilled occupations and offering relatively cheap labour. However, the global economic and political climate has altered profoundly since then, and this has changed the terrain upon which companies organise their work and their workers. Markets are increasingly constructed globally and are increasingly volatile and therefore competitive. Pressure upon company managements to address this competition in a number of ways, one of which is to lower the costs of production and the price of labour, largely through automation, grows all the time. At the same time, the break-up of the former socialist bloc in the Soviet Union and Eastern Europe (to a lesser extent in China), and of the social democratic systems in the Nordic countries, removes any alternative economic system to that of the market and signals the break-up of countervailing ideologies. It also widens the markets to which companies can orient their products and services, and widens the pool of (exploitable) female labour upon which they can draw. Then, the decline of the trade union movement in many countries also reduces the ability of labour to resist exploitation and managerial deskilling programmes. In this context, the restructuring and automation of many jobs historically performed by men has largely been accomplished, and we see managements pressing home their deskilling agendas.

Indeed, in terms of the deskilling of labour by capital, women's work is largely being rationalised and routinised. If the deskilling of craft jobs held by men was one of the first outcomes of the process of computerisation, then managements now appear to have turned their attention to intensifying the work done by women, in back offices, shops, hospitals and factories. Corporate streamlining and re-engineering programmes which are currently in vogue (see, for example, Hammer, 1990) affect women's as well as men's jobs; indeed, no area of enterprise is exempt from these latest searches for rationalisation.

One of Cockburn's (1985a) interviewees in the garment industry defined 'deskilling' very aptly as losing an 'overview of the whole production process' (1985a: 66). This, in my view, is one of the most critical aspects of work which has been lost to many people working in automated jobs: their work has been fragmented to make it amenable to machine control such that they can no longer see or control the whole process. Their abilities are becoming increasingly job specific.

> 'We used to be trained to know *why* you did a certain thing,' I was told. 'One of the problems of modernization is that people are trained to do a specific job and people don't see the whole process any more.'
> (Former craft worker in the garment industry, quoted by Cockburn, 1985a: 66)

This is a very different state of affairs from the one predicted by writers who emphasised the enskilling potential of information technologies, for men and women alike. For example, in the 'informated organization' (Zuboff, 1988), distributed systems apparently allow information to be the currency of work performance. As a result, knowledge is redistributed more equitably throughout the ranks of staff, work is largely computer-mediated, and the possibilities for 'intellective skill development' multiply. This is the antithesis of taylorism, and comes about when managements abandon their reliance on technical control and labour deskilling, and recognise that contemporary market conditions call instead for flexible, responsive organisations marked by continual learning and innovation at all levels. This implies a profound change in work organisation and skill requirements.

Zuboff's account does not deal specifically with the role of women in such an organisation, but others have since taken up this argument. Among them, Scandinavian feminist writers have suggested that in flexible organisations utilising 'teamworking' arrangements, such as Saab, the organisation of work and the absence of classical hierarchies somehow 'protect' women from conventionally discriminatory assumptions about their lack of suitability for the technical elements of a production process. Gender relations, it is suggested, play a much less divisive role in group organised work, particularly in knowledge-intensive industries (Blomqvist, 1994; Gunnarsson, personal communication). Other writers have argued that the interpersonal and social skills which are required in flexible organisations, particularly those using 'teamworking' arrangements, are skills which women have developed in abundance. As a result there are promising possibilities for the exercise of these social skills, and thus for the potential of women workers to advance (see, for example, Lie and Rasmussen, 1985, Crompton and Sanderson, 1990; Mitter, 1991; Rhodes and Carter, 1993).

Teamworking and other flexible working arrangements may indeed offer considerable experiential improvements compared to atomised and deskilled work patterns. But teamworking is often also treated somewhat uncritically, perhaps precisely because it chimes in so strongly with feminist objectives to recognise the skills which women have built up through socialisation and which have gone unrecognised until now. Teamworking is not unambiguously liberatory; it has also been shown to be highly coercive of labour and to offer little improvement upon the direct control over labour achieved through taylorism (Kamata, 1983; Garrahan and Stewart, 1992). It is totalitarian and invasive, concerning itself with workers' characters as well as with their education, training and skills (Jones, 1994).

The identification of 'interpersonal', 'communicative' skills with women often appears essentialist. Although these are skills which are learnt through socialisation (but even then are not held equally by all women), and it is on this basis that they should be acknowledged, their possession by women seems to justify a sex-typing in the new 'flexible' organisation which is reminiscent of the old 'nimble fingers' argument. This argument consigned women to low-grade occupations requiring manual dexterity and speed of working, but did not allow them access to highly valued, highly paid occupations requiring the same dexterity, which were reserved for men (Pollert, 1981; Cavendish, 1981). In a similar way, it is easy to foresee 'interpersonal skills' being used as justification for confining women to new but undervalued and underpaid teamworking functions. Instead, the interpersonal content of work is more likely to be devalued precisely because it is women who bring this into the workplace (Woodfield, 1994). In Davies and Rosser's (1986) study of clerical work in the UK National Health Service, no attempt was ever made to formalise the caring work, including the counselling, that was done by these women. Caring was seen as a quality held by the individual woman, rather than a part of the job. There are therefore reasons to be cautious about the argument that women's jobs may be enskilled in the flexible, or the 'informated' (Zuboff, 1988) organisation. Even if women's communicative abilities *are* recognised as assets in the workplace, this does not guarantee them promotion or improved job or career prospects.

There is a 'gender system' operating within workplaces and within society more broadly (Sundin, 1995), and this system conditions both the objective and the ideological components of 'skill' as it applies to women's and men's jobs. Every occupation carries a gender label which defines it as masculine or feminine work – the 'gender order' of occupations. These are constructed as such under particular 'gender regimes' within particular organisations. This concept describes the gender labels attached to all parts of the production regime (the planning and execution of production, including the recruitment and management systems) within a firm, which form a central part of the culture of an organisation:

> Gender labels can be stamped on products, processes, artefacts, places, times, etc ... The gender system ... is one of segregation and hierarchization. Consequently, women and men do not do the same thing, or at least the (unspoken) rule is that they don't ... occupational designations are amended when women take on work that was previously men's work ... Work that men do is always valued more and is less restricted in terms of space and time than women's work. Technology's active role in this connection has been analysed and documented ... Technology as such has a male label and symbolic image, although artefacts could be either male, female or mixed ... Technology plays an important role in the social construction of gender.
>
> (Sundin, 1995: 346–7)

If the gender system, within which I include the attribution of 'skill', relies on the segregation and distinction between men's and women's work, then we can always expect women to be kept in occupational ghettos (even if the ghetto boundaries shift with technological change) and women's work to be devalued and degraded (no matter how much individual jobs may objectively involve competence, skill and technological knowledge). This gender system maintains male preserves in work, and allows employers to divide work-forces and treat them as separate resources.

The gender system of many jobs is in flux in this current round of technological restructuring, and the gender relations of skill are being renegotiated. The sex-typing of so-called skilled work and so-called unskilled work is changing, as both the objective skill requirements and the skilled status of work achieved through exclusion and strong bargaining power are being undermined through the reorganisation of work and the application of technologies. As we have seen, this undermining of the skilled status of work so jealously fought for and preserved by men in craft jobs has often allowed capital to move women into these jobs. In both the garment and the print industries, for example, we see the movement of women into areas of work once only open to men with apprenticeships. There is now little skill basis in the distinction between male craftsmen and female seamstresses (West, 1990).

The deskilling of women's work, just as of all work, is not a simple process. Labour process studies show that reductions in skill hinge on many factors which are related to, though not necessarily exclusively tied in with, the application of new technologies. Size of firm or organisation, sector, and spatial location affect management strategies for the use of both labour and technologies. These strategies then determine recruitment patterns, training practices and work organisation, and the requirement of skills for jobs (Thompson, 1983; Rees, 1992). In addition to management strategies, workers organising to defend and preserve their skills is central to the extent to which skill continues to be exercised, recognised and struggled over – both between capital and labour, and between women and men. But as we have seen, 'skill' as a straightforward concept of manual dexterity is on its own insufficient to help us understand the abilities and status of, and distinctions between, men and women workers (West, 1990). In some manufacturing industries, now, there is little objective distinction between men's and women's work. Women are often engaged in more technically complex work (that is, using more complex machines) than the men they work alongside (Armstrong, 1982), though men may monopolise the more expensive capital equipment and the craft status, regardless of the level of objective skill involved. Even where women operate

---

The elasticity of 'skill'

Game and Pringle found that, as a consequence of technological change, 'men's work' may become very similar to 'women's work' but that this did not call naturalistic ideologies about suitable spheres for women and men into question. Women were allocated to some jobs, men to others, and the nature of men's and women's work redefined in order to maintain the distinction between them.

(Henwood, 1987: 103)

---

relatively complex machinery, as they do in Armstrong's study of the footwear industry, their work is defined as both unskilled and labour intensive (Armstrong, 1982: 32). Men may defend their status as skilled and technically adept, even when there is no longer any objective justification for such status. In clerical work, too, the skill distinction does not explain the division between women's (clerical) and men's (administrative) jobs (West, 1990: 249).

Skill is a socio-political label which not only *results* from the bargaining power of workers, but *helps to maintain* gender inequalities and divisions of labour in the workplace. For, even when men and women do very similar work, as has ultimately happened in many of the former craft industries, distinctions between their jobs are maintained, in order to preserve this inequality (Game and Pringle, 1984). Thus, the definition of 'skill', as well as encompassing the training to which workers have access and consequently the manual dexterity used in a job, is also highly elastic, strongly dependent upon the ability of male workers to define and redefine it in terms of their own, rather than women's competences.

Extract from an interview with a training officer of an electronics plant in South Wales

. . . young males will do the work which is very similar to the women's work. But it is very difficult to put a forty year old man, who's come out of the pits, on a fiddly little job, especially amongst a group of women, but a young bloke won't bother. It's just a difference of perception over the years. You can attempt to make the jobs more masculine by putting them on machines. It could be even a more simple job than the woman is doing on the line, but as long as he's using that machine, something powerful, he'll assume that that's a man's job and he'll do it.

(Fielder *et al.*, 1990, quoted in Rees, 1992: 144)

Skill changes therefore have a gender as well as a class dimension which the simple concept of deskilling does not capture. Moreover, the social and organisational processes by which particular skills become gendered are remarkably resistant to change and, as Fielder *et al.* (1990) show, individual men are also highly resistant to the undermining of this division, clinging firmly to their status as technically adept and therefore 'masculine' workers.

The contemporary restructuring of skill is double-edged. The female ghettos of old have also seen the entry of male labour. In many offices worldwide, men have entered secretarial occupations, becoming operators of office machines, makers of cups of coffee, and gatekeepers to their (sometimes female) bosses (Pringle, 1988). In the UK, the number of men taking secretarial jobs has risen from one in eleven in 1990 to one in six in 1995, (*The Guardian*, 19 April 1995). The gender relations of secretarial work are being redefined as, in many organisations, the secretary/typist/'office wife' created with the feminisation of routine office jobs a century ago gives way to the (male or female) computer user. Of central importance in this process is undoubtedly the computerisation of typing and the elimination of the need for the particular skills of accuracy, speed and document presentation: skills which came to be the preserve of women. However, their specific association with women has also been undermined by moves in a number of organisations to eliminate through 're-engineering' programmes their secretarial labour in all but the highest echelons and to transfer the responsibility for document preparation to the executives themselves, using personal computers. In addition, the impact of feminism over twenty-odd years has perhaps made it less acceptable overtly to require women to play the handmaid role in offices. The secretarial role is fast becoming redundant, and secretaries are increasingly a 'luxury' for which many companies, rationalising their payrolls in the 1990s, are no longer prepared to pay.

As typing loses its association with 'women's work', and becomes one of the applications of personal computers, men's former reluctance to operate the keyboard disappears. Secretarial schools now run 'breakfast time training for the busy executive' (Webster, 1993: 120). This development is often cited as indicating an increasing equalisation of men and women in the office. Typing is no longer the preserve of low paid women, and information technology has democratised the office. Vinnicombe has described this development rather less romantically: executives, she suggests, 'want to get rid of the office wife and marry the computer' (*The Guardian*, 17 June 1995). While certainly the sex-typing of typing has altered, this has by no means removed the gender inequalities in office work. Where men now operate keyboards and use word processing systems, they do so for themselves, to process their *own* words and data. This is quite different from the conventional division of labour in which female secretaries and typists process *other people's* words. Moreover, there is a technical expertise associated with the operation of a personal computer which helps to explain its appropriation by professional male employees. This appropriation is typical of the gender relations of technological expertise, and simply confirms a sexual division of labour in which skill, technical know-how and employment status are still largely the preserve of men. Indeed, in offices today, masculinity is paradoxically confirmed by closeness to the computer keyboard (and to other forms of technology: the fax, the mobile phone). No longer is it so critical to the male's status to have a secretary to do the keyboarding for him.

Overall, despite changes in the gendering of certain occupations, women are still concentrated in a few 'women's jobs', and seem set to remain so (Wilson, 1994: 27). Either sexual segregation reasserts itself once the sex-typing of jobs has settled (Cockburn, 1985a), or women enter new occupations but at comparatively low levels or at comparatively low status. In the era of the widespread application of IT and computers, women are still over-represented in service jobs – clerical work, shopwork, nursing – and under-represented in manual work or in managerial and professional jobs.

Of course, women *are* moving slowly up organisational and occupational hierarchies, into lower and middle management jobs. However, they are predominantly being employed as managers in traditional sectors of women's employment; in distribution, services, health and education. They also enjoy lower status than managers in manufacturing industry, from which women are still absent (Rubery and Fagan, 1994; Crompton, 1994). In addition, some companies are relabelling their secretaries as 'trainee executives', as the secretarial function progressively disappears in its own right (*The Guardian*, 17 June 1995). There is also evidence from the United States and Europe that some women are setting themselves up as small entrepreneurs, taking advantage of subcontracting networks and flexible automation systems to create small businesses (Gaeta *et al.*, 1992).

While these developments are certainly significant for an understanding of the totality of changes which women's employment is undergoing, they are still developments which touch the lives of only a small minority of women, and in a relatively small part of the globe. The majority of women worldwide are still to be found working as employees, in a still restricted range of occupations, with still restricted prospects. For many of these women, this is the best that can be said of their employment conditions and life chances. In several countries and industries, women continue to perform menial, repetitive and highly regimented work. They remain low paid relative to their male co-workers and they remain in jobs which carry the label of unskilled. They also remain poorly represented by their trade unions, and indeed it is where women have organised themselves that they have been most able to challenge some of the worst aspects of their working conditions (Elson, 1989; Findlay, 1989; Women Working Worldwide, 1991).

It is the situation of women such as this which makes an analysis of labour process – coupled with the insights into gender divisions in the workplace derived from feminist analysis – of continuing relevance. Although the 'labour process debate' is over two decades old, and although it has many well-known and well-documented drawbacks (its inattention to worker resistance, its gender blindness), it still offers us important conceptual tools for assessing developments in the detail of work and for evaluating the place of information technologies in these developments. The conduct and experience of work, in the ordinary, prosaic jobs which the majority of women still carry out, is not, in my view, an *issue passé*. It is precisely because the degradation of many jobs that women do is a continuing process that this degradation continues to merit, some twenty years after Braverman's death, our attention.

CHAPTER 6

Women in systems design – values, methods and artefacts

> When information technology intervenes – in work processes – in women's practices, concepts and thinking, in women's subjectivity, it is politically important for women to define information technology. By defining information technology women define also themselves, their own lives and their femininities.
>
> (Vehviläinen, 1994b: 109)

The definition of information technology systems by conventional processes has signally failed women in workplaces. There is an enormous gulf between the practice of systems designers and the world of work inhabited by women. We have already examined the computing profession, and the absence of women from the creative echelons of the profession in Chapter 3. In the sense that women are absent from the development process, their needs and concerns go unrepresented. But the issue is more than simply one of a numerical absence of women from all but the menial and routine aspects of computing work. It is also more than one of the conditions within which computing professionals work, which are antithetical to many women's lives, and of the values and culture of IT firms. The very processes and methods used in the development of computer systems are carried out in a world apart from that of the workers who are the users; the gulf between the technical-rational methods of much computer systems development and the working lives, skills and competences of women is a particularly deep one.

Computer systems developments, particularly those utilising a 'hard systems' approach, are conventionally both positivist and technicist, following in the traditions of western scientific thought (Bødker and Greenbaum, 1993). Analysts take an uncritical view of the world to be automated, concentrating their efforts on the technical capabilities and constraints of the machines. Tools and techniques for building systems become the central preoccupation, and these are often taken as the starting point for the design process. In such a technical-rational approach, information and data flows are elevated, whereas relationships between people are largely ignored. The process itself is often handled in a strictly linear fashion, as one 'phase' of development proceeds neatly from another.

On the other hand, in such projects, the organisation, its work relations and its work design, are treated unproblematically: issues of power and gender are not acknowledged, and the organisation is conceived of as a rational and harmonious entity. The work to be automated, too, is approached mechanistically, as if it were organised according to rational and neutral principles. Indeed, the failure of computer systems developers to address critically the organisation of the work they confront means that they often simply replicate oppressive systems of work organisation in automated form. Computer users – those who work at the sharp end of the system – are excluded from the process of design, because expertise is seen as residing in the heads of computing professionals and not in those who know the work process or the organisation. In all, therefore, conventional systems development is conducted in the abstract, virtually disconnected from the 'real world of work'.

Mediating between work and information technology

It was the first time that I became an interpreter, a mediator between the computing professionals and the users ... The analysts were arrogant in meetings, spoke with concepts and language that had no connection with work. The discussion was on a 'yes'–'no' level. There were no possibilities for co-operation. I thought, how can they be so helpless? I got worried about them: they were not able to explain their procedures. The meetings continually had the very same problem. There was a lack of understanding about the contents of our work. I looked for an interpreter's role in both sides. I could somehow think in both concepts.

(Eve, a Finnish systems developer, quoted in Vehviläinen, 1994b: 110)

Such criticisms of 'hard systems design' are well established, and other approaches (such as soft systems methodology and human factors approaches) have been developed in order to address these issues, in particular to allow for a recognition of organisational contexts and users' needs in the process of systems development (Friedman with Cornford, 1989). But there remain objections to the gender-blindness in this process. Since women are still largely absent from the computing professions, which remain male-dominated the world over, systems developments are still done by men, through the eyes of men. The 'objectivity' which is aspired to in the design process is in fact the viewpoint of the men who design. De Beauvoir's comment on men's representation of the world has strong resonances for feminist systems developers:

> Representation of the world, like the world itself, is the work of men; they describe it from their own point of view, which they confuse with the absolute truth.
>
> (Simone de Beauvoir, 1970, quoted in Fox-Keller, 1985: 3)

Here, women are the objects rather than the subjects of the development process, largely invisible and certainly unheard. Tijdens's (1994) survey of the automation of offices in the Netherlands found that the majority of women, particularly in the lower grades of office work, are completely bypassed in discussions over the introduction of new equipment. Belgian and French offices are also guilty of consulting their female workers to a minimal extent, and indeed making patronising assessments of the women's interest in, or ability to make, a real contribution to the innovation process (Chalude, 1984, cited in Liff, 1993). Even where issues of power and organisational politics are recognised, for example, in the 'softer' discipline of information systems, gender does not enter this discourse and organisational relations are seen in gender-neutral terms (Vehviläinen, 1994a). Gender divisions and gender relations in the workplace still go unnoticed. Human factors may be bolted on to existing methods of systems design, local and contingent knowledge of work and information handling processes held by 'users' in an amorphous sense may now even be incorporated into the systems design process, but this does not create an awareness of the way in which skills and knowledge are defined in gender-divided terms. The particular skills and forms of knowledge which women exercise in the course of their work, and which cannot always be readily articulated or codified, are still not explicitly recognised in soft systems approaches.

It is this continuing blindness to the circumstances of women workers and their skills, and their exclusion from the process of computer systems development, which has prompted feminist intervention in order to make the process more responsive to the needs of women workers. This intervention has taken the form of a range of initiatives in systems development which have been launched over the last decade in order to incorporate a recognition of women's needs and requirements, interests and values into the process of automation.

Feminist initiatives in systems design

Dominant liberal and liberal feminist thinking on the under-representation of women in the process of technological develop-

---

Systems engineering and the reproduction of gender relations

In practice the computing scientist uses a basis of some theory plus a strong pragmatic 'if it works it must be OK' element ... This practice might be acceptable if the job was simply the introduction of automation into an area dominated by white male professionals, but as we have frequently observed, automation is brought into areas of clerical work where women predominate. However, such 'unconscious' patriarchal practices which privilege traditional 'expert' forms of knowledge, also serve to reproduce gendered patterns of clerical work, albeit in a new form ... the systems engineer, with his scientifically based tools, tends not to consider workplace relations and career structures to be elements of the design. The 'natural consequence' of his designs is therefore a reproduction of gender divisions from the engineering domain to the clerical.

(Pain *et al.*, 1993: 15)

---

ment has centred around attempts to encourage women out of low-skill, feminised ghettos and into the computing profession. Barriers to women's participation are defined as: obsolete social attitudes among employers, the inappropriateness of women's qualifications, and women's lack of awareness about the opportunities available to them. Solutions to these 'problems' include encouraging women to gain technical qualifications through awareness campaigns such as the WISE (Women into Science and Engineering) campaign launched in Britain in 1984 (Henwood, 1994), increasing women's influence and participation in computerisation projects by appointing them to decision-taking committees (Bradley, 1985) and helping women to break through the 'glass ceilings' of unequal opportunities practices which prevent them from reaching the higher echelons of the computing profession. In this liberal framework, power is associated with high-level positions in technical fields, so the objective is the insertion of women into those high-level positions (Crompton, 1994).

The problems with such an approach have become increasingly apparent. The segmentation of the computing profession has remained, as we have seen in Chapter 3, deeply entrenched, and if anything it is becoming more so. In many cases, women are making informed decisions *not* to take up technological work, because of the high personal costs of entering this type of work: hostility from male co-workers, uncomfortable relationships with family and friends, and ambivalent feelings about 'masculinity' and 'femininity' which the making of such choices throws up (Cockburn, 1985b; Henwood, 1994). Moreover, women who have successfully negotiated an entry into senior positions within the industry have limited room for manoeuvre in overturning the established work practices of the companies which employ them. In fact, in locating the problem with women themselves, this approach treats technological work unproblematically and ignores the power relations which, in a remarkably flexible manner, are constantly produced and reproduced in such spheres of activity, serving to maintain the objectives of the corporations and within those to perpetuate women's subordination to men (Game and Pringle, 1984; Hacker, 1989).

In elucidating these power relations and the ways in which women's subordination to men is sustained within technological work, just as in work more generally, a number of feminists have embarked upon initiatives in systems development which go beyond the simple equal opportunities formulations, challenge the conventional gender relations of computer systems design, and place women at the centre of development projects, both as the subjects of these projects and as the agents of strategic intervention, with the purpose of creating 'woman-friendly' or 'woman-centred' technologies. These initiatives are varied in approach and emphasis: some centre upon the participation of women workers in particular projects, others use women as computer scientists in the process of development, yet others have developed innovative methods of systems development which draw out the skills and knowledge used by women in the course of their work, and others still seek somehow to incorporate 'socially-useful' or 'women-friendly' values and objectives into the process of development with the aim of producing artefacts with alternative gender relations embedded within them.

Participative approaches to woman-friendly systems development

In the early 1980s, as the first computer systems were being introduced into workplaces, many women gained a strong sense of their own exclusion from the process of decision-taking, and of the way in which computerisation was proceeding over their heads. Some fought to become involved in the process and to shape the agenda for change in their own interests. One such group of women workers was a team of secretaries and support staff faced with the introduction of work processors into the Science Policy Research Unit (SPRU) at the University of Sussex in 1982 (Huggett, 1988). Without irony, academics well versed with the implications of new technologies for women's work

---

Word processors in SPRU

The introduction of word processors was the first major contact that most of the secretaries had had with electronics in their everyday working lives. However, some had spent several years at SPRU typing reports about the implications of the introduction of new technology for jobs, skills, etc. – often highlighting possible increases in unemployment especially in areas where many women work (such as offices, assembly lines). Despite this, some of the researchers appeared very surprised about – even taken aback by – the secretaries' concern and wish to be actively involved in the process of deciding about the introduction of word processors into their offices.

(Huggett, 1988: 4)

---

assumed that their own secretaries would accept the introduction of work processing as unproblematic.

The secretaries began to collaborate and identify as a working group when it became clear to them that word processors were to be introduced into the Unit. Their participation was not, then, initially a formalised, clearly worked out affair, in which they had a clear group identity or idea of their own objectives, but rather one which the group identity and sense of an agenda emerged out of their realisation that they, the group of people most likely to be affected by the introduction of work processing, had been the least involved in the decision-making process.

As the secretaries began to gather information about the equipment, its capabilities and its potential implications, they found themselves profoundly patronised by more senior staff – in this case, academic researchers – and also by the equipment suppliers. Researchers suggested that the secretaries need not trouble themselves with technical detail, and indeed should not be involved in the computerisation process other than at a superficial level. Suppliers addressed their remarks past secretaries to their bosses, the researchers, and made assumptions that the bosses had the purchase of the word processors in their gift. The secretaries were written off as 'old fashioned' and unable to understand the complexities of the new technology, and this of course played on their own awareness of their ignorance in this respect. In addition, their inexperience in arguing a particular case in contribution to debates in Unit-wide meetings was also used to disenfranchise and dismiss them. Their understanding of their own labour processes, on the other hand, was not taken seriously from the outset, and so it was some time before they were able to convince their superiors that the nature of secretarial, as opposed to research, work should be a central consideration in the choice of equipment.

Although guidelines for the introduction of word processing and parallel work organisation practices were finally produced by the Unit, this was not a project in which the secretaries had participated in the development of the new system on an equal basis with their colleagues and superiors. Nor was it a project in which there was an adequate arena for the secretaries to explore their own patterns of work and skill and the technological options available to them. Indeed, this project was an object lesson in the need to create supportive settings in which women workers can review their work patterns and skills, articulate their interests and fears, and where these discussions will be recognised as a full part of the process of systems development.

It is now evident that the experiences of the women at SPRU are all too common. Women workers who attempt to engage in discussions and decisions concerning the computerisation of their own jobs are frequently patronised by their colleagues and by salesmen (and they are usually men). When a group of secretaries in a research institute in the University of Copenhagen decided on their own initiative to survey the market in word processing equipment, they became concerned about effects on the work environment and occupational health hazards (Morgall, 1983, 1993). In evaluating different systems, they expressed these concerns to the sales representatives. The response was a now woefully predictable one:

> ... When a secretary made a remark about the screaming green letters on a screen, she was told by the salesman that all you had to do was pull a pair of pantyhose over the screen to avoid eyestrain.
>
> (Morgall, 1983: 111)

Despite having participated closely in the introduction of the new systems, these secretaries were given negligible training in their use, and at the same time their workload was dramatically increased. This merely served to raise their consciousness of their position further, and they became active in their union and in alliances with women professional staff. However, when Morgall reviewed their position ten years afterwards, she found that half of the secretaries had disappeared, having fallen victim to technological displacement, natural wastage and university budget cuts (Morgall, 1993: 162).

It has become quite clear that simply involving women workers in conventional decision-making processes about technological change is quite inadequate to ensure that the concerns of women are addressed. Instead, it seems necessary to create arenas in which these can be explored, articulated, recognised as legitimate, and fed into the decision-making process. This has been the approach of later feminist projects on systems development. Much of this work finds its origins in the Scandinavian collective resource approaches which were developed during the 1970s and early 1980s (Ehn and Kyng, 1987). These were founded upon the recognition that a trade union intervention into the design of *both technologies and working practices* was necessary in order to influence and preserve the quality of jobs and services, and to build more progressive values into the resulting artefacts. The UTOPIA project in Sweden, involving computer scientists, social scientists and graphic workers set out to develop a computer system for newspaper page make-up and image processing, and also incorporated policy development on working practices and on general participatory design (Pain *et al.*, 1993). It was the overall principles of systems design which the project generated which were perhaps the most influential and enduring outcomes of this work. These emphasised the importance of gaining understanding of the labour process, including the tacit aspects of skill, of doing design with users rather than for them, through mutual learning in a design group, and of designing by doing.

As Pain and his colleagues point out, the Scandinavian human-centred projects concentrated on workplaces dominated by male craft workers and not on areas where women workers prevailed. However, other human-centred projects were also important: the Lucas Plan and the UMIST human-centred lathe project in Great Britain, and, from a feminist perspective, the techniques developed by Scandinavian female researchers such as Vehviläi-nen, and Olerup and her colleagues, who emphasised women's experiences, concerns and requirements of information technologies (Pain *et al.*, 1993: 22–23).

The Sheffield Hallam University Human-Centred Systems Project (Green *et al.*, 1993b), which was conducted between 1987 and 1991, focussed upon female office workers rather than upon male manufacturing workers. It was concerned with the potential deskilling of work consequent upon the implementation of office technologies, but also saw the gender relations of office work as central to the constitution both of the work and of computer systems developed to automate that work. The project was an attempt, through action research, to democratise the development of a new human-centred online library system in such a way as to place the working methods, skills, expertise and needs of the women working in a local library at the heart of the process.

The library and the local authority of which it was a department both had a long-standing commitment to improving public service provision and simultaneously improving pay and career development opportunities through work reorganisation. In recognition of gender divisions in occupational pay and status, the work done by non-professional library staff on clerical grades (almost exclusively women) was being compared against that done by professional staff (mainly men) for similarities in skills and experience. The authority was therefore making moves towards changing the organisation of work, and improving consultation and local democracy.

The project took the 'study circle' method which was pioneered in Scandinavia (Avner, 1993; Vehviläinen, 1991) as its starting point for participant involvement in defining and working on an agenda for both technical and organisational change. It was seen as providing the basis for 'sharing and comparing experiences in order to raise questions and develop new understandings', laying the basis for networks of mutual support, and enabling participants to 'gain access to new ideas, contacts and information' (Green *et al.*, 1993b: 133). The study circle method was designed to open up discussion on two fronts: first, between 'experts' and 'users' so that a genuine dialogue between them was established, and second, among the women library assistants, in order to establish and evaluate their own working knowledge and experience. This second objective was important because it attempted to counter the conventional privileging of technical expertise often held by men, and to raise the knowledge of the female staff to authoritative status.

The work of the study circle fed into the broader design team which carried out the detailed work of planning, specification and implementation of the new system. On the recommendation of a study circle, the design team was established precisely in order to be broader, more flexible and more representative than the IT Policy Development Group which had existed before. The design team consisted of not only middle management, and computing personnel, but also library assistants themselves.

The design team underwent a number of internal and external crises which delayed the project and ultimately shortened its life. Most seriously, a budgetary crisis, brought about by cuts in British central government funding of local government, meant the suspension of book purchases, redundancies and severe demoralisation throughout the authority which made it hard to justify and to carry out the project on the same basis as before. By this time, suppliers and their products had been evaluated on the basis of the work done in the study circles and design team. However, when the project was ultimately reorganised, though the prerogative of female library assistants to participate in training and job design discussions was accepted, the *technical* group formed was entirely made up of male professional staff.

The problems that arose were to some extent specific to this project, but general issues of the feasibility of this sort of approach to systems for development by, with and for women also emerged (Green, 1994), and these are examined later in this chapter. However, the project also confirmed the importance of the study circle method from several aspects. First it treated the workplace experiences and knowledge of the female library assistants as important and authoritative, rather than as marginal or even irrelevant:

> For the first time, large numbers of women library assistants took part in detailed discussions and assessments of IT possibilities, both through the study circles and through the subsequent systems demonstrations. Their views were formally expressed through study circle reports, evaluation questionnaires and contributions to the systems specification. This effectively dispelled the view, formerly held by some male managers, that women non-professional staff had become too discouraged by bad experiences of IT to make an active contribution.
>
> (Green *et al.*, 1993b: 141)

Second, the starting point for the study circles was their members' perceptions and requirements of current and future forms of computerisation. Consequently, the definition of the computer system and the associated working arrangements remained open for discussion and negotiation, and the technology was not 'taken as given'.

There were, however, clear gender patterns in the relationships of the various library staff to the process of system development which came into sharp relief during the project. There was an informal male 'techies club' which often met out of office hours, and which conferred both power and excitement upon its members. A strong part of the connection between them derived from the computer play which they engaged in and which allowed them to become intimate with, and skilled at using, the functions of the machine. This culture of computing created informally shared values and even a shared language which simultaneously reinforced their masculine identities and the male power-base of the organisation. The female library assistants, by contrast, did not have either the time or the inclination to spend hours in front of the computer screen, cruising the system. Many of them worked part-time, had children to attend to and domestic responsibilities waiting for them. They were absent from, and chose to absent themselves from, this informal network.

The Australian Taxation Office (ATO) also had a commitment to improving both service delivery and working conditions through collaboration with the labour force. On the one hand, it set out to make innovations in the ways in which income was declared and taxes were collected which provided an improved service to the public, and on the other, it aimed to automate and reorganise its internal work procedures. In 1990 it set up an organisation-wide 'modernisation' programme aimed at computerising the organisation and developing new working arrangements, and an agreement was made between the ATO and the Public Sector Union (PSU) governing union participation in this programme. The Union Research Centre on Office Technologies (URCOT) was established in Melbourne in 1991 as an independent advisory unit to the PSU (Probert and Wilson, 1993a).

This initiative drew strongly upon the legacy of the Scandinavian industrial democracy projects in which unions had won a role in the design and development of new technologies. The PSU also campaigned for the right to participate in the process of technological development and to be centrally involved in parallel negotiations over new working practices. The agenda it pursued included a suite of related issues: job protection, work organisation, occupational health and safety, job redesign and career development. However, it did not put gender at the heart of its approach to the process of system development, though gender issues have since been acknowledged to be central to the redesign of jobs and to the negotiation of change.

URCOT is an independent body which since its inception has been pursuing an action research programme for the modernisation of the ATO drawing upon the involvement of both union and ATO representatives. The first phase of the programme consisted of a series of inter-related projects. The first, on teamworking, examined the planning, communication and decision-making processes of the teams which were being established. It investigated the possibility of a transition to task-oriented flexible teams and the options for lines of control, communication, function, mobility and staff selection. The second project investigated, from a user perspective, different approaches to computer interface design for the ATO, in order to identify the most appropriate and skill-enhancing features for users of a local area network, and to overcome the problems of the unfriendliness of the existing system. The third project examined various options for work flow and job design, particularly for lower-grade clerical staff, and considered the development of integrated functions in order to minimise redundancy and deskilling. The fourth and final project concentrated on workplace planning, and with the establishment of programmes for the transfer and retraining of tax office staff displaced by computerisation or branch closure.

URCOT's aim in conducting this research was to ensure that the expertise and understanding of the ATO workplace in the performance of work came to the forefront of the modernisation programme; it was concerned to offer the workforce a point of access to the process of work reorganisation, so that it was not marginalised from the process. It therefore favoured a variant of action research entitled 'praxis research', which insists that researchers and union members work together so that control of the process, and often the conduct of the research itself, is in the hands of those directly affected by the process of change and the conflicts it throws up. This approach provides a framework for addressing the twin priorities of effective change and intellectual rigour (URCOT Investigative Work Group Handbook, n.d.).

The methodology used by URCOT for this research programme had strong similarities with the study circle method of the Sheffield Human-Centred Systems Group and other action research projects. It established a series of 'Investigative Work Groups' (IWGs), each of which undertook research related to a defined topic, for example, systems design, job design, job grading, training and so on. IWGs were based in workplaces selected after consultation with the union, and groups consisted of union members, with URCOT staff playing a facilitating role. Through this mechanism, union members could identify issues which would improve their jobs and working arrangements, and could simultaneously develop their skills and confidence in dealing with workplace problems. Recommendations from the groups were transmitted to the union to be negotiated as part of the overall modernisation programme with the ATO management.

The URCOT project was, until recently, operating within a political milieu which, as in Scandinavia, was sympathetic to trade union participation in initiatives for organisational change and to attempts to enhance the skill categories and career paths of female workers. For example, the Australian Public Service had already undergone a restructuring of the terms and conditions of clerical workers in a process of participative job redesign. A single multi-skilled career path was established for all clerical workers, which although only recognising a reality of women's work which had existed for decades, at least promised to enhance women's overall promotion prospects (Probert and Wilson, 1993a: 7). This sympathetic political climate was subsequently swept away, and replaced by one more akin to British Thatcherism. In this context, the ultimate ability of the URCOT project to influence the ATO's modernisation programme in ways which address the gender issues in computerisation, work design and grading is still open to question.

Developing a critique of conventional systems which degrade work and approaching computerisation in order to improve the quality of working life have been the objectives of a number of other feminist computer systems initiatives (Applebaum and Albin, 1989; Greenbaum, 1991; Olerup *et al.*, 1985). Although not identical, the mutual influences between feminist systems design and computer-supported co-operative work projects are clear (Hales, 1993). Again, both bodies of work have philosophical origins in the Scandinavian industrial democracy tradition, one of the central concerns of which is the distinction between taylorised automation and the development of computer systems which promote 'good work'; that is, integrated jobs which are not fragmented or monotonous, which are designed to allow workers to use and expand their skills, and which are part of an overall socially responsible system of production (Bansler, 1995). This broad approach to the design of systems has parallels with the concerns of many feminists about the interaction between ways of working and ways of living in society. So in some cases, the systems design project has become much more than one of simply ensuring that systems address the skills, needs and requirements of women in the workplace; it sees the whole social fabric as the terrain of concern and the designer's task as being one of creating new working patterns to create new ways of inter-relating on a societal level: 'developing new strategies, new methods, new organisations, new ways of living together in society' (Grønfeldt and Kandrup, 1985: 212).

Women technologists – different values, different artefacts?

Another strand of feminist work on the practical development of computer systems is concerned with the question of whether female technologists make a difference to the process and out-comes of systems development. To what extent, it is asked, do women bring peculiarly 'female' qualities and values to the process, and are these translated into artefacts with tangibly 'feminine' attributes?

It has often been observed that, since much of the work that women do is reproductive rather than simply productive labour, the 'caring' aspect of their work needs to be recognised in gendered analysis of systems design (Birkenes and Fjuk, 1994; Bjerkenes and Bratteteig, 1988; Greenbaum, 1987; Karasti, 1994; Woodfield, 1994). Sørensen (1992) has attempted to operationalise the 'caring' done by female computer scientists. He has examined the technological and political values held by engineering students at the Norwegian Institute of Technology, graduate students, and junior R&D scientists, in order to ascertain whether there were gender differences which might shape the way in which computer science was done by women as opposed to men. He concludes that the women held 'caring values', but that these were weakened when they went into employment as computer scientists by educational and workplace socialisation.

'Caring values' are what Sørensen calls the values that, according to feminist discourse, women bring to research in computer science. He defines caring values through two central concepts: *empathy*, 'the ability and willingness to perceive, explore, acknowledge and act on the needs of others'; and *rationality of responsibility*, which signals an identification with the well-being of others, attention to the consequences of one's activities for others, taking responsibility for the consequences and changing one's behaviour accordingly, and acceptance of non-reciprocity, i.e., women are responsible for their self-care (Sørensen, 1992: 9–10). In computer science, this means that women 'have a caring, other-oriented relationship to nature and to people, an integrated, more holistic and less hierarchical world-view, a less competitive way of relating to colleagues and a greater affinity to users' (1992: 10). Here, there are similarities with the findings of various other studies. Morgall (1993) draws a distinction between a context-oriented (feminist) approach to technology assessment and a technology-oriented (masculinist) approach. Women work with a strong consciousness of the social context and impacts of computer systems, rather than becoming enthralled by the technical and the abstract qualities of them. Lobet's (1995) survey of Belgian computing students finds women students overwhelmingly opting for courses in information systems rather than in pure computer science, because the information systems discipline relates to the social and organisational applications of computer systems, with which they feel more comfortable. Vehviläinen's (1991) in-depth study of a Finnish woman systems developer finds her identifying herself 'on the boundaries' (1991: 109), acting as an interpreter between other professionals and users trying to articulate their requirements. Gunnarsson (1994) finds the female systems developers in her Swedish study to be largely context-oriented, conscious of the impact of technology on society and on work. She identifies a 'responsible rationality' among female systems developers, in particular a concern with the needs of users (1994: 116). In this they become carriers, developers and transmitters of different types of knowledge, qualifications and work culture than are conventionally recognised by men in their systems design practices. In addition, such a rationality gives rise to a different approach to 'good' systems development:

> Above all it must be a person that is positive to other people so that you can make good systems. You must be able to find out what people really want, what their needs are. *You must be a judge of character to know how to behave to create a good contact with the users.* It is a very big advantage. Then of course you must be able to think in a logic way and plan your work.
>
> (Female systems developer, quoted by Gunnarsson, 1994: 117, my emphasis)

These are precisely the interpersonal skills which are learnt through an apprenticeship in womanhood and which are undervalued because they are possessed by women, deriving from and contributing to their subordination. They are the skills which some feminist initiatives set out to 'name' in women workers whose jobs are undergoing computerisation, as part of systems development projects which acknowledge and value these abilities. (I look at some of these initiatives later in this chapter.) In both female systems developers and female office workers, therefore, feminist research identifies and celebrates particular personal competences arising from women's socialisation as 'good women'. This can be both progressive and problematic. On the one hand, it starts from the reality of many women's abilities, learnt from girlhood and practised every day of their working and domestic lives. It argues for a reversal of dominant assumptions about these abilities and therefore about women's value, and a rethinking of the attribution of skill based on the socially useful labour carried out by many women rather than the highly prestigious activities of men. In this sense, it is progressive. On the other hand, it carries the danger of essentialism, and confirms the notion of women as carers and supporters. Not all women have a 'caring rationality' or engage in caring work. Moreover, as long as women continue to be identified with such attributes, even if these are recognised to be the products of socialisation, then the attributes will be regarded as unimportant precisely because they are held by women, who are regarded as unimportant. Within feminist studies of technologies, there remains an unarticulated debate on this issue.

Both Gunnarsson and Sørensen are well aware of the danger of essentialism that potentially lies in such an approach, and indeed Sørensen qualifies his argument by stating that he is in fact interested in the presence of these values *in R&D*, and in the extent to which female computer scientists act as 'diffusion agents' of these values (1992: 10). However, as he also acknowledges, values are not necessarily materialised directly in artefacts. There is a 'problem of translation' of values into design criteria and then into concrete technologies, such that:

> On the one hand, domination of 'masculine' values may have less effect on technological knowledge and artefacts than has been asserted, to the extent that they are difficult to translate and/or implement. The same difficulties of translation and implementation also imply barriers to an increased impact of caring values, since it will be difficult to be certain that such values – even if they make their way into design criteria – are realized in the development of a concrete piece of technology.
>
> (Sørensen, 1992: 13)

In her research, Shaffner (1993) sidesteps the 'problem of translation' by speculating on the question of how computers might be different if 'every man in the computer industry today was replaced by a woman' (1993: 89). Her interviewees suggested a variety of differences. Some people singled out physical differences, such as improved ergonomic design and improved paper handling in printers; Shaffner attributes these responses to the fact that women's particular experience as users of technology would lead them to place a higher priority on health and safety and on issues such as paper handling, which men tend to view as trivial. Other respondents identified aesthetic aspects of computers which they thought women would design differently: the machine would be less square or less rigid in shape, it might be decorated, the shape of the keyboard and mouse might be more pleasing to the touch. Many of Shaffner's respondents directly related computers to women's values and ways of thinking, imagining machines that would be less 'centralised' and more locally flexible, less rigidly rule-based, less gratuitously technical. One male respondent articulated a vision which consisted of more than simply computers designed by women, but of an entirely different society, 'oriented towards women's priorities and based on a radically different set of values' (1993: 97):

> The whole idea of sitting at a desk in an office and using a computer would have to change. It would have to be more like something that you could do in an environment where you could have children and babies, lovers, and community. Just using them, and not actually being owned by individuals, making negotiations about using them, or finding ways to use them simultaneously, have coordinated input. It's amazing to think of what kinds of differences you could have.
>
> (Quoted in Shaffner, 1993: 97)

In practice, however, there is scarce empirical evidence on the ways in which female computer scientists work. Sørensen asks whether perhaps they choose to work with different problems than their male colleagues, so that the resulting artefact is less important than their choice of problem and method of addressing it. His research shows that male and female computer scientists concentrate on very different tasks in the course of their work. Men, he finds, concentrate on mathematical models and computer programs while women report spending more time running experiments, collecting data, doing calculations, plotting and curve-drawing, and reading project-related scientific literature (1992: 21). This, of course, does not directly connect to caring uncaring values, but it does appear to be linked to well-documented gender differences in modes of learning and working.

The rare accounts from women inside the profession support the notion that female computer scientists may choose different problems and develop different methods for addressing them than their male counterparts. I review new methods which have been devised by female and feminist computer systems developers in the next part of this chapter. But there are also many instances of women taking a very different overall approach to systems design from those which have dominated systems thinking, and often one which is highly and explicitly political. For example, in Britain, a group of women computer scientists who emphasised the importance of feminist engagement in computer science work initiated the feminist computer collective, Microsyster, in 1982. Behind their work lies a series of political commitments – to the improvement of working conditions, to the development of systems that are usable by women, and to the empowerment of women in the use of computers. The group designs systems and teaches computing to women and women's groups, and has also worked actively in the women's movement, has written about women and computing, and has organised a conference on the computerisation of women's work in offices (Microsyster, 1988).

A similar political commitment is shared by Suchman, an anthropologist working on technology design in rather different conditions, at Xerox's research centre, Xerox PARC. She takes as her key concern the rendering visible of the generally unrecognised forms of knowledge which women users bring to bear in the course of their work. Her approach to systems design (a fuller discussion of which I return to in the next section) involves redefining this knowledge as 'authoritative' and placing it at the centre of the process, in order to break the linkage between technological innovation and the continued subordination of women and their competences (Suchman and Jordan, 1989; Suchman, 1994).

In Norway, Bratteteig and her colleagues have developed what they argue is a specifically women's discourse on computer science problems and methods. This involves using feminist principles in systems development, in particular insisting on collaboration between developers and users on an equal footing and focussing very strictly on the applicability of systems (cited in Sørensen, 1992: 22). Similarly, Thoresen, of the Norwegian Computing Centre, has developed a 'tool approach' to the design of systems (Thoresen, 1989). This approach rejects the development of 'technically elegant solutions' so beloved of many male computer scientists because of their eroticism (Thoresen, 1989; Hacker, 1990; Sørensen, 1992), and starts from an understanding of what the operator can do and how her professional competence can be augmented by the use of a system. Such feminist approaches to systems design take as their starting point a recognition of the knowledge and abilities that women exercise in the workplace. Their central concern is with developing systems that allow women to enhance their competences and their confidence in the use of systems that are appropriate to the reality of their working lives. Thus, they aim, through feminist intervention in systems design, to elevate the status of what women do, and at the same time to demystify what systems do. This is how they define the central problem to which feminist computer systems designers must address themselves. The *methods* which have been evolved to serve these objectives are explored in the next section.

'Feminist' methods of systems development

Critiques – feminist and otherwise – of conventional approaches to systems development focus on their overly positivist perspective, their tendency to privilege the abstract knowledge of computer science 'experts' over and above the local knowledge of users, and the consequent creation of a gap between design and use. Going beyond critique, however, involves developing new and different methods which recognise the local, 'real' circumstances within which systems are to be used, the working competences and also the complex personal experiences of women. Feminist innovations in systems development methods have set out to do this.

Representing the world in standardised ways for the purposes of systems design creates technologies which fail to address the complexity and ambiguity of our lives and which ignore our patterns of knowledge (Star, 1991; Suchman, 1987). In her work with Xerox PARC over the years, Suchman has worked extensively with new methods of systems design. The purpose of these is to view the knowledge held by users as central to the design process, 'taking computerization as an occasion to articulate unacknowledged forms of expertise and to take that knowledge seriously as a basis for design' (Suchman and Jordan, 1989: 158). Suchman and Jordan argue that in conventional systems design, there is a yawning gap between the technologies created by computer science experts and those which are finally put to use in real working environments. Users, they argue, 'interpret' technologies constantly with respect to their local circumstances, with the result that, in practice, the design process is only fully completed when the computer system is implemented and used. This, then, is a radical reconceptualisation of the computer systems development process which recognises the innovatory character of the implementation process and places the local expertise of users at the centre. (A similar theorisation has been developed by Fleck (1988), though he does not address gender issues of computer use and expertise.)

All this, of course, goes unrecognised by computer scientists, who work in the abstract and to whom the knowledge that female users exercise in work contexts is completely invisible. When computer systems are then appropriated by users in the workplace, in order to make them usable in local contexts, they are appropriated by men. This design/use gap therefore undermines the local competence of women, by making their familiar working environments unfamiliar and by subordinating their claims to knowledge to those of men. Technological innovation is a resource for the subordination of women in two ways: first and indirectly, 'through the representations of knowledge and expertise on which the design of new technology is based', and second, and more directly, 'in the form of ideological commitments manifest in the development and implementation of the artifacts produced' (Suchman and Jordan, 1989: 157).

Suchman therefore proposes redefining women's local knowledge, rendered invisible during the computerisation process, as legitimate and consequential, worthy of discussion. Women's 'authoritative knowledge' can be articulated through ethnographic study and interaction analysis, and can then inform the development of computer systems (Suchman and Jordan, 1989). Suchman also advocates reconceptualising the systems development process as a unified process of design and use, and recognising the 'artful integrations' which take place during the implementation process, where systems are configured and customised to incorporate technologies into everyday practices (Suchman, 1994).

Suchman's approach to computer systems design

To bring such artful integration work to light, we first need to reconceptualise systems development from the creation of discrete, intrinsically meaningful objects, to the ongoing production of new forms of meaningful practice. Reorienting to practice in turn implies moving from a preoccupation with sites of professional design practice, to an orientation to settings of technologies-in-use.

(Suchman, 1994: 8)

In her work with litigation clerks, she supports them in 'articulating' the interpretive work which they do in the course of creating a database index of legal documents, and which even they are not always conscious of. The attorneys are convinced that this is menial, routine work, partly because of their own ignorance of the complexities and capabilities of the system. The clerical workers, on the other hand, know that it is not mindless work, though it can be tedious. Suchman and her colleagues found that they share with the litigation clerks a 'design value': that of 'working toward the artful integration of new technologies and working practices in a way that recognized and honored the practical reasoning that the work involved' (Suchman, 1994: 17), and they developed a prototype system in which their work was represented and designed for.

Suchman is not alone in her emphasis on articulating and integrating into systems design the hidden knowledge and experience of women at work. This has been one of the key elements of the methods developed by feminists. In Thoresen's 'tool approach', the central criteria is that control over the tool must always lie with the operator. Thus, 'the tool designer will start with the work of the operator: what does she do, and what kind of knowledge does she have to support what she does?' (Thoresen, 1989: 128). Similarly, Wagner (1993) has argued that when computerised care plans are developed for use in hospitals, the role and work of nurses needs to be represented fully by reference to the various imperatives which guide their working patterns and their responses to these imperatives: the special needs of individual patients, the routine of the hospital ward, the orders of the doctors, and the inflow of patient information from outside the ward. And Hales (1991) has proposed the notion of 'constructive users' of computer systems, meaning office workers whose work is likely to be affected by computerisation, and who therefore should be identified and supported in reconstructing their work in ways linked to the system implementation which will provide explicit career paths for information workers.

Part of the process of articulating the patterns of knowledge which women draw upon in performing their work in order to design computer systems includes understanding how they use language in their working relations. The 'What's In A Word' project, an initiative of the Women's Adviser's Unit of the South Australian Department of Labour, strives for the recognition and recompense of female clerical workers' language skills (Poynton, 1993). This means more than identifying these skills as 'communications skills' or 'interpersonal skills', however, because the latter are conventionally regarded as generic rather than specific to particular working contexts. The point of the project is that many of the skills which women demonstrate in their work – patience, consideration, friendliness and supportiveness, for example – are too often regarded as personal attributes whereas they are in fact the interactive skills of spoken language and the literacy skills of written language. Thus, through their use of language, women perform an invaluable role in the workplace, functioning co-operatively with and supportively of those with whom they interact, and often enabling more efficient functioning by their colleagues and superiors. Not only do women's language skills go unrecognised by their male colleagues, by their employers and by society at large, but women themselves have a tendency to minimise what they do. Women themselves see their work from the perspective of their own subordination, and accept the dominant interpretation of the value of their activities. Poynton's argument is that it is therefore critical that what women say about their work is reinterpreted and their skills explicitly 'named', and this is the objective of the project.

Clearly, the interactive and linguistic skills identified here are similar to those of the NHS clerical workers highlighted by Davies and Rosser (1986), and also to those used by women working in software development jobs (Woodfield, 1994), which are not conventionally thought of as 'gendered jobs' (at least not in the feminine sense). However, valuing such skills may, paradoxically, simply serve to confirm women's positions of subordination because these skills themselves have been learnt through women's socialisation into that subordination. Furthermore, the whole exercise may simply serve to raise women's consciousness and expectations without them gaining any recognition by others for their abilities, since 'skill' does not simply connote a recognition of 'objective' abilities but has to do with power at work and is continually struggled over. Poynton argues that local interventions will at least reveal to increasing numbers of women the discrepancies between what they do and what they are paid for (Poynton, 1993: 94, 100). Davies and Rosser's recommendation is that the gender qualities of certain types of work should be seen as residing in the labour process of the work itself, rather than in the women who perform it, in order to prevent women from being excluded from skill recognition (1986: 103). However, while it is relatively straightforward to identify clerical work as a gendered job (with a feminine gender label and requiring skills learnt in womanhood), the gendering of software development is much less clear-cut and yet seems to involve some of the same competences in the hands of women as clerical jobs do. The difference is that female software developers, despite using interpersonal capabilities which are generally unrecognised, are already at the centre of the process of technical change and have relative prestige and power in their work. In clerical work, however, this is not the case, and so naming women's language skills is, at the very least, part of the critical project of explicating the reality of their working lives and of ensuring that this reality is, as far as possible, brought in from the margins of computer systems developments.

There are many other competences which women possess and routinely use at work, which can be identified as points of strength. The 'Universes of Discourse' is a tool of analysis which has been developed by Cindio and Simone for understanding office work, and most recently the skills of female office workers (Cindio and Simone, 1989, 1993). Cindio and Simone describe five universes of discourse: the *physical universe*, which is the physical environment and the movements of people within it;

the *operational universe*, which is the operations or processes performed by office workers; the *procedural universe*, consisting of the documents or products office workers have to produce and the inputs which are necessary in order to create these outputs; the *commitment universe*, people's roles, relationships and mutual commitments; and finally, the *individual universe*, people's perceptions, attitudes and expectations of the phenomena in the office. This tool provides a framework for studying various aspects of office work, including technologies and resources, and skills.

This framework is used to analyse office work from a gender perspective, crediting rather than negating women's attributes. For example, analysis of the physical universe reveals women's manual dexterity, analysis of the operational universe highlights gender differences in relationships to objects and machines (men's tendency to idealise their machines, women's tendency to treat them as tools), while in the commitment universe we see how a woman performs a number of tasks simultaneously, scheduling work in order to maximise efficiency and productivity. Some of the attributes which this method identifies and celebrates are skills which are derived from women's dual role in the paid workplace and in the domestic environment: 'multi-processing', for example, is a skill which many women develop in order to handle several workloads in the home at once. All these attributes can be regarded as points of strength which, in an era of techno-logical change, can potentially be used to confer improved career opportunities upon women since they are the kinds of abilities which are likely to be most useful and most sought after (Cindio and Simone, 1993: 182–6).

All of these methods described above still rely, to some extent, on the imported 'expertise' of the computing professional, no matter how sympathetic that person is to the situation and needs of female workers. Moreover, in identifying the possibility of an alternative 'reality' to that which is normally emphasised in conventional systems development, they may still have a tendency to objectify the work done by women and to approach women's work from a single viewpoint. In her work on the study circle method, Vehviläinen (1986, 1991, 1994a) aims to create oppor-tunities for a multiplicity of women's voices to be heard and their standpoints to be represented (in the tradition of Smith, 1987) in the process of systems development. She is concerned to draw out their subjectivities as female workers, that is, to allow them to express their everyday practices and experiences, but also with the organisational setting, politics and power relations within which technological change takes place.

Workplace study circles have their origins in the Scandinavian 'collective resource' approach to systems development, and have also been one of the techniques used by the trade union movement there. More recently, they have been taken up by some British (particularly feminist) systems developers. Study circles provide a forum in which the participants in a computerisation project can define an agenda for change, share experiences, raise questions, and provide each other with mutual support (Green *et al.*, 1993b). Vehviläinen, who has worked extensively on and strongly advocates the study circle method, sees them as a way for female office workers to define their own systems, typically moving through a number of phases of activity: studying available technologies and evaluating them from the perspective of office workers, analysing the work of the office workers, interviewing experts on the basis of this analysis, and drafting plans and definitions for information systems (Vehviläinen, 1994a: 78).

Study circles can provide support, education and new perspectives to women, and can thus serve as powerful milieux for women to develop their own politics within their workplaces. But the process of convening and working with study circles also reflects and exposes connections between relations of power, both of class and of gender, and the patterns of women's subjective experiences, including their use of existing technologies, within their organisations. Thus, for example, Vehviläinen (1991) sounds various notes of caution about the issues raised by the study circle method. Women, she points out, are still concentrated at the bottom of most organisational hierarchies, and as such they can have little formal claim to or credibility in influencing the process of computerisation. Their position also makes their relationship to computing professionals, who generally work on behalf of company managements, a vexed one. For the study circle method does not abandon the role of 'experts'; rather, it requires their contribution to the informed decision-taking of the circle. The contribution of professionals can give study circle participants a feeling that the technology is manageable, not overly remote. Yet it is often difficult for women in study circles to approach experts, to explain their problems and to enrol them in the study circle on an ongoing basis. Their work and their study circles do not have independent status in terms of progressing organisational goals; they are subordinate to the strategies and imperatives of management (Vehviläinen, 1991: 255). Organisational relations and practices thus affect the 'local' and 'situated' work analysis of the study circle, sometimes in negative ways, but sometimes in positive ones:

> ... The group was able to provide knowledge and understanding. Especially the ones who had little knowledge of computers learned from others' experiences. When, for example, Maikki described how

she used systems or programs, Kaisa could see her own alternatives. During the work analysis the group discussions of the situations, work contents and contradictions in office work helped each participant to map out her own possibilities within both organizational and technical relations. The group mediated and made visible the interconnections between the local – subjective – office work situations and information systems textualities as well as the organizational relations in them. In this way, the group supported each of the members in finding her own way in her concrete surroundings. One by one, the group members gained support for their thinking, technical language and activity.

(Vehviläinen, 1994a: 87)

Lessons emerging from feminist approaches to computer systems design

Despite the positive experiences (and, less frequently, also new artefacts) which both female systems designers and female users have derived from feminist innovations in systems development, there have been significant problems with many initiatives. These problems are worthy of consideration, for they may help us to shed some light on the question of whether it is ultimately possible to have a 'feminist approach to information technology design', or whether such a concept is doomed to failure within a society which is still capitalist and patriarchal, and within which computer systems must work.

Some of these issues concern the tactics used in developing computer systems in collaboration with women workers and users. Others are more fundamental. First, the time commitment which many participative projects demand of their members is clearly a problem. A key constraint on the ability of many female workers to become involved in systems development projects is the very nature of their work and their consequent inability simply to take time away from their pressing day-to-day tasks in order to attend meetings and study groups. This problem was first identified by Enid Mumford when she worked on participative project with a group of secretaries in ICI (Mumford, 1983). As Green *et al.* (1993b) point out, in many clerical jobs there is little time for reflection, planning and taking part in lengthy meetings, unlike in professional jobs where these are typical activities. Indeed, attendance at such meetings means that workers have to postpone their regular work, and this often causes resentment and undermines their commitment to participatory projects.

Second, the assumption that women workers and women systems designers have the same interests, simply because of their subordination to men in society generally, is highly problematic.

Female computer users, often office workers, find themselves at the bottom of organisational hierarchies in low-paid jobs. Systems designers, on the other hand, are generally professionals working in relatively privileged conditions and on relatively high salaries. By definition, their labour is pressed into the service of managerial and organisational rulers, and their work is often directly dictated by these groups. They sell their expertise to the organisation and contribute to its ruling (Vehviläinen, 1991: 249). This aspect of class and power relations is often overlooked in feminist design initiatives, where it is often assumed that all women share the same perspectives or standpoints. Such an assumption makes for a naïvety of approach; systems developers are then taken by surprise when female office workers cannot or will not readily engage in their projects on their terms. For example, as I have already noted, the project of identifying and celebrating women's skills is a very ambiguous one, with both positive and negative aspects. Sometimes the invisible aspects of women's work are the only aspects over which they retain control (Barker and Downing, 1980). In this situation, making their work visible, without an understanding of the dynamics of their jobs, simply damages them. It may even be better in some cases to use more traditional methods of systems design in order to leave some of the more satisfying aspects of their work intact (Vehviläinen, 1991). Feminist practices must always be alert to the varying contexts and dynamics of women's work.

A pervasive problem with participatory design projects in general, including feminist ones, has been their failure to 'embed' themselves within their host organisations (Clements and Van den Besselar, quoted in Green, 1994: 369). Such projects have tended to remain on the margins of organisational politics, and therefore have not always achieved their objectives. For example, in a Norwegian project to computerise public libraries, 'learning oriented group work' allowed workers to reflect on the computerisation process and its implications for their labour and skills (Bergmann, 1985: 242). In parallel with these groups, the union conducting the project, KBF (Kommunale Biblioteksarbeideres Forening), sought representation on computing project teams and created networks of workers across libraries to disseminate information on work organisation and computerisation to one another. It soon discovered that representation on computing project teams did not guarantee that the interests and needs of library workers would be properly met, as structures continually changed and teams came into and out of existence. Only by creating a range of formal and informal structures did it prove possible to develop useful material on the implications of computerisation in libraries throughout Norway, which would serve as a resource for others faced with the automation of their work. Similarly, women's support groups are not sufficient for the development of information systems within modern organisations (Vehviläinen, 1994a); women's subjectivities, experiences and definitions need to be complemented by technical and organisational work. Despite this, feminist projects have achieved other results; for example, highlighting the complexity of established power and gender relations, and revealing their impact upon the process of change (Green, 1994).

Certainly, it would seem that the achievements of most feminist initiatives, like other participative design projects, have been mainly in making innovations in *methods* of systems development rather than in *products*. Sometimes it is the impetus provided by designing a new computer system which opens up the possibility of new techniques and new channels of communication, and this is perhaps the main achievement of feminist design. Bjerkenes and Bratteteig (1987), for example, conclude that one of the major achievements of their 'Florence' project for the development of a computer system for nurses was the way in which it allowed the nurses to explicate the communicative and caring aspects of their work, and to press for a new system which enshrined these qualities and so reflected their efforts to get themselves recognised as being more than simply 'doctor's assistants'.

It remains difficult to imagine how feminist objectives would be realised in an artefact, other than in creating something more usable by women (who often lack confidence with computers or the desire to 'play' with them) than many existing systems are. But usable technologies are now the concern of the entire IT industry, not least in the traditional profit-oriented corporations (Friedman and Cornford, 1989). There are, consequently, increasingly striking similarities between the results of participatory or feminist projects and traditional profit-oriented design:

> Many people feel the Macintosh is an excellent example of what politically progressive, user-centred, accessible computers should look like; yet it was designed by large companies without any special participatory techniques.
>
> (Shaffner, 1993: 194)

A more fundamental issue which must be of concern to feminists involved in systems development is the broader social and economic context within which projects are conducted, and the way in which this can undermine the progressive achievements of such projects. There is a real danger of feminist systems practitioners simply presiding over a process of raising the exploitation of workers. For example, there is a very thin dividing line between study circles, which have been used in genuinely empowering ways in feminist systems development projects, and

Losing sight of the managerial objectives

We should have made use of the women's union, as they were all
organised and as they had a union club in the Department. We totally
lost sight of the long-range planning of management and system
developers. We were so absorbed in just making this particular
system work better that it came as a shock to all the women when,
by chance, they were informed that this system was only the start of
a development towards the totally automated office where their work
would be performed by professionals, and where there would be no
need of a special registry department. We could not encounter this
problem by just getting better in the technical field; this was pure
politics and as such the only way to work on this problem would be
through the union. But the way we worked in the group did not
ensure that long range aspects of new technology would be taken
into account.

(Grønfeldt and Kandrup, 1985: 216)

quality circles, which can be highly exploitative of workers by
getting them to collaborate in their own subordination in the
workplace (Garrahan and Stewart, 1992). Similarly, the objective
of achieving systems 'usability' can easily be diverted into simple
ergonomics concerns with speedier operation of equipment –
concerns which are central in classical taylorised work systems.
Fundamentally, how should feminist designers participate in a
process of computerisation which is designed to reduce, or which
at least coincides with the reduction of, staff in the long term?
Once a women-friendly computer system has been negotiated
over, fewer women are needed to work it. In the University of
Copenhagen, where Morgall did a technology assessment study
with secretaries (Morgall, 1993), the secretaries' own intervention
in the process of computerisation, and their consequent politicis-
ation and unionisation, still finally could not prevent their numbers being reduced by half over the years as academic staff
progressively undertook more and more of their own word processing and secretarial staff budgets were cut. Similarly, in the
local authority within which Green and her colleagues conducted
their work (Green *et al.*, 1993b), a subsequent budgetary crisis
resulted in many redundancies, widespread demoralisation and
some undermining of their efforts in the development of a
human-centred computerised library system. Grønfeldt and Kandrup (1985) had a still more shocking experience, working with
female employees in the registry department of the Danish Direc-
torate of Labour. For them, even this public sector organisation
in comparatively 'enlightened' Scandinavia provided an object
lesson in the need for a political appreciation of the class, as

well as the gender, relations of power operating in processes of computerisation.

Despite these problems, feminist approaches to computer systems design have given women workers a clearer voice in the process of computerisation. As good practice alone this is important, and may influence broader systems design approaches in the longer term. Already, the CSCW movement shares many of the features and techniques of feminist systems design, and this may allow some of the latter's central tenets to be taken up more broadly. Certainly, in so far as feminist practices resemble Scandinavian democratic design practices, challenging objectified modes of analysis and the inevitability of taylorist or fordist applications of computer systems, they are applicable not only in arenas of women's work but also in men's jobs (Vehviläinen, 1991). Furthermore, women are generally unused to having their experiences in the workplace privileged and accorded value; feminist systems developments are important for the ways in which they challenge dominant notions of expertise and for their emphasis on the gendering of knowledge and competence. In revealing the gender relations of skill and in pressing for a rethinking of women's skills, they perhaps offer the most promising opportunity for addressing and reshaping the everyday reality that is women's working lives.

The gender relations of the 'techies club' at 'city libraries'

And once you've done that [spent hours in front of screens] ... you'd know there were things you could exchange, a level of hints and tips, but more deeply a level of understanding, shared language ... but they [those men] don't look around and see the absence of women, they don't perhaps think that they are creating a language, and perhaps, as it's expressed at work, a power-base which is exclusive. And they don't realise that they are where they are because the computing industry is designed for them. It's designed for people who *have* got hours to spare: in the garage, or the shed, or the attic, cracking the code.

(Male library research officer, quoted in Green *et al.*, 1993b: 145–6)

CHAPTER 7

The lessons of feminist research on women's work and IT

Women's labour is both an important contributor to the development of technologies, and crucially affected by those technologies, and in this book I have examined how the gender relations of information technologies and the technological relations of women's work are evolving and how they are implicated in one another. My aim has been to draw out the lessons of nearly two decades' worth of research on these themes which has been conducted around the world. Women's work and women's relationship to technology have been central to my own life throughout this period, first in my role as an office worker, then as a student, and finally as a researcher into, and teacher of, the subject of 'women and technology'.

These two decades of my personal development have also coincided with a resurgence of the hegemony of neo-classical political economy and a vicious restructuring of the UK economy. This has involved increasing concentration and conglomeration of corporate ownership, the privatisation of large swathes of the British public sector, and the progressive under-resourcing and dismantling of the welfare state. These developments, together with a progressive restructuring within organisations, have often taken place with the assistance of management methods imported from the United States and applied as articles of faith. In the British political arena, trade unionism and oppositional politics have largely broken down. Much feminist thinking is increasingly depoliticised, focussed on the individual and not the social, and refusing to confront the serious structural issues taking place in society at large.

Such a depressing political and economic context inevitably shapes my thinking on the dynamics of women's work, and on their relationship to technological change in that work. However, the evidence of the research which I have reviewed in this book into the detailed workings of the process of technological change in women's jobs seems to bear out this kind of thinking. For what does the accumulated body of research (feminist and otherwise) tell us about the shape of women's working lives, now and to come?

The insights offered by feminist research

First, it is clear that women are as excluded now as they have always been from the formal endeavour of designing and shaping information technologies. They are marginal to the professional echelons of this work, and more and more, given the hostility of the IT workplace culture to women, they are electing not to enter it. This is the pattern in all countries of the world, even those which have a relatively strong record of women's participation in IT professions (the Nordic countries, for example). On the other hand, the menial and extremely hazardous work of assembling IT systems is almost exclusively female, and much of it is consigned to women who live and work in desperate poverty in the non-developing countries of the Third World. In this respect, IT work is no different from any other type of work. Women are absent not only from the higher echelons of technological work, but in many spheres, even those in which they might be expected to have better representation: in art, in literature, in poetry, in music, and in education (CSO, 1995). In other words, women are systematically under-represented in influential positions across all walks of society, and in most societies of the world (UN, 1995).

Does the answer therefore lie in increasing women's representation? Would it improve matters to bring more women into the IT professions? Would this make IT a more equitable endeavour, and would it address the masculine culture of information technology? Liberal (feminist) initiatives in Britain and elsewhere have been founded on precisely the assumptions that getting more women into IT is a desirable objective both to address the inequality of women's access to professional jobs and to solve employers' problems of skills shortages. Such initiatives have been extremely limited in their success on either front. Moreover, were they to be successful, they would overwhelmingly benefit professional middle-class women who can take advantage of better employment opportunities because of their educational backgrounds, but would make little difference to the position of those women in low-skilled IT jobs. These are different women altogether, and their position would not be alleviated by initiatives aimed at addressing the gender imbalance in the IT professions. In fact, such initiatives might well serve to reinforce the class inequalities in IT occupations, between women and between men (Wickham and Murray, 1987).

How, then, is the masculinity of technology and the confinement of women within low-level IT work to be addressed? The varied feminist and democratic systems development projects have done promising work in developing new participatory development methodologies which aim to be much more sensitive than conventional methods to the situation of women workers. In particular, their value lies in their emphasis on the requirements of workers given local and specific systems of work organisation, rather than on the rarified and abstract expertise of IT professionals. Feminist design projects allow for a recognition of the tacit skills and knowledge which women deploy in the course of their work but which are rarely acknowledged, and they allow for the design and configuration of IT systems to suit these patterns of skill and local working arrangements.

However, these artefacts still have to be applied and put to work in conventional organisations with capitalist social relations of production. In these settings, some feminist initiatives have foundered, and it is clear that technological systems cannot be constructed in the interests of women in specific workplaces in isolation from the wider dynamics of capitalist production which circumscribe the application and use of these systems. It has also been found that the artefacts which have resulted from feminist systems development projects are often not qualitatively different from those which emerge from more conventional design processes, particularly those in which 'usability' is a central objective. Are these projects therefore really 'feminist' or simply 'democratic' in a more general sense, and what is the difference, if any, between the two?

Feminist research into the development of IT systems points to the serious lack of regard for women's needs and priorities in the process of systems design, which has prompted these attempts to create more woman-friendly systems. However, although it is possible to assert this absence of understanding of women's needs, it is rather more difficult to identify precisely what 'women's needs and priorities' actually are. First of all, they are of course not uniform across all women or across all social classes, nationalities and cultures. Then, making the link between women's needs and the consequently desirable features of an IT system is a vexed question, and one that is too often dealt with in an essentialist manner by reference to the supposedly universal characteristics of women IT users (for example, as lacking in confidence with computers, as disinterested in computers except as tools, as caring and sociable rather than rational and technical). Feminist design initiatives have often encountered this difficulty. Most have addressed it by focussing away from the eventual characteristics of the IT *products* which they shape, and towards the *processes* of shaping which offer scope for permanently redefining the role of female users in systems design.

There is an overall problem concerning the connection between the factors shaping the development of information technologies and the characteristics of the IT artefacts that result. In Chapter 3, we saw that the process of technological development is male-dominated and that there is a sharp sexual division of labour in the process. But what does this tell us about the gendering of artefacts? Women's exclusion from technological design does not necessarily translate into masculine technologies in a direct way. How, then, does the translation happen?

The process of IT development is complex and many faceted. Gendering takes place at many levels and at many stages in the process, and capturing this shaping is a difficult affair. So, the domination of men and the absence of women from the design process is *one* factor which creates technologies which are closely geared to the needs of men and which are inappropriate to women's requirements. But before a technology is even on the drawing board, it is taking shape in the minds of its owners and controllers. Technologies arise from the programmes of company managements and capitalist entrepreneurs, as ways of pressing home their objectives for the control of markets, the conduct of production, the organisation of work and the control of labour (Noble, 1984). The application of information technologies to female jobs, in order to control both female and male labour, and labour costs, is one part of the managerial vision which can shape the development of technologies. This is how workplace technologies emerge in their very earliest conceptions, and in these situations it is for the designers and producers of technologies to put these visions into practice. But systems designers come to the job with their own methodologies and bodies of expertise which also shape technological developments, as we saw in Chapter 6. In particular, they may employ highly technical-rational (or scientific management) methods which privilege data and information above inter-relationships between workers. These methods underline and confirm managerial programmes for work rationalisation, but they do not necessarily generate the same artefacts as those envisioned in management thinking. Designers also add to their work assumptions about the users of technologies and the capabilities of those users, sometimes deliberately to circumvent those assumed capabilities (when the overall objective is to deskill) and sometimes to address a presumed lack of expertise with technologies (when the objective is to automate work done by those with little technological competence). These assumptions are among other things gendered. Often unskilled users are presumed to be women, and skilled people to be deskilled are assumed to be men. Often, too, though not always, these assumptions are proved correct.

Jobs have 'gender labels' and are part of a broader 'gender system' in the workplace which is both structural and symbolic, as we saw in Chapter 5. These gender labels, then, contribute to the shaping of the design and marketing of workplace technologies – the ways in which they are constructed to address women's and men's work – and to appeal to those who buy and implement technologies. However, users also have a hand in the shaping of the technologies which they use – configuring systems in particular ways, preferring some applications over others – and sometimes subverting the intentions of their initiators and designers. It is important to recognise this aspect of the process of technological innovation, for not only does it give a truer picture of the process than one which concentrates purely on the design and manufacture of new technologies, but it also reveals the role and requirements of women who are so often overlooked in conceptions of technological development.

The gendering of technological artefacts is therefore an extremely complex and often long-run process. It is difficult to discern the effects of one aspect of the process on the final outcome, given the variety of factors at work. In Chapter 3, I discussed these various aspects of the gendering of information technologies as they are dealt with in feminist studies of technology, but they remain separately articulated and not coherently analysed in individual research studies. As a result, the complexity of the gendering of technologies does not always emerge clearly from feminist research, and, with some notable exceptions, the process is often over-simplified into an asserted link between these social relations and the consequent masculinity of technology. Håpnes and Sørensen have argued that the precise working of this link is inadequately articulated in feminist discussions of the gendering of technologies, and that:

> Masculinity or maleness becomes a pre-given factor that shapes technology, independent of the process of design and development. The task is thus reduced to establishing the correlation between the given features of maleness and (some of) the characteristics of the resulting technology.
>
> (Håpnes and Sørensen, 1995: 174)

It has been argued that there is a tendency within feminist studies of technology to blackbox gender relations and technology, and to repeatedly assert the exclusion of women from technology. This makes much feminist research predictable and uninspiring (Linn, 1987; Hirschauer and Mol, 1993, quoted in Gill and Grint, 1995: 20). If feminist studies of technology are to address this criticism, then feminist research must begin to investigate more closely the link between masculine technological practices and gendered artefacts, and to treat the process of technological development and implementation much more critically. The concept of 'technology' needs to be unpacked, and the precise circumstances of the design, manufacture, marketing and implementation of particular artefacts need to be examined. Cockburn and Ormrod's (1993) study of the development of the microwave oven and Chabaud-Rychter's (1994) study of the development of the food processor provide good examples of such an approach applied to domestic technologies, but this type of work also needs to be done in the sphere of employment.

It is certainly true that a great deal of feminist research into technology has been concerned with demonstrating the exclusion of women from technology in various fields. This book is no exception to that project. However, this in itself is an important objective, if we remember back to the gender-blindness of most early social research on new technologies. Feminist accounts of women's exclusion from both science and technology have historically been consigned to the margins of social science. Furthermore, the importance of demonstrating women's exclusion from technology, predictable as it might now seem, has not diminished simply because that exclusion is now more widely acknowledged than it was in the past. While it may be well-understood by feminist researchers in this field, there are many other spheres in which it still needs to be asserted. In particular, there is a role for research which empirically relates that exclusion to the range of spheres of technological endeavour, and explores the reasons for it. Equally, it is important to identify areas of technology where women are not excluded and to develop programmes for women's active engagement in the processes of technological design and use. This, indeed, has been the direction which some recent feminist studies have taken, as we saw in Chapter 6, and in restoring agency to women in technology they are to be welcomed.

What of the *effects* of information technologies on women in the workplace? Have women indeed been as vulnerable to displacement by information technologies as was feared? Did the segregation of women in typically 'women's jobs', and at the bottom of organisational hierarchies, work against them when it came to the implementation of information technologies? Or has this segregation of women in occupational ghettos been broken down to any extent with the application of information technologies and the redefinition of work?

We have seen the difficulties in assessing the job losses associated with the diffusion and use of information technologies in Chapter 4. We know, too, that studies of technological unemployment have been as gender-blind as other social studies of technological change, and often fail to differentiate between trends in employment tenure for women and for men. However, the evidence that has been collected specifically on the effects of information technology implementation on women's employment suggests that women *are* vulnerable because they are concentrated in routine jobs which have been drastically reduced, and that on the other hand, women do not benefit from new job creation in professional technological fields to the same extent that men do.

It is also apparent that in the large economies of the USA and countries of the European Union, information technologies are being used to underpin forms of organisational and corporate restructuring which allow employers to reduce their dependence upon labour, and certainly upon *expensive* labour. No category of employee is now secure from displacement or casualisation of their employment, but there are contradictory implications for women specifically. Some groups of women have clearly benefited from the relocation and 'temporization' (Greenbaum, 1994) of work. For example, the closure of offices in city centres and metropolitan areas, and the opening of new offices in the suburbs and regions has created employment for suburban women, but at the expense of women in cities (who are more likely to be black and working-class). Similarly, the development of offshore information processing has improved the employment prospects of women in poorer countries. Particularly in the service industries which are based upon the processing, buying and selling of information, telecommunications and satellite technologies have eliminated the necessity to locate processing operations physically near to end markets. Instead the information and data processing functions that were once performed by women in the First World are now being exported to low cost economies.

Computer-based technologies have not, therefore, had a uniform impact on women's employment across industry sectors or across countries; rather, the significance of these technologies for women's work lies in their offering corporations greater choice in the optimal location of their manufacturing or information processing operations, the better to meet their strategic and operational objectives. Women workers the world over can more than ever be treated as company resources to be utilised or dispensed with, depending on the extent to which they meet the strategic needs of corporations at particular times, and new technologies make them much more flexible resources than hitherto. It therefore seems that the diffusion and application of information technologies has on the whole served to confirm the tenuous relationship of women to the labour market rather than providing exciting new employment and career opportunities for women. Because it allows employers to be much more flexible than hitherto in the way they locate and organise employment, it makes the labour market more competitive. This in turn shifts the burden of employment onto workers, and makes work insecure.

So, although employment opportunities have been created for

women in new geographical areas, they have equally readily been removed as IT makes the location of work more and more immaterial to its efficient and cost-effective performance. Some communities have experienced very short-term benefits of employment growth, rapidly reversed as corporations move their activities on to other sites which offer more appropriate resources to meet their strategic and tactical objectives. A case in point is that of women working in the clothing industry in the Third World, whose work I considered in Chapters 4 and 5. While they benefited in employment terms from the location of production in their home countries, they subsequently suffered, when some companies withdrew their operations and relocated closer to home markets, producing garments using computer-based technologies instead of cheap labour. With this, the vulnerability of these women was clarified. The benefits of new job creation or of employment relocation are very fragile, and even being a cheap source of labour does not protect women from displacement. Microelectronics-based technologies are particularly problematic in this respect because they offer much cheaper forms of automation than ever before and therefore undermine even the cheaper labour which has often escaped displacement in earlier rounds of technological change.

It would seem that, as Kirkup has argued, this innovatory technology has not so far contributed to a significant reduction in inequality between the rich and poor countries of the world. Neither has it been used to restructure established sexual divisions of labour, or unequal race or gender relations (1992: 281). The research discussed in this book provides no evidence of a breakdown in the sexual division of labour, or of significant new employment opportunities for women. Instead, the persistence of sexual segregation in employment is confirmed. Wider evidence collected and published by the United Nations for the Fourth World Conference on Women in Beijing in September 1995 bears out this conclusion. Although there is some movement of women into professional and technical jobs in certain countries (particularly in the Nordic countries, and in Canada and the United States), women are still under-represented in managerial work and heavily over-represented in clerical and sales jobs. (The United Kingdom does not have a good record on equal opportunities for women: it is ranked eighteenth on the United Nations' scale of human development.) The United Nations report argues that in general there is little evidence of a fundamental change in the traditional pattern of women's employment and that consequently 'the doors to economic and political opportunities are barely ajar' (1995: 4).

This absence of change in the fortunes of women should not surprise us. The class and gender inequalities of capitalist societies remain in place, and these are not threatened by the introduction throughout economies of information technologies, though they may be expressed differently in such environments. Access to, and control of, technologies is constitutive of both class and gender, as we have seen. But it remains in the interests of capital to segment workforces and divide labour; it also remains in the interests of men to attempt to preserve as far as possible their ghettos of privilege and their source of domestic labour by preserving the exclusion of women from sections of the labour market and confining them to others.

The use of information technologies may alter the means of achieving these ends, but not the overall dynamics of tension between capital and labour, and between women and men. So, in Britain and in the US, successful attacks on labour by capital have allowed employers to alter the gender composition of the labour force, by permitting women into the labour force as 'flexible' workers. The increased participation of women in these roles has, as Walby has pointed out, been supported by changes in gender relations outside employment:

> ... In access to education, in marriage and divorce, in political citizenship and in household structure (which) improve women's access to paid work on a long-term basis.

> (Walby, 1989: 140)

This increasing participation of women in the labour market simply means that women increasingly shoulder a double burden of paid and unpaid work, and their labour is consequently hugely undervalued. In all countries of the world women earn less than men (on average around three-quarters). Women's poverty is worsening; because of their unequal labour market position and their status in the family, women constitute 70 per cent of those who live in poverty in both industrial and developing countries and this proportion is growing (UN, 1995: 36).

In this context, far from providing new opportunities for women in new fields of employment, information technologies seem to have simply facilitated the double burden which women carry, allowing them to combine paid labour and domestic labour in new ways. Women have always needed to find ways of managing their domestic responsibilities whilst in employment, and ICT-supported forms of working, such as teleworking, as well as other 'contingent' forms of employment, such as part-time work, offer them the means to do this. To the extent that ICTs provide the wherewithal for carrying these casual forms of employment to new heights of sophistication, they are an important mechanism in the confirmation of women's marginal relationship to the labour market.

But ICTs can also directly allow women to handle paid and

unpaid work simultaneously. A simple example is the cellphone. Frissen (1995) suggests that it allows working women to transform the double burden of home and work into a parallel burden, allowing them to multitask and manage their domestic responsibilities better (from a distance). Other feminist research on domestic technologies confirms this argument, showing how technologies like the washing machine have simply increased the number of tasks a woman can do simultaneously, rather than being labour saving devices which free women from the drudgery of work (Wacjman, 1991). In fact, it is disheartening to see how the double burden is primarily being accommodated through technical innovations, rather than being challenged or addressed head on through political change. It is, after all, only through political change that women's relationship to the labour market and their problems in developing meaningful jobs and careers can be improved.

What can we conclude about the labour processes of women working with technologies from this now very substantial body of feminist research? Have women's jobs changed and have the gender relations of women's workplaces been transformed? The combined insights of feminist research here do not, in my view, suggest very encouraging prospects for the majority of women. Individual studies certainly show that there are important variations in the nature of women's work. These variations are confirmed by research done by Rees (1992) which suggests that there are many reasons for organisations to apply computer systems, and these shape women's experiences of automated work:

> ... Some are concerned to reduce labour costs or to rationalise work, while others use it simply as an instrument to improve productivity, gain more control over their work processes or to improve quality.

> (Rees, 1992: 139)

Rees goes on to add that UK companies tend to use IT to cut costs rather than for other objectives, but this objective itself can be met both directly by making people redundant and indirectly by deskilling, dividing the craft to cheapen the parts, as Babbage had it. The OECD confirms this variation in management strategies in using new technologies, though it sees skills increases as the likely outcome of the widespread use of IT:

> The relationship between new technology and work organisation is characterised by great diversity as well as mutual dependence. New technology promises to revolutionise the way work is organised in many institutions – and has at times already done so. The direction and extent of change, however, is difficult to predict in particular cases as it depends on a range of factors – among which managerial

strategy stands out as the most important. In practice, skill-using modes of implementation prove more common than skill-reducing ones, although there is reason for concern over loss of worker autonomy and initiative. At the aggregate level, where microprocessor-based innovation continues the upgrading of demands made on the skills of the labour force in a wide range of areas, skill enhancement is expected to prove the rule (*outside the personal service sector at least*).

(OECD, 1988: 87–9, my emphasis)

The OECD's conclusions that the overall trend is towards an upskilling of labour may be somewhat optimistic, and they are particularly questionable in the case of women's work. As the report itself suggests, in the personal service sector a different pattern of skill change may be observable, and this is, after all, an important site of women's employment. Overall, feminist studies present a very different picture, of a marked trend towards the degradation of women's jobs, and in particular, jobs which inherently have a distinctly routine aspect to them: clerical jobs, typing jobs, supermarket jobs and semi-skilled manufacturing jobs. And, after all, these are the jobs in which the bulk of women in non-agrarian work are employed – are *still* employed.

To some extent, new occupations have been opened up to women in areas from which they were previously excluded. Just as some predicted, the application of computer-based technologies has allowed women to enter jobs which were in the past monopolised by men and which were bastions of craft skill or male privilege. But this is not so much an indication of the potential of computer technologies to create equal opportunities in the workplace; rather it is a signal of the deskilling of these jobs, and the consequent lowering of the barriers to feminisation. It is a trend which has been revealed in a number of industries and occupations, and it marks a redefinition, a reshaping and a re-gendering of jobs in clerical occupations (Feldberg and Glenn, 1983), in the printing industry (Cockburn, 1983), in garment manufacture (Cockburn, 1985a; Phizacklea, 1990), and in telecommunications engineering (Hacker, 1990). All of these spheres are marked by a sexual division of labour in flux.

However, Feldberg and Glenn (1983) and Hacker (1990) have found this to be a temporary stage in a longer-term process of restructuring in which these jobs are being readied for complete automation and elimination, and it is only in this context that women are permitted to enter these fields. This argument is confirmed by much of the empirical research in this field, and is not an optimistic view of women's prospects for gaining new skills and entering new areas of technological work. It is not a picture of enskilling, of the acquisition of expertise, or of training for new work on a systematic basis which might create new job or career paths. On the contrary, it is confirmation of the marginality and vulnerability of the women who move into these jobs, like so many of their counterparts in more traditionally 'female' areas of work. In this context, female labour is being used as a particular form of dispensable resource within the capitalist labour process at the point in the process of work reorganisation and technological change when skilled labour has been eliminated, and less skilled labour is required on a temporary basis.

I have discussed earlier in the book the difficulties with assessing skill changes in women's work, given the ideological connotations which attach to the concept of 'skill'. These barriers to the acknowledgement of women's work as skilled simply serves to confirm my pessimism about women's prospects for advancing into new and more highly graded areas of work. For, no matter what objective skills women acquire in particular spheres of employment with technological change and the reorganisation of work (such as the ability to operate particular computing applications, or new responsibilities for handling customers), feminist studies show that their skills are not defined as skills, are rarely if ever remunerated on this basis, and are unlikely to lead to promotion prospects or opportunities for career advance. Instead, invariably when women move into new areas of skilled work, these areas themselves become redefined as non-skilled, no matter what expertise is required or what the technical content of the work is. The feminisation of skilled work, rather than benefiting the women who move there, simply detracts from the socially ascribed status of the work itself.

In Chapter 5, I considered developments in the gender relations of workplaces, and in particular in forms of patriarchal control over women workers. It had been supposed that information technologies would, among other things, lead to a transformation of patriarchal relations of control over women in the workplace into more mechanically-based forms of control (Barker and Downing, 1980). This contention has not been borne out by empirical studies, and this may be because the two forms of control are not mutually exclusive to start with. Many women's jobs have always been subject to the technical control of the machine, particularly in semi- and unskilled assembly work, but also to a certain extent in low-grade clerical work where a routine is imposed. In these sorts of jobs, women are largely working beside other women (Martin and Roberts, 1984), and so patriarchal control assumes a particular, remote form and operates from a distance. However, it does operate, and it conditions the roles that women play in the workplace in relation to each other – as girls and wives working together – in relation to skilled men elsewhere in the workplace and in trade unions, and in relation to their supervisors and management (Pollert, 1981; Cavendish, 1981; Westwood, 1984).

Patriarchal control over women in offices generally takes a more direct form (the use of secretaries as 'office wives' to perform domestic types of tasks, and the overt sexism often directed at typists in pools). But, contrary to expectations, it has not been swept away with the automation of office work (Webster, 1993). Even the entry of a small number of men into this work has not altered the central dynamic of patriarchal control (Pringle, 1988). Both patriarchal and technical control coexist side by side, and as elements in a wide repertoire of control techniques available to management, they fulfil specific functions in specific instances rather than being exclusive systems.

This is not to deny that the gender relations of many workplaces are in flux as technological change takes place alongside innovations in patterns of work, new modes of allocating workers to work roles and new definitions of skill. There is clearly *potential* here for women to benefit from shifts away from established patterns of work organisation; for example, teamworking *could* operate in women's favour and undermine conventional practices of task allocation, new skill definition *could* be harnessed to revalue the work which women do, and the roles which women and men play in workplaces *could* be transformed by a redefinition of the value of women's work. And these changes *are* observable in isolated instances, for example, in the UK building society industry where women have been able to move into new roles involving customer service functions (Crompton and Sanderson, 1990). But changes in the gender relations of work and workplaces are principally political, not technical, changes. They rely on a broader climate of equal opportunities and on changes in women's role in the domestic sphere as well as in the workplace, for women's domestic labour is critical to their employment position. And here there are national variations in the position of women. In the Scandinavian countries (and particularly Sweden), for example, access to childcare and to social services, the sexual division of labour in the home, and the employment policies of firms are all (still) relatively helpful to women in paid work. (This is rapidly changing, however.) A global perspective is not so encouraging. As long as women the world over continue to hold responsibility for the domestic sphere, because men's contribution remains relatively minimal (UN, 1995), they will be unable to benefit in a systematic way from the potential opportunities in the workplace which information technologies might otherwise offer them. As Kirkup has argued, few women up to now have been actively involved in IT developments either in employment or in the home, and they may be even more peripheral in the future than they have been in the past (1992: 267).

Feminist versus 'malestream' social studies of technology – any intellectual exchange?

When feminist researchers began to address the social issues surrounding the development and application of new technologies and their implications for women, they were moving into a conceptual world which was largely gender-blind. As we have seen throughout this book, studies of the social relations of technology and the social construction of technology signally failed to differentiate those social relations. As Horn (1994) puts it:

> "Seamlessness" seems to leave little room for the articulation of *difference*, and . . . society . . . is . . . unrent by the politics of identity . . . (G)ender and race remain invisible, which might move some to worry whether "actors" lead us everywhere "we" might want to go. However, the issue is not simply that women and others do not get to count as "relevant social groups". It is also that such issues as the gendering of the technological . . . are never engaged . . . (We) are left to wonder whether those engaged in constructivist projects and in cultural and feminist studies of technology will have more rather than less to say to each other in the future.
>
> (Horn, 1994: 387–8)

In this context, it was not surprising that feminist studies repeatedly emphasised women's exclusion from technological endeavour, for this had not occurred to the social constructivists as they theorised technology and society into a seamless web, or to the labour process theorists as they examined the processes of technological change in men's working lives. The history of feminist studies of technology is in some ways therefore a story of feminists compensating for, and offering a corrective to, decades of social scientific blindness to the divisions within society.

But this lack of vision has improved a little. Social shaping and social constructivist perspectives have begun, slowly, to see and to analyse the gender components in the creation and consumption of technologies. This improvement has partly come from within these traditions, as a new focus on the sphere of use rather than simply on the design of technological artefacts brings more women into view (Silverstone and Hirsch, 1992; Kline and Pinch, 1995). It is also encouraged by the writings of feminist researchers who have taken up a social constructivist approach and used it to highlight the gender relations contributing to the design, manufacture, marketing and use of artefacts (Cockburn and Ormrod, 1993; Chabaud-Rychter, 1994; Shaffner, 1993). Labour process studies of women's work and of the implications of technological change for their jobs, as we saw in Chapter 2, now abound.

It would be wrong, therefore, to conclude that feminist studies of technological development and application have not informed the larger body of 'malestream' research in this field. There are clear indications of some intellectual exchange, and of a greater awareness of the existence of women as a 'relevant social group' implicated, in various ways, in the creation of technologies (Grint and Gill, 1995). Equally, feminist thinking has benefited from constructivist thinking; the concept of 'technology' itself is much less taken for granted and subject to 'unpacking', just as 'gender' is seen as 'socially constructed ... and under construction' (Wajcman, 1991: 9), a 'discursive construct' (Van Zoonen 1992: 12), and a 'social achievement' (Cockburn, 1992: 39). But there remains a worrying marginalisation of feminist studies of information technologies in practical spheres – in curricula, in conferences, and in publications – and a still great preponderance of research which concerns itself with processes of innovation but not with the divisions between the social groups which generate those processes. As long as this remains the case, there will continue to be a need for feminists to point up women's exclusion, not only from technological work but also from the academy which is concerned with that work.

Where should future feminist studies of women in workplaces go, and how can they respond to this enduring problem? Many feminists have argued that, despite their exclusion from technologies, women's relationship to technology is not entirely negative. On the one hand, according to writers such as Autumn Stanley (1983), women have simply been written out of historical accounts of the development of technologies. According to Lie (1995), contemporary women are increasingly becoming users of technological artefacts, some of which were previously male domains, such as cars and motorbikes (and, we might add, computers). Lie argues that women increasingly strive for competence and knowledge in relation to the technical artefacts they use, and Henwood (1993) has found that women also enjoy the power and status which accompanies some forms of technological work. In this book, we have seen the many spheres of work in which women are everyday users of computer technologies in their jobs. As women work more with computing systems, could their own and men's images of femininity be altered and extended to include capacities which traditionally have not been associated with being a woman? And even if they were to be, could this in any way improve the position of women in the workplace and in relation to technology? Or will women's computing expertise remain without status, while men continue to monopolise computing jobs with prestige and power? These issues need to be pursued by feminist researchers interested in understanding long-term developments in women's technological work.

Equally, in advancing feminist initiatives for systems which meet the needs of women, we have to answer the question which is continually put in this context: is there such a thing as an 'appropriate' technology for women, and can it be specified on behalf of them? A 'rationality of caring' has been advanced as a central element in women's labour which IT systems need to support (Sørensen, 1992; Gunnarsson, 1994). Brun (1994) has similarly argued that the creation and protection of human life should be the point of departure for technological development for women:

> Women's ethics ... is not sentimental. It is practical. It implies a concrete and holistic consideration of people's need for a sustainable environment and that basic security which is the precondition for common responsible action ... A step by step process ... makes the protection of the weak its highest priority: creating social solidarity and collective security in a sustainable manner from below. This must go hand in hand with a gradual reduction of the importance of wage labour in the shape of a collective re-appropriation of control over the means of subsistence ... In the context of such a process new technology must be invented, old technologies transformed or abandoned.
>
> (Brun, 1994: 79)

This is an eloquent plea for a programme of progressive social technological change, but how far are the objectives expressed really those of all women? Perhaps they are only the values of *some* women, those with a democratic or socialist conscience. Women are not an undifferentiated social group; class and race interests divide us and our dreams of social progress. Nor are all women mothers whose first priority is the protection of children. So feminist studies of technology, particularly those concerned with identifying 'women's values' for the purposes of systems design, need to be extremely careful not to lapse into universal or essentialist assumptions about women's interests, or to assume that there are appropriate systems for all women which can be specified in advance and on their behalf.

Despite these differences in the consciousness of women, women's lives have much in common. Most women perform their technological work in capitalist societies, in relatively powerless and peripheral positions in most public spheres of those societies and certainly in the workplace. In this arena, the tools of their trade are developed first and foremost by and for those holding power in those societies – the owners of capital, their managerial representatives, male professionals. Can these power and gender relations of technology be simply overturned by 'good practice' – feminist systems design? What is the likelihood that systems can really be designed to serve the interests of women workers within patriarchal capitalist societies which generally develop and use technologies for efficient industrial production and corporate organisation and not for the development of human potential? And, if it is possible to do so, how can this best be achieved? By highlighting and detailing the factors which shape technological development, and particularly by showing the loopholes in the process, social constructivist analyses have identified the areas where there are real possibilities for democratic intervention. Here are lessons which feminist and other democratic systems design initiatives can, and have, drawn upon.

Political engagement is, after all, surely the priority of most feminist studies of technology. As Gill and Grint (1995) have argued, feminist research in this area is an emancipatory project, and I believe that it must continue to be so. There is a danger lurking in some contemporary feminist post-modernist work that any definition of the reality of women's lives is abandoned in favour of analysis of texts, for no one account of truth has any primacy over another (Rose, 1994). I would argue, as Rose does, that the value of feminist post-modernist accounts has been in the recognition of diversity between women which they allow, in the possibility for a post-colonial discourse which goes beyond the perspective of white, Western women and considers the standpoints of black women, Asian and Hispanic women. They too have their experiences of technologies in their workplaces, and, as we have seen throughout this book, we cannot properly understand the gender dynamics of contemporary technological development without discussing their working lives.

The concepts of class, power, technology and even gender which featured in many structuralist accounts of social, economic and technical change are more usefully seen as social *relations* rather than simply as social entities. In this way, we can begin to understand the ways in which they are constantly reconstituted and evolved through interaction with one another, and we can see more clearly the dynamism of patriarchal capitalist endeavours with technology. If we are serious about using feminist analysis for political engagement, then rather than lapsing into apolitical relativism, we need to draw upon the insights of post-modernist feminism, but recognise that there is indeed a reality to be grasped and addressed, and for many women working the world over, it is an enduringly grim one.

REFERENCES

Appelbaum, E. (1987) 'Restructuring work: temporary, part-time and at home employment', in H. Hartmann, R. Kraut and L. Tilly (eds) (1987) *Computer Chips and Paper Clips: Volume II*, Washington, DC: Academy Press.

Appelbaum, E. (1992) 'Structural change and the growth of part-time and temporary employment', in V. L. duRivage (ed.) (1992) *New Policies for the Part-time and Contingent Work-force*, Armonk, New York: M. E. Sharpe.

Appelbaum, E. and Albin, P. (1989) 'Computer rationalization and the transformation of work: lessons from the insurance industry', in S. Wood (ed.) (1989) *The Transformation of Work?* London: Unwin Hyman.

Armstrong, P. (1982) 'If it's only a woman it doesn't matter so much', in J. West (ed.) (1982) *Work, Women and the Labour Market*, London: Routledge.

Arnold, E. and Faulkner, W. (1985) 'Smothered by invention: the masculinity of technology', in W. Faulkner and E. Arnold (eds) (1985) *Smothered by Invention: Technology in Women's Lives*, London: Pluto Press.

Atkinson, J. and Meager, N. (1986) 'New forms of work organisation', *IMS Report No. 121*, Brighton: Institute of Manpower Studies.

Avner, E. (1993) 'Trade unions, IT and equal opportunities in Sweden', in E. Green, J. Owen and D. Pain (eds) (1993) *Gendered by Design: Information Technology and Office Systems*, London: Taylor and Francis.

Bangemann Group (1994) *Europe and the Global Information Society: Recommendations to the European Council*, Brussels: European Commission.

Bansler, J. (1995) 'Information Systems and Empowerment', Panel presented to *European Conference on Information Systems*. Athens, Greece, June 1–3.

Barker, J. and Downing, H. (1980) 'Word processing and the transformation of the patriarchal relations of control in the office', *Capital and Class*, **10**: 64–99.

Beatson, M. (1995) *Labour Market Flexibility*, Research Series No. 48. Sheffield: Employment Department.

Beech, C. (1991) 'Women and WIT', in I. V. Eriksson, B. Kitchenham and K. G. Tijdens (eds) (1991) *Women, Work and Computerization: Understanding and Overcoming Bias in Work and Education*, Amsterdam: North-Holland.

Beechey, V. (1977) 'Some notes on female wage labour in capitalist production', *Capital and Class*, **3**: 45–66.

Beechey, V. (1982) 'The sexual division of labour and the labour process: a critical assessment of Braverman', in S. Wood (ed.) (1982) *The Degradation of Work? Skill, Deskilling and the Labour Process*, London: Hutchinson.

Belussi, F. (1992) 'Benetton Italy: Beyond Fordism and flexible specialisation. The evolution of the network firm model', in S. Mitter (ed.) (1992) *Computer-aided Manufacturing and Women's Employment: The Clothing Industry in Four EC Countries*, London: Springer-Verlag.

Benet, M. K. (1972) *Secretary: an Enquiry into the Female Ghetto*, London: Sidgwick and Jackson.

Berg, A. J. (1994) 'Technological flexibility: Bringing gender into technology (or was it the other way round?)', in C. Cockburn and R. Fürst Dilic (eds) (1994) *Bringing Technology Home: Gender and Technology in a Changing Europe*, Buckingham: Open University Press.

Berg, A. J. and Lie, M. (1995) 'Feminism and constructivism: Do artifacts have gender?', *Science, Technology and Human Values*, **20**(3): 332–51.

Berger, S. and Piore, M. (1980) *Dualism and Discontinuity in Industrial Societies*, Cambridge: Cambridge University Press.

Bergouignan, M-C., Cameleyre, M-J. and Rouyer, M-C. (1989) 'Impact of the introduction of new technologies on women's work in South West France: Women's critical assessment and suggested strategies', in K. Tijdens, M. Jennings, I. Wagner and M. Weggelaar (eds) (1989) *Women, Work and Computerization: Forming New Alliances*, Amsterdam: North-Holland.

Bergmann, T. (1985) 'Not only windmills. Female service workers and new technologies', in A. Olerup, L. Schneider and E. Monod (eds) (1985) *Women, Work and Computerization: Opportunities and Disadvantages*, Amsterdam: North-Holland.

Beynon, H. (1973) *Working For Ford*, Harmondsworth: Penguin.

Bijker, W. E., Hughes, T. P. and Pinch, T. (eds) (1987) *The Social Construction of Technological Systems*, London: MIT Press.

Bird, E. (1980) *Information Technology in the Office: The Impact on Women's Jobs*, Manchester: Equal Opportunities Commission.

Birkenes, T. and Fjuk, A. (1994) 'A feminist approach to design of computer systems supporting co-operative work – the troublesome issue of co-operation seen from a women's perspective', in A. Adam, J. Emms, E. Green and J. Owen (eds) (1994) *Women, Work and Computerization: Breaking Old Boundaries – Building New Forms*, Amsterdam: North-Holland.

Bjerkenes, G. and Bratteteig, T. (1988) 'Computers – utensils or epaulets? The application perspective revisited', *AI and Society*, **2**(3): 258–266.

Blaxall, M. and Regan, B. (eds) (1976) *Women and the Workplace: The Implications of Occupational Segregation*, Chicago: University of Chicago Press.

Blomqvist, M. (1994) 'Gender hierarchies challenged: Women in knowledge-intensive companies', Uppsala: University of Uppsala unpublished PhD thesis.

Blomqvist, M., Mackinnon, A. and Vehviläinen, M. (1994) 'Exploring the gender and technology boundaries: an international perspective', in T. Eberhart and C. Wächter (eds) (1994) *Proceedings of the Second European Feminist Research Conference on Feminist Perspectives on Technology, Work and Ecology*, Graz, Austria, July.

Bloomfield, B. (1989) 'On speaking about computing', *Sociology*, **23**(3): 409–26.

Bødker, S. and Greenbaum, J. (1993) 'Design of information systems: Things versus people', in E. Green, J. Owen and D. Pain (eds) (1993) *Gendered by Design: Information Technology and Office Systems*, London: Taylor and Francis.

Bradley, G. (1985) 'Computers and work content, work load and stress – analyses and women's participation strategies', in A. Olerup, L. Schneider and E. Monod (eds) (1985) *Women, Work and Computerization: Opportunities and Disadvantages*, Amsterdam: North-Holland.

Bradley, G. and Bergstrom, C. (1986) *The Secretary Role and Word Processing – Office Profession in Transition*, Stockholm: University of Stockholm.

Bradley, H. (1989) *Men's Work, Women's Work*, Cambridge: Polity Press.

Braverman, H. (1974) *Labor and Monopoly Capital*, New York: Monthly Review Press.

Bruegel, I. (1989) 'Sex and race in the labour market', *Feminist Review*, **32**: 49–68.

Brewster, C. and Hegewisch, A. (1994) *Policy and Practice in European Human Resource Management*, London: Routledge.

Bridges, W. (1995) *Jobshift*, London: Allen and Unwin.

Brun, E. (1994) 'Technology appropriate for women?', in E. Gunnarsson and L. Trojer (eds) (1994) *Feminist Voices on Gender, Technology and Ethics*, Luleå: University of Technology Centre for Women's Studies.

Bulletin on Women and Employment in the EU, No. 4, April 1994, Brussels: European Commission DGV.

Bulletin on Women and Employment in the EU, No. 5, October 1994, Brussels: European Commission DGV.

Bulletin on Women and Employment in the EU, No. 7, October 1995, Brussels: European Commission, DGV.

Butler, D. (1988) 'Secretarial skills and office technology', in E. Willis (ed.) (1988) *Technology and the Labour Process: Australasian Case Studies*, Sydney: Allen and Unwin.

CAITS (1987a) *Flexibility – Who Needs it?*, London: Polytechnic of North London, Centre for Alternative Industrial and Technological Systems.

CAITS (1987b) *Retailing – A Sectoral Analysis for the London Borugh of Islington*, London: Polytechnic of North London, Centre for Alternative Industrial and Technological Systems.

Campbell-Kelly, M. (1993) *Data Processing and Technological Change: the Post Office Savings Bank 1861–1930*, University of Manchester, Centre for the History of Science, Technology and Medicine mimeo.

Cast, M. (1995) 'Competitive advantage through Indian software services', *Computer Bulletin*, **7**(5): 14–16.

Cavendish, R. (1981) *Women on the Line*, London: Routledge.

Central Statistical Office (CSO) (1995) *Social Focus on Women*, London: HMSO.

Chabaud-Rychter, D. (1994) 'Women users in the design process of a food robot: Innovation in a French domestic appliance company', in C. Cockburn and R. Fürst-Dilic (eds) (1994) *Bringing Technology Home: Gender and Technology in a Changing Europe*, Buckingham: Open University Press.

Chiesi, M. (1992) 'On using women as resources: Italian unions' strategies towards information technology and new organisation of work', in S. Mitter (ed.) (1992) *Computer-aided Manufacturing and Women's Employment: the Clothing Industry in Four EC Countries*, London: Springer-Verlag.

Child, J. and Tarbuck, M. (1988) 'The introduction of new technologies: Managerial initiatives and union response in British banks', *Industrial Relations Journal*, **16**(3): 19–33.

de Cindio, F. and Simone, C. (1989) 'A framework for understanding (women's) work and its computerization', in K. Tijdens, M. Jennings, I. Wagner and M. Weggelaar (eds) (1989) *Women, Work and Computerization: Forming New Alliances*, Amsterdam: North-Holland.

de Cindio, F. and Simone, C. (1993) 'The universes of discourse for education and action/research', in E. Green, J. Owen and D. Pain (eds) (1993) *Gendered by Design: Information Technology and Office Systems*, London: Taylor and Francis.

Clark, J. (ed.) (1993) *Human Resource Management and Technical Change*, London: Sage.

Cockburn, C. (1983) *Brothers: Male Dominance and Technological Change*, London: Pluto.

Cockburn, C. (1985a) *Machinery of Dominance: Men, Women and Technical Know-how*, London: Pluto.

Cockburn, C. (1985b) 'Caught in the wheels: the high cost of being a female cog in the male machinery of engineering', in D. MacKenzie and J. Wajcman (eds) (1985) *The Social Shaping of Technology*, Milton Keynes: Open University Press.

Cockburn, C. (1992) 'The circuit of technology: gender, identity and power', in R. Silverstone and E. Hirsch (eds) (1992) *Consuming Technologies*, London: Routledge.

Cockburn, C. and Ormrod, S. (1993) *Gender and Technology in the Making*, London: Sage.

Collinson, D. and Collinson, M. (1995) 'The remasculinization of financial services', Paper presented to the conference on Gender and Life in Organizations, University of Portsmouth, 9 September.

Commission of the European Communities (CEC) (1994) *Growth, Competitiveness, Employment: The Challenges and Ways Forward into the 21st Century*, White Paper, Brussels: Commission of the European Communities.

Conference of Socialist Economists (CSE) Microelectronics Group (1980) *Microelectronics: Capitalist Technology and the Working Class*, London: CSE Books.

Confederation of British Industry (CBI)/Coopers and Lybrand (1995) *Financial Services Survey*, No. 22, March, London: CBI/Coopers and Lybrand.

Cowan, R. S. (1985) 'Gender and technological change', in D. MacKenzie and J. Wajcman (eds) (1985) *The Social Shaping of Technology*, Milton Keynes: Open University Press.

Cowan, R. S. (1987) 'The consumption junction: A proposal for research strategies in the sociology of technology', in W. E. Bijker, T. P. Hughes and T. Pinch (eds) (1987) *The Social Construction of Technological Systems*, London: MIT Press.

Coyle, A. (1982) 'Sex and skill in the organisation of the clothing industry', in J. West (ed.) (1982) *Work, Women and the Labour Market*, London: Routledge and Kegan Paul.

Coyle, A. (1984) *Redundant Women*, London: The Women's Press.

Cringely, R. X. (1992) *Accidental Empires – How the boys of Silicon Valley make their millions, battle foreign competition, and still can't get a date*, Harmondsworth: Penguin.

Crompton, R. (1994) 'Occupational trends and women's employment patterns', in R. Lindley (ed.) (1994) *Labour Market Structures and Prospects for Women*, Manchester: Equal Opportunities Commission.

Crompton, R. and Jones, G. (1984) *White Collar Proletariat: Deskilling and Gender in Clerical Work*, London: Macmillan.

Crompton, R. and Sanderson, K. (1990) *Gendered Jobs and Social Change*, London: Unwin Hyman.

Daniel, W. W. (1987) *Workplace Industrial Relations and Technical Change*, London: Frances Pinter.

David, P. A. (1985) 'Clio and the economics of QWERTY', *American Economic Review*, **75**(2): 332–7.

Davies, C. and Rosser, J. (1986) 'Gendered jobs in the health service', in D. Knights and H. Willmott (eds) (1986) *Gender and the Labour Process*, London: Macmillan.

Davies, M. (1979) 'Woman's place is at the typewriter: the feminization of the clerical labor force', in Z. Eisenstein (ed.) (1979) *Capitalist Patriarchy and the Case for Socialist Feminism*, New York: Monthly Review Press.

De Kadt, M. (1979) 'Insurance: A clerical work factory', in A. Zimbalist (ed.) (1979) *Case Studies on the Labor Process*, New York: Monthly Review Press.

Dicken, P. (1992) *Global Shift*, London. Paul Chapman.

Donato, K. M. and Roos, P. A. (1987) 'Gender and earnings inequality among computer specialists', in B. D. Wright (ed.) (1987) *Women, Work and Technology*, Ann Arbor, Michigan: University of Michigan Press

Easlea, B. (1983) *Fathering the Unthinkable: Masculinity, Scientists and Nuclear Arms Race*, London: Pluto.

Ehn, P. and Kyng, M. (1987) 'The collective resource approach to systems design', in G. Bjerkenes, P. Ehn and M. Kyng (eds) (1987) *Computers and Democracy: A Scandinavian Challenge*, Aldershot: Avebury.

Eisenstein, Z. (1979) *Capitalist Patriarchy and the Case for Socialist Feminism*, New York: Monthly Review Press.

Elger, T. (1987) 'Flexible futures? New technology and the contemporary transformation of work', *Work, Employment and Society*, **1**(4). 528–40.

Elling, M. (1985) 'Remote work/telecommuting', in A. Olerup, L. Schneider and E. Monod (eds) (1985) *Women, Work and Computerization: Opportunities and Disadvantages*, Amsterdam: Elsevier.

Elson, D. (1989) 'The cutting edge: Multinationals in the EEC textiles and clothing industry', in D. Elson and R. Pearson (eds) (1989)

Women's Employment and Multinationals in Europe, London: Macmillan.

Elson, D. and Pearson, R. (1989) 'Introduction', in D. Elson and R. Pearson (eds) (1989) *Women's Employment and Multinationals in Europe*, London: Macmillan.

European Trade Union Institute (ETUI) (1979) *The Impact of Microelectronics on Employment in Western Europe in the 1980s*, Brussels: ETUI.

Falck, M., Steensma, L., Van Oost, E. and Owen, J. (1991) 'Women in EDP jobs – working group report', in I. V. Eriksson, B. Kitchenham and K. G. Tijdens (eds) (1991) *Women, Work and Computerization: Understanding and Overcoming Bias in Work and Education*, Amsterdam: North-Holland.

Fearfull, A. (1992) 'The introduction of information and office technologies: The great divide?', *Work, Employment and Society*, 6(3): 423–42.

Feldberg, R. L. and Glenn, E. N. (1983) 'Technology and work degradation: Effects of office automation on women clerical workers', in J. Rothschild (ed.) (1983) *Machina ex Dea: Feminist Perspectives on Technology*, New York: Pergamon Press.

Felstead, A. (1995) *Vocational Qualifications: Gender Barriers to the Certification of Work-related Skills*, University of Leicester; Centre for Labour Market Studies mimeo.

Fielder, S., Rees, G. and Rees, T. (1990) 'Regional restructuring, services and women's employment: Labour market change in South Wales', *Institutional Determinants of Employers' Training Strategies, Project Paper No. 3*, Cardiff: University of Wales College of Cardiff Social Research Unit.

Figes, K. (1994) *Because of her Sex: The Myth of Equality for Women in Britain*, London: Macmillan.

Fincham, R., Fleck, J., Procter, R., Scarbrough, H., Tierney, M. and Williams, R. (1994) *Expertise and Innovation: Information Technology Strategies in the Financial Services Sector*, Oxford: Clarendon Press.

Findlay, P. (1989) 'Fighting plant closure: Women in the Plessey occupation', in D. Elson and R. Pearson (eds) (1989) *Women's Employment and Multinationals in Europe*, London: Macmillan.

Fleck, J. (1988) *Innofusion or Diffusation? The Nature of Technological Development in Robotics*, Edinburgh: Edinburgh PICT Working Paper No. 4.

Fleck, J. (1993) 'Configurations: Crystallising contingency', *International Journal of Human Factors in Manufacturing*, 3(1): 15–36.

Fleck, J., Webster, J. and Williams, R. (1987) 'The organisational shaping of integrated automation', Paper presented to the PICT National Conference, UMIST, December.

Fleck, J., Webster, J. and Williams, R. (1990) 'Dynamics of information technology implementation: A reassessment of paradigms and trajectories of development', *Futures*, 22(6): 618–40.

Fothergill, A. (1994) 'Telework: Women's experiences and utilisation of information technology in the home', in A. Adam, J. Emms, E. Green and J. Owen (eds) (1994) *Women, Work and Computerization: Breaking Old Boundaries – Building New Forms*, Amsterdam: North-Holland.

Fox-Keller, E. (1985) *Reflections on Gender and Science*, Yale: University Press.

Frances, J. and Garnsey, E. (1995) 'Re-engineering the food chains: A systems perspective on UK supermarkets and BPR', Paper presented to the Workshop on Critical Studies of Organisations and Management Innovations, Brussels, May 8–9.

Francis, A. (1986) *New Technology at Work*, Oxford: Clarendon Press.

Freeman, C. and Soete, L. (1994) *Work for All or Mass Unemployment: Computerised Technical Change into the 21st Century*, London: Pinter Publishers.

Friedman, A. L. with Cornford, D. S. (1989) *Computer Systems Development: History, Organization and Implementation*, Chichester: Wiley.

Frissen, V. (1995) 'Gender is calling: Some reflections on past, present and future uses of the telephone', in K. Grint and R. Gill (eds) (1995) *The Gender-Technology Relation: Contemporary Theory and Research*, London: Taylor and Francis.

Fröbel, F., Heinrichs, J. and Kreye, O. (1980) *The New International Division of Labour*, Cambridge: Cambridge University Press.

Fuentes, A. and Ehrenreich, B. (1983) *Women in the Global Factory*, Boston, Mass.: South End Press.

Gaeta, R., Belussi, F. and Mitter, S. (1992) 'Pronta moda: new business ventures for women in Italy', in S. Mitter (ed.) (1992) *Computer-aided Manufacturing and Women's Employment: The Clothing Industry in Four EC Countries*, London: Springer-Verlag.

Game, A. and Pringle, R. (1984) *Gender at Work*, London: Pluto.

Garrahan, P. and Stewart, P. (1992) *The Nissan Enigma*, London: Mansell.

Gerver, E. (1989) 'Computers and gender', in T. Forester (ed.) (1989) *Computers in the Human Context: Information Technology, Productivity and People*, Oxford: Blackwell.

Gill, C. (1985) *Work, Unemployment and the New Technology*, Cambridge: Polity Press.

Gill, R. and Grint, K. (1995) 'Introduction', in K. Grint and R. Gill (eds) (1995) *The Gender-Technology Relation: Contemporary Theory and Research*, London: Taylor and Francis.

Gillespie, A., Richardson, R. and Cornford, J. (1995) *Review of Telework in Britain: Implications for Public Policy*, Newcastle: University of Newcastle Centre for Urban and Regional Development Studies Report prepared for the Parliamentary Office of Science and Technology.

Glenn, E. N. and Feldberg, R. L. (1979) 'Proletarianizing clerical work: Technology and organizational control in the office', in A. Zimbalist (ed.) (1979) *Case Studies on the Labor Process*, New York: Monthly Review Press.

Glenn, E. N. and Tolbert, C. M. (1987) 'Technology and emerging patterns of stratification for women of color: Race and gender segregation in computer occupations', in B. Wright (ed.) (1987) *Women, Work and Technology*, Ann Arbor, Michigan: University of Michigan Press.

Glogau, M. (1985) 'Office computerization and work structures: A challenge to women', in A. Olerup, L. Schneider and E. Monod (eds)

(1985) *Women, Work and Computerization: Opportunities and Disadvantages*, Amsterdam: North-Holland.

Glucksmann, M. (1990) *Women Assemble: Women Workers and the New Industries in Inter-War Britain*, London: Routledge.

Glucksmann, M. (1995) 'Why "work"? Gender and the "total social organization of labour" ', *Gender, Work and Organization*, 2(2): 63–75.

Goldstein, N. (1989) 'Silicon glen: Women and semiconductor multinationals', in D. Elson and R. Pearson (eds) (1989) *Women's Employment and Multinationals in Europe*, London: Macmillan.

Goodman, S. E. and Perby, M-L. (1985) 'Computerization and the skill in women's work', in A. Olerup, L. Schneider and E. Monod (eds) (1985) *Women, Work and Computerization: Opportunities and Disadvantages*, Amsterdam: North-Holland.

Gray, M. (1993) 'BT's Inverness teleworking experiment: Sending the inbound call centre home', Paper presented to the *Telecommute '93* Conference, Washington DC, 20–21 October.

Green, E. (1994) 'Gender perspectives, office systems and organizational change', in A. Adam, J. Emms, E. Green and J. Owen (eds) (1994) *Women, Work and Computerization: Breaking Old Boundaries – Building New Forms*, Amsterdam: North-Holland.

Green, E., Owen, J. and Pain, D. (eds) (1993a) *Gendered by Design: Information Technology and Office Systems*, London: Taylor and Francis.

Green, E., Owen, J. and Pain, D. (1993b) ' "City Libraries": Human-centred opportunities for women?'', in E. Green, J. Owen and D. Pain (eds) (1993) *Gendered by Design: Information Technology and Office Systems*, London: Taylor and Francis.

Green, K., Coombs, R. and Holroyd, K. (1980) *The Effects of Microelectronic Technologies on Employment Prospects: A Case Study of Thameside*, Farnborough: Gower.

Greenbaum, J. (1976) 'Division of labour in the computer field', *Monthly Review*, 28(3): 40–55.

Greenbaum, J. (1979) *In the Name of Efficiency*, Philadelphia: Temple University Press.

Greenbaum, J. (1987) 'The head and the heart', Aarhus University, Department of Computer Science paper.

Greenbaum, J. (1991) 'Toward participatory design: The head and the heart revisited', in I. V. Eriksson, B. Kitchenham and K. G. Tijdens (eds) (1991) *Women, Work and Computerization: Understanding and Overcoming Bias in Work and Education*, Amsterdam: North-Holland.

Greenbaum, J. (1994) 'Windows on the workplace: The temporization of work', in A. Adam, J. Emms, E. Green and J. Owen (eds) (1994) *Women, Work and Computerization: Breaking Old Boundaries – Building New Forms*, Amsterdam: North-Holland.

Greenbaum, J. (1995) *Windows on the Workplace: Computers, Jobs and the Organization of Office Work in the Late Twentieth Century*, New York: Monthly Review Press.

Grint, K. and Gill, R. (eds) (1995) *The Gender-Technology Relation: Contemporary Theory and Research*, London: Taylor and Francis.

Grint, K. and Woolgar, S. (1995) 'On some failures of nerve in constructivist and feminist analyses of technology', in R. Gill and K. Grint (eds) (1995) *The Gender-Technology Relation: Contemporary Theory and Research*, London: Taylor and Francis.

Grundy, F. (1994) 'Women in the computing workplace: Some impressions', in A. Adam, J. Emms, E. Green and J. Owen (eds) (1994) *Women, Work and Computerization: Breaking Old Boundaries – Building New Forms*, Amsterdam: North-Holland.

Grønfeldt, J. and Kandrup, S. (1985) 'Women, work and computerization', in A. Olerup, L. Schneider and E. Monod (eds) (1985) *Women, Work and Computerization: Opportunities and Disadvantages*, Amsterdam: North-Holland.

Gunnarsson, E. (1994) 'Women and men – Different rationalities?', in E. Gunnarsson and L. Trojer (eds) (1994) *Feminist Voices on Gender, Technology and Ethics*, Luleå: University of Technology Centre for Women's Studies.

Gunter, K. (1994) 'Women and the information revolution: Washed ashore by the third wave', in A. Adam, J. Emms, E. Green and J. Owen (eds) (1994) *Women, Work and Computerization: Breaking Old Boundaries – Building New Forms*, Amsterdam: North-Holland.

Hacker, S. (1987) 'Feminist perspectives on computer based systems and democracy at the workplace', in G. Bjerkenes, P. Ehn and M. Kyng (eds) (1987) *Computers and Democracy: A Scandinavian Challenge*, Aldershot: Avebury.

Hacker, S. (1989) *Pleasure, Power and Technology*, London: Unwin Hyman.

Hacker, S. (1990) (D. E. smith and S. M. Turner (eds)) *Doing It the Hard Way: Investigations of Gender and Technology*, London: Unwin Hyman.

Haddon, L. (1988) 'The home computer: The making of a consumer electronic', *Science as Culture*, 2: 7–51.

Haddon, L. and Silverstone, R. (1993) *Teleworking in the 1990s: A View from Home*, Brighton, SPRU CICT Report Series No. 10.

Hakim, C. (1979) Occupational Segregation, Research Paper No. 9, Department of Employment, London, HMSO.

Hakim, C. (1981) 'Job segregation: Trends in the 1970s', *Employment Gazette*, **89**(12): 521–9.

Hakim, C. (1987) 'Trends in the flexible work-force', *Employment Gazette*, **95**(11): 549–60.

Hales, M. (1991) 'A human resource approach to information systems development – The ISU (Information Systems Use) design model', *Journal of Information Technology*, 6: 140–61.

Hales, M. (1993) 'Human-centred systems, gender and computer supported co-operative work', in B. Probert and B. Wilson (eds) (1993) *Pink Collar Blues: Work, Gender and Technology*, Melbourne: Melbourne University Press.

Hammer, M. (1990) 'Reengineering work: Don't automate, obliterate', *Harvard Business Review*, July/August: 104–12.

Handy, C. (1989) *The Age of Unreason*, London: Arrow Books.

Håpnes, T. and Sørensen, K. H. (1995) 'Competition and collaboration in male shaping of computing: A study of a Norwegian hacker culture', in R. Gill and K. Grint (eds) (1995) *The Gender-Technology*

Relation: Contemporary Theory and Research, London: Taylor and Francis.

Haraway, D. (1985) 'A manifesto for cyborgs: Science, technology and socialist feminism in the 1980s', *Socialist Review*, **80**: 65–107.

Harding, S. (1986) *The Science Question in Feminism*, Milton Keynes, Open University Press.

Hayes, D. (1989) *Behind the Silicon Curtain: The Seductions of Work in a Lonely Era*, London: Free Association Books.

Heeks, R. (1993) 'Software subcontracting to the third world', in P. Quintas (ed.) *Social Dimensions of Systems Engineering*, London: Ellis Horwood.

Henderson, J. (1989) *The Globalisation of High Technology Production*, London: Routledge.

Henwood, F. (1987) 'Microelectronics and women's employment: an international perspective', in M. J. Davidson and C. L. Cooper (eds) (1987) *Women and Information Technology*, Chichester: Wiley.

Henwood, F. (1993) 'Establishing gender perspectives on information technology', in E. Green, J. Owen and D. Pain (eds) (1993) *Gendered by Design: Information Technology and Office Systems*, London: Taylor and Francis.

Henwood, F. (1994) 'WISE choices? Understanding occupational decision-making in a climate of equal opportunities for women in science and technology', University of East London, Innovation Studies Working Paper No. 2.

Herzog, M. (1980) *From Hand to Mouth*, Harmondsworth: Penguin.

Hirata, H. (1989) Production relocation: an electronics multinational in France and Brazil', in D. Elson and R. Pearson (eds) (1989) *Women's Employment and Multinationals in Europe*, London: Macmillan.

Hoel, B. (1982) 'Contemporary clothing sweatshops', in J. West (ed.) (1982) *Work, Women and the Labour Market*, London: Routledge and Kegan Paul.

Hofmann, J. (1994) 'Two versions of the same: The text editor and the automatic letter writer as contrasting conceptions of digital writing', in A. Adam, J. Emms, E. Green and J. Owen (eds) (1994) *Women, Work and Computerization: Breaking Old Boundaries – Building New Forms*, Amsterdam: North-Holland.

Hofmann, J. (1995) 'Writers, texts and writing acts – constructed realities in word processing software', Paper presented to the International Workshop on 'The Mutual Shaping of Gender and Technology', Twente University, The Netherlands, 6–8 October.

Horn, D. G. (1994) 'Review of W. Bijker and J. Law (eds) *Shaping Technology/Building Society*', in *Science, Technology and Human Values*, **19**(3): 386–7.

Howells, J. and Hine, J. (eds) (1993) *Innovative Banking: Competition and the Management of a New Network Technology*, London: Routledge.

Hoyles, C. (1988) *Girls and Computers*, London: Bedford Way Papers.

Huggett, C. (1988) *Participation in Practice: A Case Study of the Introduction of New Technology*, Watford: Engineering Industry Training Board.

Hutton, W. (1995) *The State We're In*, London: Jonathan Cape.

Huws, U. (1982) *Your Job in the Eighties: A Woman's Guide to New Technology*, London: Pluto Press.

Huws, U. (1984) 'The new homeworkers: New technology and the changing location of white-collar work', London, Low Pay Unit Pamphlet No. 28.

Huws, U. (1993) *Teleworking in Britain*, Sheffield: Employment Department Research Series No. 18.

Jaeckel, M. (1989) 'Home based telework – Selected highlights from a case study in the Federal Republic of Germany', in K. Tijdens, M. Jennings, I. Wagner and M. Weggelaar (eds) (1989) *Women, Work and Computerization: Forming New Alliances*, Amsterdam: North-Holland.

Jenson, J. (1989) 'The talents of women, the skills of men: Flexible specialization and women', in S. Wood (ed.) (1989) *The Transformation of Work?*, London: Unwin Hyman.

Joeman, L. (1992) 'Teleworking in Britain', London: Department of Employment Working Paper No. 1.

Jones, L. (1995) Skills and Deskilling in the Typing Labour Process, University of East London Department of Innovation Studies, unpublished undergraduate project.

Jones, M. (1994) 'Don't emancipate, exaggerate: Rhetoric, "reality" and reengineering', in R. L. Baskerville, S. Smithson, O. Ngwenyama and J. I. De Gross (eds) (1994), *Transforming Organizations with Information Technology*, Amsterdam: North-Holland.

Kamata, S. (1983) *Japan in the Passing Lane*, London: George Allen and Unwin.

Karasti, H. (1994) 'What's different in gender oriented ISD? Identifying gender oriented information systems development approach', in A. Adam, J. Emms, E. Green and J. Owen (eds) (1994) *Women, Work and Computerization: Breaking Old Boundaries – Building New Forms*, Amsterdam: North-Holland.

Karpf, A. (1987) 'Recent feminist approaches to women and technology', in M. McNeil (ed.) (1987) *Gender and Expertise*, London: Free Association Books.

Kheng, L. G. (1989) 'Women's participation in the computer industry in Singapore', in K. Tijdens, M. Jennings, I. Wagner and M. Weggelaar (eds) (1989) *Women, Work and Computerization: Forming New Alliances*, Amsterdam: North-Holland.

Kirkup, G. (1992) 'The social construction of computers: Hammers or harpsichords?', in G. Kirkup and L. S. Keller (eds) (1992) *Inventing Women: Science, Technology and Gender*, Cambridge: Polity Press.

Kirkup, G. and Keller, L. S. (eds) (1992) *Inventing Women: Science, Technology and Gender*, Cambridge: Polity Press.

Kline, R. and Pinch, T. (1995) 'Taking the black box off its wheels: The social construction of the car in the rural United States', Paper presented to the International Workshop on 'The Mutual Shaping of Gender and Technology', Twente University, The Netherlands, 6–8 October.

Knie, A. (1992) 'Yesterday's decisions determine tomorrow's options: The case of the mechanical typewriter', in M. Dierkes and U. Hoffmann (eds) (1992) *New Technology at the Outset: Social Forces in the Shaping of Technological Innovations*, Frankfurt: Campus Verlag.

Knights, D. and Sturdy, A. J. (1987) 'Women's work in insurance: IT and the reproduction of gendered segregation of work in insurance', in M. Davidson and C. L. Cooper (eds) (1987) *Women and Information Technology*, Chichester: Wiley.

Knights, D. and Sturdy, A. (1990) 'New technology and the self-disciplined worker in the insurance industry', in I. Varcoe, M. McNeil and S. Yearley (eds) (1990) *Deciphering Science and Technology: The Social Relations of Expertise*, London: Macmillan.

Knights, D. and Willmott, H. (eds) (1990) *Labour Process Theory*, London: Macmillan.

Kraft, J. and Siegenthaler, J. K. (1989) 'Office automation, gender and change: An analysis of the management literature, *Science, Technology and Human Values*, **14**(2): 195–212.

Kraft, P. (1977) *Programmers and Managers: The Routinization of Computer Programming in the United States*, New York: Springer-Verlag.

Kraft, P. and Dubnoff, S. (1983) 'Software Workers Survey', *Computer World*, **XVII**: 3–13.

Lane, C. (1988) 'New technology and clerical work', in D. Gallie (ed.) (1988) *Employment in Britain*, Oxford: Basil Blackwell.

Leeds Trade Union and Community Resource and Information Centre (TUCRIC) (1982) *New Technology and Women's Employment: Case Studies from West Yorkshire*, Manchester: Equal Opportunities Commission.

Lehto, A. M. (1989) 'Women's labour market position from the perspective of technological change', in K. Tijdens, M. Jennings, I. Wagner and M. Weggelaar (eds) (1989) *Women, Work and Computerization: Forming New Alliances*, Amsterdam: North-Holland.

Lie, M. (1985) 'Is remote work the way to "the good life" for women as well as for men?', in A. Olerup, L. Schneider and E. Monod (eds) (1985) *Women, Work and Computerization: Opportunities and Disadvantages*, Amsterdam: North-Holland.

Lie, M. (1995) 'Technology and masculinity: The case of the computer', *European Journal of Women's Studies*, **2**(3): 379–94.

Lie, M. and Rasmussen, B. (1985) 'Office work and skills', in A. Olerup, L. Schneider and E. Monod (eds) (1985) *Women, Work and Computerization: Opportunities and Disadvantages*, Amsterdam: North-Holland.

Liff, S. (1986) 'Technical change and occupational stereotyping', in D. Knights and H. Willmott (eds) (1986) *Gender and the Labour Process*, Aldershot: Gower Publishing.

Liff, S. (1990) 'Gender and information technology: Current research priorities, strengths, gaps and opportunities', Paper presented to the 2nd PICT workshop on Gender and Information Technology, November/December 1989.

Liff, S. (1993) 'Information technology and occupational restructuring in the office', in E. Green, J. Owen and D. Pain (eds) (1993) *Gendered by Design: Information Technology and Office Systems*, London: Taylor and Francis.

Lin, V. (1987) 'Women electronics workers in south east Asia: The emergence of a working class', in J. Henderson and M. Castells (eds) (1987) *Global Restructuring and Territorial Development*, London: Sage.

Linn, P. (1987) 'Gender stereotypes, technology stereotypes', in M. McNeil (ed.) (1987) *Gender and Expertise*, London: Free Association Books.

Littek, W. (1987) 'Administrative work and the impact of new information technologies – an overview of recent trends', in W. Littek and U. Heisig, Papers on the Rationalization of White-collar Work and Employee Reactions, University of Bremen Discussion Paper.

Littek, W. and Heisig, U. (1987) 'Papers on the Rationalization of White-collar Work and Employee Reactions,' University of Bremen Discussion Paper.

Lloyd, A. and Newell, L. (1985) 'Women and computers', in W. Faulkner and E. Arnold (eds) (1985) *Smothered by Invention: Technology in Women's Lives*, London: Pluto Press.

Lobet, C. (1995) 'Is the future female?', Panel presentation to European Conference on Information Systems, Athens, Greece, June 1–3.

Lovering, J. (1994) 'Employers, the sex-typing of jobs, and economic restructuring', in A. MacEwen Scott (ed.) (1994) *Gender Segregation and Social Change*, Oxford: Oxford University Press.

Machung, A. (1984) 'Word processing: Forward for business, backward for women', in K. Sacks and D. Remy (eds) (1984) *My Troubles are Going to Have Trouble with Me*, New Brunswick: Rutgers University Press.

Machung, A. (1988) ' "Who needs a personality to talk to a machine?": Communication in the automated office', in C. Kramarae (ed.) (1988) *Technology and Women's Voices: Keeping in Touch*, London: Routledge and Kegan Paul.

MacInnes, J. (1988) 'New technology in Scotbank: Gender, class and work', in R. Hyman and W. Streeck (eds) (1988) *New Technology and Industrial Relations*, Oxford: Basil Blackwell.

Mackay, H. and Gillespie, G. (1992) 'Extending the social shaping of technology approach: Ideology and appropriation', *Social Studies of Science*, 22(4): 685–716.

MacKenzie, D. and Wajcman, J. (eds) (1985) *The Social Shaping of Technology*, Milton Keynes: Open University Press.

Magdoff, H. (1992) 'Globalization: To what end?', in R. Millband and L. Panitch (eds) (1992) *Socialist Register 1992: New World Order?*, New York: Monthly Review Press.

Martin, M. (1991) *Hello, Central? Gender, Technology and Culture in the Formation of Telephone Systems*, London: McGill-Queen's University Press.

Martin, J. and Roberts, C. (1984) *Women and Employment: A Lifetime Perspective*, London: HMSO.

Marx, K. (1954) *Capital Volume 1*, London: Lawrence and Wishart.

Massey, D. (1984) *Spatial Divisions of Labour*, London: Macmillan.

McLoughlin, I. and Clark, J. (1988) *Technological Change at Work*, Milton Keynes: Open University Press.

McNally, F. (1979) *Women for Hire*, London: Macmillan.

McNeil, M. (1987a) 'It's a Man's World', in M. McNeil (ed.) (1987) *Gender and Expertise*, London: Free Association Books.

McNeil, M. (ed.) (1987b) *Gender and Expertise*, London: Free Association Books.

Microsyster (1988) *Not Over our Heads: Women and Computers in the Office*, London: Microsyster.

Mitter, S. (1986) *Common Fate, Common Bond*, London: Pluto.

Mitter, S. (1991) 'Computer-aided manufacturing and women's employment: A global critique of post-Fordism', in I. V. Eriksson, B. Kitchenham and K. G. Tijdens (eds) (1991) *Women, Work and Computerization: Understanding and Overcoming Bias in Work and Education*, Amsterdam: North-Holland.

Mitter, S. (1992) (ed.) *Computer-aided Manufacturing and Women's Employment*, London> Springer-Verlag.

Monod, E. (1985) 'Telecommuting – a new word, but still the same old story?', in A. Olerup, L. Schneider and E. Monod (eds) (1985) *Women, Work and Computerization: Opportunities and Disadvantages*, Amsterdam: North-Holland.

Morgall, J. (1983) 'Strengthening group solidarity of clericals: A case study of office automation', in D. Marsall and J. Gregory (eds) (1983) *Office Automation*, Cleveland: Working Women Education Fund.

Morgall, J. (1993) *Technology Assessment: A Feminist Perspective*, Philadelphia: Temple University Press.

Morgan, K. and Sayer, A. (1988) *Microcircuits of Capital: 'Sunrise' Industry and Uneven Development*, Cambridge: Polity.

Mörtberg, C. (1994) 'Computing as masculine culture', in E. Gunnarsson and L. Trojer (eds) (1994) *Feminist Voices on Gender, Technology and Ethics*, Luleå: Luleå University Centre of Women's Studies.

Moyal, A. (1992) 'The gendered use of the telephone: An Australian case study', *Media, Culture and Society*, **14**(1): 51–72.

Mumford, E. (1983) *Designing Secretaries*, Manchester: Manchester Business School.

Mumford, E. and Banks, O. (1967) *The Computer and the Clerk*, London: Routledge and Kegan Paul.

Murray, F. (1987) 'Reconsidering clerical skills and computerisation in UK retail banking', Sheffield: Sheffield City Polytechnic Human Centred Office System Project Working Paper.

Murray, F. (1993) 'A separate reality: Science, technology and masculinity', in E. Green, J. Owen and D. Pain (eds) (1993) *Gendered by Design: Information Technology and Office Systems*, London: Taylor and Francis.

Murray, P. and Wickham, J. (1982) 'Technocratic ideology and the reproduction of inequality: The case of the electronics industry in the Republic of Ireland' in G. Day with L. Caldwell, K. Jones, D. Robbins and H. Rose (eds) (1982) *Diversity and Decomposition in the Labour Market*, Aldershot: Gower.

Neathey, F. and Hurstfield, J. (1995) *Flexibility in Practice: Women's Employment and Pay in Retail and Finance*, Research Discussion Series No. 16, London: Industrial Relations Services.

Nelson, K. (1986) 'Labor demand, labor supply and the suburbanization of low-wage office work', in A. J. Scott and M. Storper (eds) (1986) *Production, Work and Territory: The Geographical Anatomy of Industrial Capitalism*, Massachusetts: Allen and Unwin.

Newton, P. (1991) 'Computing: An ideal occupation for women?', in J.

Firth-Cozens and M. A. West (eds) (1991) *Women at Work*, Milton Keynes: Open University Press.

Noble, D. (1984) *Forces of Production: A Social History of Industrial Automation*, New York: Knopf.

Noyes, I. (1983) 'The QWERTY keyboard: a review', *International Journal of Man–Machine Studies*, **18**: 265–281.

Olerup, A. (1985) 'Office automation, work and skill', in A. Olerup, L. Schneider and E. Monod (eds) (1985) *Women, Work and Computerization: Opportunities and Disadvantages*, Amsterdam: North-Holland.

Olerup, A., Schneider, L. and Monod, E. (eds) (1985) *Women, Work and Computerization: Opportunities and Disadvantages*, Amsterdam: North-Holland.

OECD (1988) *New Technologies in the 1990s: A Socio-economic Strategy*, Paris: Organisation for Economic Co-operation and Development.

OPCS (1991) *Census of Population*, London: HMSO.

Pain, D., Owen, J., Franklin, I. and Green, E. (1993) 'Human-centred systems design: A review of trends within the broader systems development context', in E. Green, J. Owen and D. Pain (eds) (1993) *Gendered by Design: Information Technology and Office Systems*, London: Taylor and Francis.

Patel, P. and Pavitt, K. (1993) *Uneven (and Divergent) Technological Development amongst Countries and Firms: Evidence and Explanations*, Brighton: Science Policy Research Unit.

Pearson, R. (1986) 'Female workers in the first and third worlds: The "Greening" of women's labour', in K. Purcell, S. Wood, A. Waton and S. Allen (eds) (1986) *The Changing Experience of Employment: Restructuring and Recession*, London: Macmillan.

Pearson, R. (1989) 'Women's employment and multinationals in the UK: Restructuring and flexibility', in D. Elson and R. Pearson (eds) (1989) *Women's Employment and Multinationals in Europe*, London: Macmillan.

Phillips, A. and Taylor, B. (1980) 'Sex and skill: Notes towards feminist economics', *Feminist Review*, **6**: 79–88.

Phizacklea, A. (1988) 'Gender, racism and occupational segregation', in S. Walby (ed.) (1988) *Gender Segregation at Work*, Milton Keynes: Open University Press.

Phizacklea, A. (1990) *Unpacking the Fashion Industry: Gender, Racism and Class in Production*, London: Routledge.

Phizacklea, A. and Wolkowitz, C. (1995) *Homeworking Women: Gender, Racism and Class at Work*, London: Sage.

Pinch, T. J. and Bijker, W. E. (1987) 'The social construction of facts and artifacts: Or how the sociology of science and the sociology of technology might benefit each other', in W. E. Bijker, T. P. Hughes and T. Pinch (eds) (1987) *The Social Construction of Technological Systems*, London: MIT Press.

Piore, M. J. and Sabel, C. F. (1984) *The Second Industrial Divide: Possibilities for Prosperity*, New York: Basic Books.

Pollert, A. (1981) *Girls, Wives, Factory Lives*, London: Macmillan.

Pollert, A. (1988) 'Dismantling flexibility', *Capital and Class*, **34**: 42–75.

Pollert, A. (1990) 'Conceptions of British employment restructuring in the 1980s', in I. Varcoe, M. McNeil and S. Yearley (eds) (1990)

Deciphering Science and Technology: The Social Relations of Expertise, London: Macmillan.

Posthuma, A. (1987) 'The internationalisation of clerical work: A study of offshore office services in the Caribbean', Brighton: Science Policy Research Unit Occasional Paper No. 24.

Poynton, C. (1993) 'Naming women's workplace skills: Linguistics and power', in B. Probert and B. Wilson (eds) (1993) *Pink Collar Blues: Work, Gender and Technology*, Melbourne: Melbourne University Press.

Pringle, R. (1988) *Secretaries Talk*, London: Verso.

Probert, B. and Hack, A. (n.d.) *Remote Office Work and Regional Development: The Australian Securities Commission in the La Trobe Valley*, Melbourne: CIRCIT.

Probert, B. and Wilson, B. (1993a) 'Gendered work', in B. Probert and B. WQilson (eds) (1993) *Pink Collar Blues: Work, Gender and Technology*, Melbourne: Melbourne University Press.

Probert, B. and Wilson, B. (eds) (1993b) *Pink Collar Blues: Work, Gender and Technology*, Melbourne: Melbourne University Press.

Rajan, A. (1985) 'New technology and jobs: the counter argument', *Personnel Management*, **17**(7): 36–9.

Rakow, L. F. (1988) 'Women and the telephone: The gendering of a communications technology', in C. Kramarae (ed.) (1988) *Technology and Women's Voices*, London: Routledge and Kegan Paul.

Rees, G. (1994) 'IT and vocational education and training in Europe: An overview', in K. Ducatel (ed.) (1994) *Employment and Technical Change in Europe*, Aldershot: Edward Elgar.

Rees, T. (1992) *Women and the Labour Market*, London: Routledge.

Rees, T. (1994) 'Information technology skills and access to training opportunities: Germany and the UK', in K. Ducatel (ed.) (1994) *Employment and Technical Change in Europe*, Aldershot: Edward Elgar.

Rhee, H. A. (1968) *Office Automation in Social Perspective*, Oxford: Blackwell.

Rhodes, E. and Carter, R. (1993) 'EDI and supply chain innovation: Emerging production options in textiles, and the implications for changing patterns of gender and skill in apparel manufacture', Paper presented to COST/ESRC Workshop on EDI, Edinburgh, April.

Rhodes, E. and Carter, R. (1995) 'The impact of EDI and related ICTs on production divergence and convergence', in R. Clarke, J. Cricar and J. Novak (eds) (1995) *Electronic Commerce for Trade Efficiency*, Proceedings of the eighth international conference on EDI/IOS, Kranj, Slovenia, Moderna Organizacija.

Richardson, R. (1993) 'Back officing front office functions: New telemediated back offices and economic development', Paper presented to the PICT National Conference, Kenilworth, 19–21 May.

Richardson, D. and Robinson, V. (1994) 'Theorizing women's studies, gender studies and masculinity: The politics of naming', *European Journal of Women's Studies*, **1**(1): 11–27.

Roberts, B. (1994) *Minority Ethnic Women: Work, Unemployment and Education*, Manchester: Equal Opportunities Commission.

Rose, H. (1994) 'Feminist standpoints on science and technology', in E.

Gunnarsson and L. Trojer (eds) (1994) *Feminist Voices on Gender, Technology and Ethics*, Luleå: University of Technology Centre for Women's Studies.

Rubery, J. and Fagan, C. (1994) 'Occupational segregation: Plus ça change . . .?', in Lindley, R. (ed.) (1994) *Labour Market Structures and Prospects for Women*, Manchester, Equal Opportunities Commission.

Salminen-Karlsson, M. (1995) 'Reforming a masculine bastion from above: State-supported reform of engineering education', Paper presented to the conference on 'Doing Feminist Research on Technology and Society', Vadstena, Sweden, May 23–24.

Scottish Education and Action for Development (SEAD) (1985) *Electronics and Development: Scotland and Malaysia in the International Electronics Industry*, Edinburgh, SEAD.

Senker, J. and Senker, P. (1994) 'Skills implications of technical change in the service sector', in K. Ducatel (ed.) (1994) *Employment and Technical Change in Europe*, Aldershot: Edward Elgar.

Shaffner, J. (1993) 'Gender and Politics in the Machine: Computer Scientists and social change', University of Edinburgh, unpublished MPhil thesis.

Shapiro, G. (1994) 'Informal processes and women's careers in information technology management', in A. Adam, J. Emms, E. Green and J. Owen (eds) (1994) *Women, Work and Computerization: Breaking Old Boundaries – Building New Forms*, Amsterdam: North-Holland.

Siegel, L. (1980) 'Delicate bonds: The global semiconductor industry', *Pacific Research*, **11**: 1–26.

Siltanen, J. (1994) *Locating Gender: Occupational Segregation, Wages and Domestic Responsibilities*, London: UCL Press.

Silverstone, R. (1974) 'The office secretary', London: City University, unpublished PhD thesis.

Silverstone, R. and Hirsch, E. (eds) (1992) *Consuming Technologies: Media and Information in Domestic Spaces*, London: Routledge.

Sleigh, J., Boatwright, B., Irwin, P. and Stanyon, R. (1979) *The Manpower Implications of Micro Electronic Technology*, London: HMSO.

Smith, D. (1987) *The Everyday World as Problematic: A Feminist Sociology*, Toronto: University of Toronto Press.

Smith, S. (1988) 'How much change at the store? The impact of new technologies and labour processes on managers and staff in retail distribution', in D. Knights and H. Willmott (eds) (1988) *New Technology and the Labour Process*, London: Macmillan.

Smith, S. and Wield, D. (1987a) 'Banking on the new technology: Co-operation, competition and the clearers', in L. Harris (ed.) (1987) *New Perspectives on the Financial System*, London: Croom Helm.

Smith, S. and Wield, D. (1987b) 'New technology and bank work: Banking on IT as an "organisational technology" ', in L. Harris (ed.) (1987) *New Perspectives on the Financial System*, London: Croom Helm.

Softley, E. (1985) 'Word processing: new opportunities for women office workers?', in W. Faulkner and E. Arnold (eds) (1985) *Smothered by Invention: Technology in Women's Lives*, London: Pluto.

Sonnentag, S. (1994) 'Team leading in software development: A comparison between women and men', in A. Adam, J. Emms, E. Green and

J. Owen (eds) (1994) *Women, Work and Computerization: Breaking Old Boundaries – Building New Forms*, Amsterdam: North-Holland.

Sørensen, K. (1992) 'Towards a feminized technology? Gendered values in the construction of technology', *Social Studies of Science*, **22**(1): 5–31.

SPRU, Women and Technology Studies (1982) *Microelectronics and Women's Employment in Britain*, Brighton: University of Sussex Science Policy Research Unit.

Stabile, C. A. (1994) *Feminism and the Technological Fix*, Manchester: Manchester University Press.

Stanley, A. (1983) 'Women hold up two-thirds of the sky: Notes for a revised history of technology', in J. Rothschild (ed.) (1983) *Machina ex Dea: Feminist Perspectives on Technology*, New York: Pergamon Press.

Stanworth, J. and Stanworth, C. (1989) 'Home truths about teleworking', *Personnel Management*, November, 48–52.

Star, S. L. (1991) 'Invisible work and silenced dialogues in knowledge representation', in I. V. Eriksson, B. Kitchenham and K. G. Tijdens (eds) (1991) *Women, Work and Computerization: Understanding and Overcoming Bias in Work and Education*, Amsterdam: North-Holland.

Storey, J. (1987) 'The management of new office technology: Choice, control and social structure in the insurance industry', *Journal of Management Studies*, **24**(1): 43–62.

Strober, M. H. and Arnold, C. L. (1987) 'Integrated circuits/segregated labor: Women in computer-related occupations and high-tech industries', in H. I. Hartmann, R. E. Kraut and L. A. Tilly (eds) (1987) *Computer Chips and Paper Clips: Technology and Women's Employment*, Washington, DC: National Academy Press.

Sturdy, A. (1992) 'Clerical consent: "shifting" work in the insurance office', in A. Sturdy, D. Knights and H. Willmott (eds) (1992) *Skill and Consent: Contemporary Studies in the Labour Process*, London: Routledge.

Suchman, L. (1987) *Plans and Situated Actions: The Problem of Human–Machine Communication*, Cambridge: Cambridge University Press.

Suchman, L. (1994) 'Supporting articulation work: Aspects of a feminist practice of technology production', in A. Adam, J. Emms, E. Green and J. Owen (eds) (1994) *Women, Work and Computerization: Breaking Old Boundaries – Building New Forms*, Amsterdam: North-Holland.

Suchman, L. and Jordan, B. (1989) 'Computerization and women's knowledge', in K. Tijdens, M. Jennings, I. Wagner and M. Weggelaar (eds) (1989) *Women, Work and Computerization: Forming New Alliances*, Amsterdam: North-Holland.

Sundin, E. (1995) 'The social construction of gender and technology: A process with no definitive answer', *European Journal of Women's Studies*, **2**(3): 335–53.

Swords-Isherwood, N., Zmroczek, C. and Henwood, F. (1984) 'Technical change and its effect on employment opportunities for women', in P. Marstrand (ed.) (1984) *New Technology and the Future of Work and Skills*, London: Frances Pinter.

Taft, P. (1963) 'Organized labor and technical change: a backward look', in G. Somers (ed.) (1963) *Adjusting to Technological Change*, New York: Harper and Row.

The Rising Tide: A Report on Women in Science, Engineering and Technology (1994) London: HMSO.

Thompson, P. (1983) *The Nature of Work: An Introduction to Debates on the Labour Process*, London: Macmillan.

Thoresen, K. (1989) 'Systems development: Alternative design strategies', in K. Tijdens, M. Jennings, I. Wagner and M. Weggelaar (eds) (1989) *Women, Work and Computerization: Forming New Alliances*, Amsterdam: North-Holland.

Tierney, M. (1995) 'Negotiating a software career: Informal work practices and "The lads" in a software installation', in K. Grint and R. Gill (eds) (1995) *The Gender–Technology Relation: Contemporary Theory and Research*, London: Taylor and Francis.

Tijdens, K. (1991) 'Women in EDP Departments', in I. V. Eriksson, B. Kitchenham and K. G. Tijdens (eds) (1991) *Women, Work and Computerization: Understanding and Overcoming Bias in Work and Education*, Amsterdam: North-Holland.

Tijdens, K. (1994) 'Behind the screens: the foreseen and unforeseen impact of computerization on female office workers' jobs', in T. Eberhart and C. Wächter (eds) (1994) *Proceedings of the 2nd European Feminist Research Conference – Feminist Perspectives on Technology, Work and Ecology*, Graz, Austria, July.

Tjänstemännens Centralorganisation (TCO) (1987) *At a Suitable Distance – Distance Work, Pro et Contra*, Stockholm: TCO.

Trades Union Congress (TUC) (1980) *Employment and Technology*, London: TUC.

Truman, C. and Keating, J. (1988) 'Technology, markets and the design of women's jobs: The case of the clothing industry', *New Technology, Work and Employment*, 3(1): 21–9.

Turkle, S. (1984) *The Second Self: Computers and the Human Spirit*, London: Granada.

Turkle, S. (1988) 'Computational reticence: Why women fear the intimate machine', in C. Kramarae (ed.) (1988) *Technology and Women's Voices: Keeping in Touch*, London: Routledge and Kegan Paul.

United Nations Development Programme (1995) *Human Development Report 1995*, Oxford: Oxford University Press.

URCOT (n.d.) *Investigative Work Group Handbook*, Melbourne: Union Research Centre on Office Technology.

Van Oost, E. (1992) 'The masculinization of the computer: A historical reconstruction', Paper presented to the international conference on Gender, Technology and Ethics, Luleå, Sweden, 1–2 June 1992.

Van Zoonen, L. (1992) 'Feminist theory and information technology', *Media, Culture and Society*, 14(1): 9–29.

Vedel, G. and Gunnarsson, E. (1985) 'Flexibility in women's remote office work', in A. Olerup, L. Schneider and E. Monod (eds) (1985) *Women, Work and Computerization: Opportunities and Disadvantages*, Amsterdam: North-Holland.

Vehviläinen, M. (1986) 'A study circle approach as a method for women to develop their work and computer systems', Paper presented to the IFIP Conference on Women, Work and Computerisation, Dublin, August.

Vehviläinen, M. (1991) 'Gender in information systems development – a women office workers' standpoint', in I. V. Eriksson, B. Kitchenham and K. G. Tijdens (eds) (1991) *Women, Work and Computerization: Understanding and Overcoming Bias in Work and Education*, Amsterdam: North-Holland.

Vehviläinen, M. (1994a) 'Women defining their information technology – Struggles for textual subjectivity in an office workers' study circle', *European Journal of Women's Studies*, **1**(1): 73–93.

Vehviläinen, M. (1994b) 'Living through the boundaries of information systems expertise – a work history of a Finnish woman systems developer', in A. Adam, J. Emms, E. Green and J. Owen (eds) (1994) *Women, Work and Computerization: Breaking Old Boundaries – Building New Forms*, Amsterdam: North-Holland.

Vinnicombe, S. (1980) *Secretaries, Management and Organisations*, London: Heinemann.

Virgo, P. (1994) *The Gathering Storm: 1994 IT Skills Trends Report*, Sidcup: Institute of Data Processing Management/Computer Weekly/ Women into IT Foundation.

Wagner, I. (1985) 'Women in the automated office', in A. Olerup, L. Schneider and E. Monod (eds) (1985) *Women, Work and Computerization: Opportunities and Disadvantages*, Amsterdam: North-Holland.

Wagner, I. (1993) 'Women's voice: The case of nursing information systems', *AI and Society*, **7**(4): 295–310.

Wajcman, J. (1991) *Feminism Confronts Technology*, Pennsylvania: Pennsylvania State Press.

Wajcman, J. (1995) 'Feminist theories of technology', in S. Jasanoff, G. E. Markle, J. C. Petersen and T. Pinch (eds) (1995) *Handbook of Science and Technology Studies*, London: Sage.

Wajcman, J. and Probert, B. (1988) 'New technology outwork', in E. Willis (ed.) (1988) *Technology and the Labour Process: Australian Case Studies*, Sydney: Allen and Unwin.

Walby, S. (1986) *Patriarchy at Work*, Cambridge: Polity.

Walby, S. (1989) 'Flexibility and changing sexual division of labour', in S. Wood (ed.) (1989) *The Transformation of Work?*, London: Unwin Hyman.

Webster, J. (1986) 'The effects of word processing on secretarial and typing work', PhD thesis, University of Bradford.

Webster, J. (1990) *Office Automation: The Labour Process and Women's Work in Britain*, Hemel Hempstead: Harvester Wheatsheaf.

Webster, J. (1993) 'From the word processor to the micro: Gender issues in the development of information technology in the office', in E. Green, J. Owen and D. Pain (eds) (1993) *Gendered by Design: Information Technology and Office Systems*, London: Taylor and Francis.

Webster, J. (1995) 'Networks of collaboration or conflict? Electronic data interchange and power in the supply chain', *Journal of Strategic Information Systems*, **4**(1): 31–42.

Weizenbaum, J. (1976) *Computer Power and Human Reason*, Harmondsworth: Penguin.

Wernecke, D. (1983) *Microelectronics and Office Jobs: The Impact of the Chip on Women's Employment*, Geneva: International Labour Office.

West, J. (1978) 'Women, sex and class', in A. Kuhn and A. M. Wolpe (eds) (1978) *Feminism and Materialism*, London: Routledge and Kegan Paul.

West, J. (1990) 'Gender and the labour process: A reassessment', in D. Knights and H. Wilmott (eds) (1990) *Labour Process Theory*, London: Macmillan.

Westwood, S. (1984) *All Day Every Day: Factory and Family in the Making of Women's Lives*, London: Pluto Press.

Wickham, J. and Murray, P. (1987) *Women in the Irish Electronics Industry*, Dublin: Employment Equality Agency.

Williams, K., Cutler, T., Williams, J. and Haslam, C. (1987) 'The end of mass production?', *Economy and Society*, 1(3): 404–39.

Williams, R. and Edge, D. (1992) 'The social shaping of technology: Research concepts and findings in Great Britain', in M. Dierkes and U. Hoffmann (eds) (1992) *New Technology at the Outset: Social Forces in the Shaping of Technological Innovations*, Frankfurt: Campus Verlag.

Wilson, R. A. (1994) 'Sectoral and occupational change: Prospects for women's employment', in R. Lindley (ed.) (1994) *Labour Market Structures and Prospects for Women*, Manchester: Equal Opportunities Commission.

Winner, L. (1993) 'Upon opening the black box and finding it empty: social constructivism and the philosophy of technology', *Science, Technology and Human Values*, 18(3): 362–78.

Women's Voice Word Processor Pamphlet (1979) *Job Massacre at the Office*, London: Women's Voice.

Women Working Worldwide (1991) *Common Interests: Women Organising in Global Electronics*, London: Women Working Worldwide.

Woodfield, R. (1994) 'An ethnographic exploration of some factors which mediate the relationship between gender and skill in a software R& D unit', University of Sussex, unpublished D Phil thesis.

Young, B. (1977) 'Science is Social Relations', *Radical Science Journal*, 5: 65–131.

Zimbalist, A. (ed.) (1979) *Case Studies on the Labor Process*, New York: Monthly Review Press.

Zuboff, S. (1988) *In the Age of the Smart Machine*, Oxford: Heinemann Professional Publishing.

INDEX